THE ORIGINS OF THE GOTHIC REVIVAL

THE ORIGINS
OF THE
GOTHIC
REVIVAL

Michael McCarthy

Published for the Paul Mellon Centre for Studies in British Art
by Yale University Press · New Haven and London 1987

Designed by Mary Carruthers and set in Linotron Baskerville
Printed and bound at The Bath Press, Avon

Library of Congress Cataloging-in-Publication Data

McCarthy, Michael J., 1939–
    The origins of the Gothic revival.

    Based on the author's thesis (Ph.D.)—University
of London, Courtauld Institute of Art, 1972.
    Bibliography: p.
    Includes index.
    1. Gothic revival (Architecture)—Great Britain.
2. Architecture, Modern—17th–18th centuries—Great
Britain.   3. Architecture, Modern—19th century—
Great Britain.   4. Architecture—Great Britain.
I. Title.
NA966.5.G66M33   1987   720′.942   86–28119
ISBN 0–300–03723–6

Contents

Dedicated to G. STEPHEN VICKERS, Professor Emeritus,
University of Toronto

Photographic Acknowledgments

Avery Architectural and Fine Arts Library, Columbia University, New York 40–62; British Library 5, 8–11, 30, 31, 73, 80, 187, 188, 210, 212–4; Country Life 20, 21, 25, 127, 128, 180–2, 184–6; Daventry, Lord 154, 155, 167–72, 175–9, 207; English Heritage 211, XI; Greater London Record Office 207; Hampshire County Record Office 18, 75–8, 84, 85, 118, 126, 131–4, 222; Lewis Walpole Library, Farmington, Connecticut 1–4, 6, 12–15, 17, 27, 32–8, 74, 79, 81–3, 86–92, 94–101, 105–9, 113, 115, 119–21, 139–50, 165, 166, 191, 194, 216, 217, 220, 221, 223, 224, I–IX; Metropolitan Museum of Art, New York 69; Musées Royaux des Beaux Arts, Brussels 16; National Trust 19, 110, 112, 122–4, 129, 135–7, 219; Oxford City Libraries 174; Paul Mellon Centre, London 129, 135–8, 151, 219; Plymouth City Art Gallery 7; Richmond Public Libraries 151; Rousham House, Oxon. 26; Royal Academy, London 19, 154; Royal Commission on the Historic Monuments of England 22–4, 29, 63–8, 70–2, 125, 130, 152, 153, 156–63, 192, 193, 195–9, 204–6, 208, 215, 218, X; Royal Institute of British Architects 28, 164, 183; Sir John Soane's Museum 190; Stowe School 189; University of Toronto, courtesy of John Glover 93, 101, 102–4, 111, 114, 116, 117, 209; Victoria and Albert Museum, London 173, 200–3; Warwick County Record Office 167–72, 175–9.

Acknowledgments

The research for this book began with my doctoral thesis, which was submitted to the Courtauld Institute of Art, University of London, in 1972. My first acknowledgment is to the thesis supervisor, the late Professor Pevsner, and my second to the then Director of the Institute, who initiated the research, the late Professor Blunt. Neither the thesis nor the book would have been possible without the friendship and generosity of the founder of the Lewis Walpole Library, Farmington, Connecticut, and I wish to make special acknowledgment to the late Wilmarth Sheldon Lewis. In England, Lord Daventry has been particularly generous in providing access to the Newdegate papers in the Warwick County Record Office and in Arbury Hall to facilitate research into the architectural and other interests of Sir Roger Newdigate.

The curators of these collections, Michael Farr and Monica Ory in Warwick and Catherine Jestin, Joan Sussler and Karen Peltier in Farmington, deserve special mention because I have had occasion to trouble them so frequently and have consistently met with kindness and encouragement. I trust that my acknowledgment to them will stand as a mark of my gratitude to the curators of the collections mentioned in the first section of the bibliography and to the keepers of the photographic archives which are credited individually in the captions to the plates.

Acknowledgment to previous writers on this subject will be found in the notes to the text at appropriate points, but I may take this opportunity to thank Howard M. Colvin and John Harris for the continuing stimulus that their research and publications have afforded me. Among recent writers I have found the works of James Macaulay and John Frew particularly stimulating, and I owe special thanks to Teresa Badenoch-Watts and Loftus Jestin for permitting access to their recent theses on Johann Heinrich Müntz and Richard Bentley respectively. I have also profited much from the researches of Clive Wainwright, Michael Snodin and Stephen Calloway, who were responsible for the exhibition devoted to Horace Walpole at Richmond-on-Thames in 1980. I wish to thank the editors of the *Journal of Garden History* for allowing me to repeat the substance of the article on Thomas Wright's gothic drawings, first published in their journal, and the editor, John Dixon Hunt, who did much to improve that article.

Professor Patricia Brückmann of Trinity College, University of Toronto, kindly read the first draft of this book and suggested corrections, and Ann Hilty of the Department of Fine Art, Universty of Toronto, edited the manuscript for presentation to the publisher. I am most grateful to Elly Miller for the kindness with which she undertook the reading of the manuscript and introduced it and me to Yale University Press, to the staff of which I am grateful for their care of the book's production and publication. The personal encouragement and practical assistance of Professor Emeritus G. Stephen Vickers, University of Toronto, is acknowledged in the dedication of the book.

The travel involved in research for the book was aided by grants and fellowships from the Social Sciences and Humanities Research Council of Canada, the Office of Research Administration, University of Toronto, and Trinity College, University of Toronto. Finally I wish to thank the Directors of the Paul Mellon Centre in London, which has sponsored the publication.

Introduction

This book is born of the conviction that the beginnings of the gothic revival in architecture have hitherto been presented to the public in an incomplete and therefore mistaken manner. The source of the incompleteness is found in Horace Walpole, who played such a large part in the revival that he cast himself in the role of its originator and with considerable justice, as I seek to show. But he was also its recorder and publicist and remains a primary source of information on the subject; personal and political antipathies prejudiced him against the work of major practitioners of the style, however, and though some of their works have been treated in periodical literature, this book brings more evidence to bear on the subject and seeks to correct the imbalance caused by Walpole's sometimes culpable omissions.

The standard history of the movement is that published in 1872 by C. L. Eastlake and re-issued with a lengthy introduction and valuable supplement by J. M. Crook at the University of Leicester Press in 1970. The standard interpretation of the movement is K. Clark, *The Gothic Revival*, first published in 1928 and frequently re-issued though not revised. Recent books include those by G. Germann (1972), T. Davis (1974) and J. Macaulay, *The Gothic Revival 1745–1845* (1975). The last would appear to make this book superfluous, but its title is misleading, since it deals only with manifestations of the gothic revival in Scotland and the north of England; the origins of the revival are to be found in the south of England and the Midlands, and it is with buildings in these areas from 1740 to 1770 that this book will be concerned.

Part of the reason for the incompleteness of current accounts of this movement in architecture, which was to become a principal style of building in the nineteenth century throughout the world, is that a considerable amount of the evidence for its origins, in the form of drawings for eighteenth century buildings, had found its way into American collections, principally into the Lewis Walpole Library (now part of the Yale University system) and the Avery Architectural and Fine Arts Library of Columbia University. My endeavour has been to study these in co-ordination with the evidence remaining in English collections and archives, and with evidence to be gathered from buildings on the spot, or from the photographic records of buildings now demolished, to form a more complete account of the movement than is possible by studying them separately from relevant drawings and manuscripts in older collections.

Walpole's initiative in rebuilding and expanding Strawberry Hill was of first and lasting importance in introducing asymmetry into domestic architecture and historicism into the gothic revival. Precedents for the first of these innovations can be found in the work of Sir John Vanbrugh at Greenwich, and for the second in Batty Langley's publication of 1742, *Gothic Architecture Restored and Improved*, Plates A and B of which extrapolate from columns in Westminster Abbey the proportional system proposed for new buildings in the revived style or the restoration of older buildings. Neither Vanbrugh nor Langley, however, expressed such consciousness of their innovations as did Walpole; nor did Walpole seem conscious of their work as precedents for his own program, which he deliberately effected as an ideal for emulation. This book seems to demonstrate that the ideal was shared by a larger number of his contemporaries than the writings of Walpole have led us to believe.

Even the most neo-classical architects of the period, Sir William Chambers and Robert Adam, occasionally designed in the gothic style, as had the Palladian architects of the preceding generation. But it was not until James Wyatt established his practice in London in the 1770s that building in the gothic revival style became a major concern of a professional architect. Walpole recognised in Wyatt the torch-bearer of the revolution in architecture he had sought to effect, and he recognised in Wyatt's Lee Priory, Kent, "a child of Strawberry, prettier than the parent". Prettiness is perhaps the last of the qualities sought by an architect, but it is a consistent characteristic of Walpole's references to his achievement at Strawberry Hill that he couches them in diminutive terms. This should not mislead us into an underestimation of the size and clarity of his architectural ambition, which will be discussed in the third chapter.

Wyatt's work at Lee Priory and other country houses, especially the monumental Fonthill Abbey in Wiltshire, was marked by fidelity to the letter and the spirit of antique precedents, which he had derived from his continuing study for restoration purposes of the gothic cathedrals. The rapidity with which commissions for buildings and rebuildings in the gothic style overtook commissions for classical buildings with which his practice had started, demonstrated that his work struck a responsive chord in patrons of a much wider range than the amateur and antiquarian circle associated with Walpole. Undoubtedly there were nationalistic reasons for this and some snobbery too, but most important was the compatibility of his style with the formulation by Edmund Burke in 1757 of the Sublime as an aesthetically defensible objective. The writings of Uvedale Price and Richard Payne Knight were to interpose the aesthetic of the picturesque between those of the Beautiful and Sublime, providing theoretical sanction for the application of irregularity to buildings and sites that could not make claim to the qualities necessary for sublimity, especially that of scale.

It was Wyatt's achievement to give architectural form to the wishes of patrons conditioned by this body of aesthetic writing, but neither the historicism of his architecture nor its asymmetry came about in a vacuum, nor can Strawberry Hill alone account for the establishment of the gothic revival as a practicable alternative to domestic architecture in the classical style. The works of the amateurs and architects discussed in the second part of the book, particularly those whom Walpole for his own reasons chose to omit from his account of contemporary architecture, Sir Roger Newdigate, Henry Keene and Johann Heinrich Müntz, had demonstrated the practicability of a revival of the gothic style and form a necessary prelude to the adoption of that style on a larger and wider scale in the succeeding decades.

The theoretical writings referred to above had direct relevance to landscape painting and landscape design rather than to architecture, and Walpole's way of thought seems to have been comparable, since he derived irregularity in architectural design from the practice of William Kent in landscape design. For this reason the design of garden buildings is most important to the understanding of the origins of the gothic revival and a separate chapter is devoted to the subject here. As in the cases of domestic and ecclesiastical architecture, the popularity of the gothic revival in garden buildings was more widespread than has been supposed and affected patrons in a much wider circle than the writings of Walpole would suggest. The works of Palladian architects and of Sanderson Miller and Thomas Wright of Durham are examples to the point. Walpole's insight led him to apply asymmetry and gothic form simultaneously in a domestic rather than a landscape context. The results of this perception can hardly be overestimated in importance, and in succeeding decades they were manifest particularly in the practice of John Nash as well as James Wyatt.

It seemed unnecessary to discuss the aesthetic writings that form the background to the gothic revival, since that has been done so well so often. But there is an interesting body of pattern-book literature accompanying the beginnings of the movement that deserved a closer look than it has hitherto received. There is also a small body of critical writing that has not received the attention it merits, and a larger body of writing that may be classed as historical research or historical speculation. Some of this writing remained in manuscript form, but it was well known to the early practitioners in the style and is therefore considered in the first chapter, along with the published works of criticism and pattern-books, to provide the specifically architectural background in literature that clarifies the intent of the revival. It demonstrates that the historical or antiquarian impulse behind the revival was vigorous and continuous from the start, and this of course was to be the principal factor that informed the revival in the nineteenth century. Though mercifully untainted by the religious dogmatism that characterised the work of Pugin and the Ecclesiologists a century later, the gothic revival of the middle of the eighteenth century saw the beginnings of the historicism that informed the later monuments of the style.

I. The Literature of the Revival

Professional pattern-books, books of architectural criticism and studies in antiquarianism form the literary background to the revival of the gothic style in architecture in the middle decades of the eighteenth century.[1] Some of the antiquarianism was known only in manuscript form, and one important contribution, that of Sanderson Miller, never went beyond the planning stage. But the expectations aroused by these fugitive pieces of literature afford us an insight into the endeavours of the small band of amateurs, architects and antiquaries who were the originators of the architectural style which was to be predominant throughout the western world for most of the nineteenth century.[2]

PATTERN-BOOKS

The most prolific supplier of pattern-books at the beginning of the eighteenth century was Batty Langley, whose career has been clarified in recent studies by Alistair Rowan and by Eileen Harris.[3] His name is justly linked to the revival of the gothic style because of his publication in 1742 of *Ancient Architecture Restored and Improved by a Great Variety of Grand and Useful Designs, entirely New in the Gothick Mode for the Ornamenting of Buildings and Gardens*.[4] This was re-issued in 1747. It must be said at once that this famous book is a minor item in the list of publications of Batty Langley, slimmer in substance and less successful in its circulation than his typical works.

Born in 1696, Batty was the son of Daniel Langley, a landscape gardener from Twickenham. Before turning his attention to architecture, Batty followed his father's profession and also became a publicist for the art of landscape gardening. He began to publish architectural books in 1726 and in 1734 he assumed the role of architectural critic with a series of bitter articles in the *Grub Street Journal* directed against Lord Burlington's sponsorship of the cult of Andrea Palladio and Inigo Jones in architecture. It might be assumed therefore that his publishing of gothic designs in 1742 constituted a continuation of his anti-Burlington crusade and a conscious attempt to undermine Palladianism and propose an alternative architectural mode for modern building. Such an assumption is not warranted, however, by the history of his publications, among which *Ancient Architecture Restored and Improved* was to remain exceptional though Batty Langley continued a feverish career in architectural publishing till his death in 1751.

By 1741 Batty Langley had established himself in a house in Meard's Court, in Dean Street, Soho, where he founded, with the help of his brother Thomas, who illustrated his books, a school of architectural draughtsmanship. He had published thirteen books by this date, four on the art of landscape gardening and nine on architecture. The latter met with particular success, three having been reprinted twice by 1741 and one having had three editions. After opening his school he wrote nine further works on architecture, one of which was published posthumously. The most successful was *The Builder's Jewel, or the Youth's Instructor and Workman's Remembrancer* of 1741, which reached its eleventh edition in 1768 and was to be reissued again in 1787 and 1808. There was also an American edition, published at Charleston in 1800.[5]

Success such as this can be understood only against the background of the need which existed for instruction in architectural draughtsmanship. Art training of any sort in England in the eighteenth century was, to quote Wittkower, "disgraceful".[6] Practising architects were fully aware of the scandalous absence of facilities for instruction of draughtsmen, and of the inevitability of plagiarism in the absence of such instruction. The most authoritative voice of the age is that of John Gwynn, whose writings will be discussed later in this chapter. "If they can form no designs on their own," he pointed out, "they are constantly obliged to copy those of better Artists".[7] The truth of his observation is only too apparent in the architectural literature of the period, and particularly in the publications of Batty Langley, whose working methods are described by Eileen Harris: "Hurriedly, designs were copied, engraved and printed, some upside down and mis-numbered, several with as many different pieces as possible on a single sheet. Provided with an equally slap-dash, piratical text by Batty, they were issued whole or in parts to carpenters, joiners, masons, cabinet-makers and other craftsmen."[8] The inadequacy of the training of professional architects explains to some extent the importance of the role of the amateur in the eighteenth century.[9] One amateur wrote to another in 1754: "I would never draw a line more, if I did not see much worse in the shocking designs of common workmen."[10]

English architectural literature of the eighteenth century has not yet received the detailed study it deserves, but some analysis has been offered by Wittkower.[11] He sees the works of Batty Langley as contributing to the vulgarisation of architectural theory. Its appeal lay partly in promoting simplified methods of mensuration and partly in that the emphasis on mensuration related it to a tradition of rational and mathematically based writings on surveying or architecture that already existed in England. It is from this context of debased vulgarisations of classical treatises on architecture that Batty Langley's *Ancient Architecture Restored and Improved* emerged in 1742 as an exceptional and none-too-successful item in a long list of works dedicated to promulgation of the ideals and forms of classical architecture. Batty Langley would surely regard it as a cruel trick of fate to be associated primarily with the revival of the gothic style, when the majority of his books were classical in nature, and the corner-stone of his teaching was emphatically purist in emphasising the importance of the canonical orders. He wrote in 1745: "The first work to be done in order thereto, is perfectly to understand the Five Orders of Columns, which here I have placed precedent to the designs for that purpose; and which I peremptorily admonish be well understood, before any Proceeding be made to attempt the Art of Designing."[12]

The title *Ancient Architecture Restored and Improved* is absurdly pretentious to us, since we have long appreciated the gothic style as an artistic phenomenon independent of the classical canons. But it was the accepted wisdom in Batty Langley's time that gothic architecture was a corrupt version of Roman architecture and therefore capable of improvement by the application of principles derived from study of Roman architecture by Vitruvius and his many followers, principally Palladio. An appreciation of the gothic style on premises that were separate from those applied to classical architecture was first posited by Richard Hurd in an aside in his *Letters on Chivalry and Romance* in 1762:

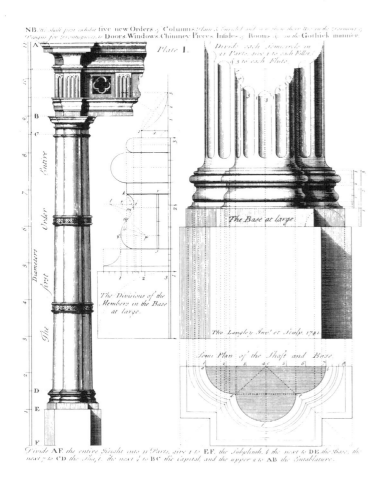

When an architect examines a gothic structure by Grecian rules he finds nothing but deformity. But the gothic has its own rules, by which when it comes to be examined, it is seen to have its merit, as well as the Grecian. The question is not, which of the two is conducted in the simplest or truest taste: but, whether there be not sense and design in both, when scrutinised by the laws in which each is projected.[13]

Hurd is quite exceptional, and even practitioners of the gothic revival did not share his clear-sightedness.[14] In 1742, the date of Batty Langley's book, the fifth edition of *Chamber's Cyclopaedia* defined "gothic architecture" as "that which deviates from the proportions, characters etc. of the antique", and the "gothic column" was quite simply described as "any round pillar in a gothic building, either too thick, or too small for its height".[15]

It is probably fairer to emphasise the "Restored" rather than the "Improved" in the title of Batty Langley's book. There was a continuing need for the restoration of the numerous gothic buildings which still stood in England, and these restorations would have to be effected by the members of the building trades to which this book, like all of Batty Langley's books, was addressed. He set about teaching them in a very sound pedagogical manner by proceeding from the known to the unknown, adapting the mathematical formulae of the classical canon to apply them to the gothic style. Hence the five orders of gothic columns and other transferences, so that quatrefoils, for instance, are made to function as metopes (Plates 1 and 2). The result, as Wittkower says, is a travesty of the classical canon.[16] Historians of the gothic revival from Walpole to Eastlake have condemned his proceeding as a travesty of the gothic style.[17] But this is to misunderstand

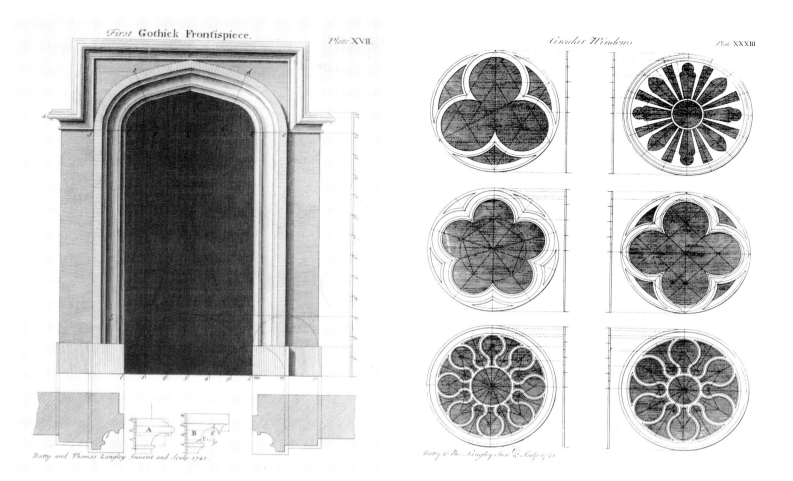

Batty and Thomas Langley Invent and Sculp 1741.

Batty & Tho. Langley Invt & Sculp 1741.

the nature of Langley's publication and the limitations of the age. Batty Langley undoubtedly thought he was paying the gothic style a handsome compliment in proposing that it could be analysed in terms derived from the classical style.

Langley certainly had no intention that his book should be the manifesto of a revolution in architecture.[18] The designs he included are all for slight buildings intended as ornaments in a landscape garden, or for architectural details, such as doors, windows and chimney-pieces (Plates 3 and 4). Its content, method and influence have been detailed by Alistair Rowan, and it is clear from the scarcity of records of its influence that it was not very influential at all.[19] A promise of a second volume sparked no noticeable interest in his reading public and was never to be fulfilled, and, in an age of rampant pirating of designs, only William Pain in 1765 and T. C. Overton in 1766 paid Langley the compliment of plagiarising his book.[20] Among his own publications it has the distinction of being the most original of his productions. But it is not original in architectural history, for the gothic mode had been established in fashionable circles ten years earlier by William Kent, and as Rowan asserts, Langley responded to a fashion rather than led it.[21] Indeed, there is considerable justification for regarding his book as a systematising of the Kent version of the gothic style.[22]

Wittkower's analysis has shown that the Palladian canon had never been as pure in England as Lord Burlington might have wished.[23] Kent's excursions into gothic can be parallelled in the works of other architects of the Burlington circle, Roger Morris, for example, and Isaac Ware.[24] Robert Morris, who was related to the architect Roger, went so far in a lecture read on 12 November, 1730, as to rank the cathedral of Florence with the best works of Palladio, though, as we shall see, he was severely critical of English

3. (*left*) Plate 17 of Batty and Thomas Langley, *Ancient Architecture*, 1742. Courtesy of the Lewis Walpole Library, Farmington, Connecticut.

4. (*right*) Plate 33 of Batty and Thomas Langley, *Ancient Architecture*, 1742. Courtesy of the Lewis Walpole Library, Farmington, Connecticut.

cathedrals.[25] Classical architects not so closely connected with Lord Burlington who provided designs in the gothic style include James Gibbs, James Paine and John Carr.[26] Carr even set his students the exercise of making copies of the designs in Batty Langley's book.[27] It is quite possible, of course, that as a supplier of cheap "books for the trade", Langley was beneath the notice of authors of the great architectural studies of the century, such as Isaac Ware. He is probably a chief target of the many objections to the unjustified assumption of the title of architect by tradesmen that we find in the writings of Robert Morris, John Gwynn and Stephen Riou. But we find no criticism of the gothic content of his book in professional writings.[28]

More important for the first phase of the gothic revival was the reception afforded to *Ancient Architecture Restored and Improved* by the amateur architects of the period. Horace Walpole and Thomas Gray were to be responsible for the institution of Batty Langley as the villain of the style in their letters of the mid-1750s;[29] but Walpole and his friend John Chute each acquired a copy of the book, and their indebtedness to it in the creation of Strawberry Hill will be demonstrated in a later chapter.[30] Even in his unexecuted designs for the remodelling of his country seat, The Vyne in Hampshire, John Chute shows a close dependence on the gothic designs of Batty Langley.[31]

Sanderson Miller of Radway also obtained a copy of Langley's book, and the delight it afforded him was evidently communicated to his friend Richard Jago, who in turn told William Shenstone of The Leasowes. Shenstone wrote to Jago seeking further inform-ation so that he could draw inspiration from Miller's source:

> Did you not tell me of a treatise that your Mr. Miller had, where the author endeavours to vindicate and establish Gothic architecture? And does not the same man explain it also by draughts on copper plates? That very book, or rather the title and the author's name, I want.—I shall never, I believe, be entirely partial to Goths or Vandals either. But I think, by the assistance of some such treatise, I could sketch out some charming Gothic temples and Gothic benches for garden-seats.[32]

Langley's book was of such assistance to Shenstone that by 30 July, 1749, he had completed his first gothic building at The Leasowes, and felt able to declare by the end of that year: "I conceive the mechanic part of architecture to be a science easily acquired; and that a tolerable good native taste is generally what gives the *distinction*." In this same letter we read that he has sent away for Batty Langley's *Builder's Jewel*.[33]

Like Horace Walpole and Sanderson Miller, who was a close neighbour in Warwick-shire, William Shenstone maintained an extensive correspondence with gentlemen anxious to improve their estates.[34] Another neighbour of his was Lord Stamford at Enville in Staffordshire, and both Sanderson Miller and William Shenstone were to advise him, in person as well as by correspondence, on the erection of gothic buildings on his estate.[35] Miller also travelled quite widely advising his friends on their gardens and garden buildings, besides directing their planning and erection by letter and by the loan of his building handyman (or "mason *a latere*", as Edward Turner called him), William Hitchcox.[36] Walpole too was a fervent propagandist for the revival of the gothic style. He wrote of the alterations to his friend Dicky Bateman's house and grounds at Old Windsor: "I preached so effectively that his every pagoda took the veil."[37] His correspondence was frequently the vehicle for the promotion of the gothic revival style in building.[38] By these personal contacts among amateur architects and landowners, each of whom had set an example by himself erecting gothic buildings on his own estate,[39] the designs in *Ancient Architecture Restored and Improved* gained a currency that was every bit as important for the early stages of the gothic revival as the direct influence of the book upon professional builders and architects. Their enthusiasm for the gothic of Batty Langley did not last long into the 1750s, as we have noticed; but their first steps in the gothic revival were demonstrably guided by his "draughts on copper plates".

In pattern-book publishing of the middle decades of the century the closest follower of the lead given by Batty Langley was his contemporary rival in the architectural publications business, William Halfpenny. Batty Langley referred to him slightingly as "*alias* Hoare, lately of Richmond in Surry, carpenter";[40] but in fact he is of considerably more importance as a practising architect than is Langley, with several buildings attributable to him, principally in the Bristol area.[41] For some reason, his popular *Builder's Pocket Companion* of 1728 was published under the pseudonym Michael Hoare, but the rest of his books, about twenty in number, were issued under his true name, and in 1752 his son John Halfpenny was first listed as co-author. This was the year which saw the publication of two volumes, *Rural Architecture in the Gothic Taste* and *Chinese and Gothic Architecture properly Ornamented*. It is important again to note that these are exceptional items in the Halfpenny output; as in the case of Batty Langley the bulk of Halfpenny's production is classical in character, and he never displayed the anti-Burlington bias of Langley. These books did not reach a second edition and received no notice in later professional literature or amateur correspondence, so they must be judged to have been less influential than the *Ancient Architecture Restored and Improved*. John Harris has remarked upon the old-fashioned character of his designs,[42] and indeed, his understanding of gothic represents a variation upon Kent's practice of the style rather than any development of it .[43]

The most prolific pattern-book authors besides Langley and Halfpenny were Robert Morris and Abraham Swan, and they include no gothic designs in their publications.[44] Thomas Wright of Durham published in 1755 *Six Original Designs of Arbours* and in 1758 *Six Original Designs of Grottoes*. These contain gothic motifs but are different in kind from the pattern-book examples, as we would expect since he is an amateur architect of distinction.[45] Something of his charm and whimsy and his feeling for natural materials is evident in Paul Decker's *Gothic Architecture Decorated*, published in two parts in 1759. This line of design in the gothic manner culminates in 1767 in a delightful volume by William Wrighte, the title of which is sufficiently descriptive to merit quotation in full: *Grotesque Architecture or Rural Amusement, consisting of Plans, Elevations and Sections for Huts, Retreats, Summer and Winter Hermitages, Terminaries, Chinese, Gothic and Natural Grottos, Cascades, Mosques, Moresque Pavilions, Grotesque and Rustic Seats, Greenhouses, etc., many of which may be executed with Flints, Irregular Stones, Rude Branches and Roots of Trees.*[46] Nothing is known of the architectural careers of Paul Decker (which may be a pseudonym derived from a German architect who died in 1713) or of William Wrighte, and they did not publish any other pattern-books, so they cannot be considered to have had a significant influence on the development of the gothic revival.

Of the same nature as the books by Thomas Wright, Paul Decker and William Wrighte is Charles Over's *Ornamental Architecture in the Gothic, Chinese and Modern Taste*, of 1758, and Charles Over is comparable to Decker and Wrighte in the obscurity that shrouds his career.[47] Thomas Overton is not quite so obscure. He is the author of *The Temple Builder's Most Useful Companion* of 1766.[48] This contains fifty plates, eighteen of which show gothic designs. Three of these may well have been erected.[49]

One plate by Thomas Overton appears in a compilation of designs by T. Milton, J. Crunden and P. Columbani, also of 1766, *The Chimney-Piece Maker's Daily Assistant*. But of the fifty-four designs in this collection only two are in the gothic style.[50] Similarly, John Crunden's book of 1770, *Convenient and Ornamental Architecture*, contains only two gothic designs out of a total of seventy.[51] Crunden reappears as the contributor of six plates to Robert Manwaring's *The Carpenter's Complete Guide to the Whole System of Gothic*

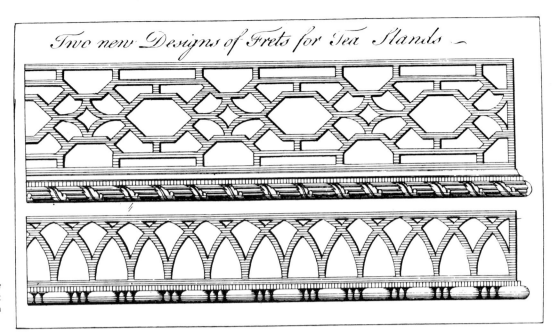

Two new Designs of Frets for Tea Stands

5. Johann Heinrich Müntz, Plate 5 of *The Carpenter's Complete Guide* by Robert Manwaring, 1765. Courtesy of the British Library.

Railing, published in 1765, which is noteworthy because it includes four designs by Johann Heinrich Müntz (Plate 5),[52] and also because it is the only book of designs for woodworkers exclusively devoted to the gothic style.[53] But as the level of designing thus shows a decline from the art of architecture to the manual crafts, so too does the level of presentation and the discrimination of style. The title of the unsigned Plate 14, *Mosaick Gate Gothick Stile*, is sufficient to convey the tone of this publication.[54]

One of the more substantial contributions to the gothic revival in pattern-book literature of this period is by Timothy Lightoler, *The Gentleman and Farmer's Architect*, published in 1764. Of the twenty-five plates, seven show gothic motifs. These start quite lamely with the fourth plate, "Two Small Farm-Houses", which have almost identical plans, but the second of which is a gothic variation on the classical facade of the first. It is lighted by pointed windows and has a half-quatrefoil in the implied pediment, which, like the rest of the roof-line, is battlemented. Other gothic designs in the book are applied to out-buildings, and the most delightful as well as revealing of them are the final two plates of the collection. Plate 24 is titled "Design for a Sheep Coat to be built on a hill, which, seen from a Genteel house, forms an agreeable object". This is the spirit also of the final plate, "Facades to place before disagreeable objects". The disagreeable objects are barns and other subsidiary farm buildings, here shown fronted by ruinated walls and crumbling towers. This is a pleasant flirtation with the gothic style, but it does not seem to have exerted any traceable influence on the gentlemen and farmers to which it was addressed and by that date these designs are symptoms of a fashion well established.

By 1770 architectural writers were concerned with the more pressing theoretical issue of the revival of the Greek style, which aroused far more passionate feelings in the profession than the gothic revival ever aroused till the days of Pugin.[55] Antiquarians, on the other hand, were concerned rather with scholarship in the history of the gothic style, especially as it affected the restoration of the cathedrals and churches of England.[56] The gothic style drops out of the pattern-books of the last three decades of the century almost completely. The gothic books of Langley and Halfpenny were not to be reissued after 1760, though some of their classical books were in regular demand. An exceptional publication of little merit and no known influence is that of the obscure N. Wallis, *The*

Carpenter's Treasure, a collection of sixteen plates divided between gothic temples and Chinese fences, which appeared in 1773 but seems to have had an earlier edition which is no longer traceable.[57] William Thomas was a well-known professional architect of the end of the century, and it is symptomatic of the lack of interest in gothic designs that his *Original Designs in Architecture* (1783) contains only one gothic plate.[58] Robert Adam's draughtsman, George Richardson, was the most prolific author of designs in this period and produced many very splendid books. None of them contain gothic designs, however, and this is all the more striking in that he was a designer of gothic churches.[59]

Gothic designs were to reappear in ever-increasing number from the first decade of the nineteenth century, but they were to be different in inspiration and intention from those published in the eighteenth century. This review of the pattern-book literature prior to 1800 will have demonstrated that it was small in scale and in circulation, and that its major impact was upon amateur patrons rather than upon the members of the building trades or the architectural profession.

CRITICAL LITERATURE

The theoretical and critical literature of architecture in the eighteenth century in England takes very little notice of gothic architecture. Most of the influential treatises are explicitly partisan in their promotion of Palladianism[60] or of the Greek revival,[61] but even writers with more general concerns—John Gwynn, Robert Morris and Stephen Riou—display considerable inconsistency of attitudes and judgment when they touch on the subject of the gothic style, and this inconsistency is probably the result of indifference. In French architectural literature, by comparison, one can trace a growing appreciation of gothic cathedrals from the work of Félibien des Avaux (1707) to that of Louis Avril (1774).[62] This does not seem to have had any impact on the appreciation of gothic architecture in England, though the French treatises were readily available to English architects in translation.[63]

Robert Morris may be taken as representative of the Palladian school of thought, and his praise of Florence cathedral has already been mentioned.[64] He was far less generous in his analysis of English cathedrals, as the following passage on Westminster Abbey demonstrates:

> . . . it appears only a heavy, lumpish, unrefined mass of materials jumbled together, without design, regularity or order; the middle isle is too long and too high for its breadth: the symmetry of the external part has no analogy to the internal; the multitude of little pillars have no proportion to the parts to which they are connected; the windows are performed without rule, without beauty, or design; and if they happen to start into a kind of proportion, it is only blind chance which inadvertently leads them to it.[65]

Stephen Riou was an apologist of the Greek revival, which he saw as a refinement of existing practice by the application of principles derived from the origins of architectural orthodoxy.[66] His attitude is one of patronising condescension rather than outright dismissal:

> I do not absolutely condemn these extravagancies in the inner decorations and furniture of some particular apartments of a building, or of such works as are made of timber, to be dispersed in different parts of a garden, park, etc. In such situations they afford an agreeable contrast and pleasant variety.—But then let their beauties be always considered as accidental, and not positive.[67]

Clearly the kind of gothic structures and designs proposed in the pattern-books examined in the previous section posed no threat to the interests of Riou. He does show concern, however, about the argument, which was evidently gaining currency by 1760, for the structural superiority of the gothic style, and he dismissed the argument on aesthetic grounds:

> Gothic arches are of so barbarous an aspect, that it is sufficient to condemn them upon that account alone.—The inspection of their summit shows, that this arch is made up of mangled portions of two curves intersecting one another with a harshness as grating as the most repugnant lines in nature.—The superiority of their strength, alledged by some, is not a sufficient motive, all things considered, to render them acceptable.[68]

Arches were the subject of particular interest in 1760, the year of publication of Riou's *Short Principles*, because of controversy between the two great bridge-builders of the age, Robert Mylne and John Gwynn.[69] Although he favoured the semi-circular arch and even induced his friend Dr Johnson to write in support of this position in the arch controversy, Gwynn's writings constitute the most sustained and eloquent advocacy of the gothic style in the eighteenth century.[70]

Gwynn's earliest published comment on the subject, found in his *Essay on Design* (1749), goes a long way towards the position articulated more fully by Hurd in 1762, quoted earlier: "Our Gothic Structures, bad as we esteem them, in comparison with those built after the models of Greece and Rome, are yet generally complete, according to the original Idea of their respective Architects."[71] Although this is a half-hearted defence of the gothic style, Gwynn's genuine concern for the cathedrals is evident in the anger with which he later protests against the cluttering of Westminster Abbey with modern tombs in the classical style.[72] By the date of publication of his most important book, *London and Westminster Improved* (1766), his convictions had strengthened considerably, and Gibbs's building at King's College, Cambridge, provides the occasion for heavy sarcasm directed against the great universities:

> This custom of mixing Gothick and Modern architecture in the same pile of buildings, has also been practised in the University of Oxford, with great success, and serves to show that very little attention is paid to taste and elegance in places where one would expect to find hardly anything else. If these things are suffered to be done merely because they produce variety, they should be told that variety may be produced in Gothick architecture without changing the stile, and that at the same time, a harmony may be produced without destroying the connection of what is already built; in short, very great, noble and elegant things may be done in the Gothick taste, and, with proper attention, not prove so expensive as imagined.[73]

This positive respect for the gothic style is one reason for attributing to John Gwynn the authorship of a very rare book, *English Architecture: or the Public Buildings of London and Westminster*, published in 1758.[74] The preface explains that the work has been undertaken for the instruction of the architectural student, its critical notices of the buildings being intended to establish true taste in judgment of works of architecture and incidentally to establish an outline of the history of the art in England. It is divided into six sections, dealing respectively with churches, palaces, bridges, gates, public buildings, and the City of London. The text consists of 120 double-columned pages, and there are 123 illustrations, twelve of which are fold-outs.[75] A history of each building precedes critical analysis of its architectural features.

Of particular interest is the analysis of Gibbs's St Martin's in the Fields, declared to be "a lasting memorial of the good taste the English had in the science in the eighteenth century''.[76] Gibbs, of course, was the outstanding exception to the Palladian norm of the first half of the century,[77] and Gwynn takes advantage of the opportunity to comment upon the effects of the Palladian movement:

> One book has, with the generality of modern builders, taken the place of all others; and in a manner denied the employment of genius and invention. This is Palladio's: it has made its way into all hands under a variety of forms, and being considered by the generality as the sole model of truth and perfection, stops the progress of the science, and gives a dull sameness to all our buildings.
>
> Perhaps Palladio has in this sense done as much hurt to architecture as in the preventing absurdities and errors he has been of service.
>
> If we allow nothing is faulty that is found in this author, still it does not follow that nothing is beautiful but what is there. Architecture is of great extent; it can adopt great variety without extending the bounds of truth or support of authority; and it is in these liberties the genius of the architect is to shew itself.[78]

In the light of this passage and others quoted above from Gwynn's later work, it is not so surprising that Westminster Abbey, the first building to be examined, should be seen in a very different light from that in which Robert Morris had viewed it in 1734.[79] Gothic architecture, Gwynn declares in the opening sentence of his book, should not be superseded entirely by Grecian architecture, particularly in religious buildings. The triumph of the Greek style has been ''too absolute'', though its pre-eminence is allowed ''by all who have a taste for proportion, dignity or beauty''. He proceeds to relate the history of the Abbey, dwelling particularly upon the beauty of the Chapel of King Henry VII, and comes to the promised analysis of the faults as well as the virtues of the gothic style. The passage is so important for its bearing upon eighteenth-century thought and practice that it warrants quotation in full:

> Although there want in this, and in all Gothick structures, that decent regularity and composed perfection we trace in those edifices, late hands have learned to raise from the Italians, and they from antient Rome and Greece, there is yet a magnificence peculiar to this style which their cold rules cannot reach: this is the character of true, pure, and antient Gothick: and this the practical architect must carefully distinguish from the wild, false, and fantastick modern architecture of that name. This he will see in all its glory in the Abbey; and this, if he be ever employed in Gothick work, he should introduce; avoiding the vain and trifling superfluities.
>
> Let him form a building that has this nobleness of the true Gothick air, banish all those grotesque ornaments: they never fail to draw the censure of little minds that have not genius to comprehend its beauties, or piety to receive the religious impressions it gives of the Deity.
>
> Let him not introduce into his Gothick structure ornaments purely Roman, nor into the temple of the true God symbols of heathen sacrifices: these would be equally absurd. On the contrary, let it be his care to suit the ornaments at once to the architecture, and to the subject.
>
> In examining those which are truly Gothick, he will find always something to admire, as well as to condemn: there is freedom and delicacy in them, though there wants simplicity and nature. These characters let him introduce, while he preserves others; let him retain the elegance of form, and observe nature in the ornaments. This is the method of improvement; and he who shall execute it happily will have the praise of shewing this style of building in its full perfection, without its blemishes, and with all its beauty.

The misfortune of all who have of late attempted the Gothic manner is, that they have too closely copied those who went before them: and in all imitation faults are more sure to be preserved than beauties. We see the errors, and yet continue to practice them. On the contrary, if we would allow in these buildings a little more light, and distribute it better, we should in that improve the manner without deviation from its proper character; and we might somewhat reduce the height of the antient Gothick arches retaining yet enough of their magnificence.

There is an additional praise to the Gothick of which all perhaps are not aware. Many of its old inventions have been copied under the name of new discoveries; and men have had the honour for reviving what their ancestors neglected or exploded. The French, as well as ourselves, have taken many hints from the old Gothick sculpture. It is easy to see wherein it has been absurd or ridiculous, but there is in it a great deal of freedom of drawing which has given the best hints to many a modern hand: the art of adopting the good and separating it from the bad is one of the greatest secrets in the power of an artist.

Nor is it only in the article of drawing that our people have found their advantage in models of the Gothick stile. We value ourselves upon the paper ceilings and ornaments imitating carved wood, formed of that light and cheap wrought material. But it is certain this which we call a new invention in softened and pressed paper formed into figures, is as old as this venerable building. The roses of the principal arch, which appear wood to the eye, are paper.

Let not the reader suppose we are on this occasion setting the Gothick upon a level with the Grecian architecture: we only say that each kind has its place; and lay down the rational manner of employing this, with the true sources of improvement.[80]

The disclaimer of the final paragraph hardly mitigates the surprise of such a lengthy appreciation of the gothic style in architecture and sculpture. The terms in which it is couched are vague and groping, but the comparisons with recent practice show a desire to grasp the qualities of gothic architecture which is very different from the dismissive attitude of Morris or the patronising tone of Riou. Even the freedom of gothic ornament is defended, and ingenuity comparable to the most recent innovations in fashionable architecture is attributed to the gothic architects. Structural considerations play no part in the appreciation, but there is clear perception of ''magnificence'', ''delicacy'', and even ''elegance''.

In differentiating between the true gothic and ''the wild, false, and fantastick modern architecture of that name'' it is possible that Gwynn is denouncing the works of Langley and Halfpenny and other pattern-book authors. Like Robert Morris and Stephen Riou, he was quick to condemn the pretensions of carpenters and gardeners to expertise in architectural design. But it is more likely that he used the term ''modern'' to cover Elizabethan and Jacobean architecture, characterised by the mingling of styles against which he constantly inveighed.[81] Support for this reading comes from John Aheron's *A General Treatise on Architecture* (1754), which thus defines ''modern'': ''this Word in its genuine Meaning, is only applicable to such Architecture as partakes partly of the Gothic, retaining somewhat of its Delicacy and Solidity; partly of the Antique, whence it borrows Members and Ornaments without any Proportion or Judgment.'' The same author's definition of gothic is a useful reminder that Gwynn's appreciation of the style was exceptional: ''Gothic architecture is that which is far removed from the Manner and Proportions of the Antique, having its Ornaments wild and chimerical, and its Profiles incorrect.''[82]

6. E. F. Burney, *Portrait of Thomas Gray*, 1799. Courtesy of the Lewis Walpole Library, Farmington, Connecticut.

AMATEUR AND ANTIQUARIAN STUDIES

Walpole is at the centre of amateur and antiquarian studies in the eighteenth century, and his writings on the subject of the gothic style parallel closely those of John Gwynn in pleading passionately for a detailed study of the style:

> Considering how scrupulously our architects confine themselves to antique precedent, perhaps some deviations into Gothic may relieve them from that servile imitation. I mean that they should study both tastes, not blend them; that they should dare to invent in the one, since they will hazard nothing in the other. When they have built a pediment and portico to the Sibyl's circular temple, and tacked the wings to a house by a colonnade, they seem *au bout de leur latin*. [83]

Before this splendid denunciation of current Palladian practice, however, Walpole, like Gwynn, made it quite clear that he implied no comparison between "the rational beauties

7. Joshua Reynolds, *Portrait of Thomas Pitt*, oil on canvas, Courtesy of the Plymouth City Art Gallery.

of regular architecture, and the unrestrained licentiousness of that which is called Gothic''. Nor did he condone recent attempts at gothic architecture, criticising those of Inigo Jones, Sir Christopher Wren and William Kent.[84] But his criticism ended with a haunting question—''Is an art despicable in which a great master cannot shine?''

The uneasy tension which their simultaneous respect for the classical heritage of architecture and devotion to the national heritage of the gothic style imposed upon the amateurs and antiquaries of the eighteenth century is evident in the ambidexterity of their architectural efforts. All of the amateurs designed buildings in the classical style as well as in the gothic style, and Sanderson Miller, who is most closely associated with the gothic revival, was far more competent in the designing of Palladian architecture.[85] The tension also appears in the correspondence of the amateurs and antiquarians. Thomas Gray (Plate 6), for instance, had a major influence on the study of gothic architecture, yet when he heard that Thomas Wharton was proposing some gothic alterations to his house in 1754, he wrote: ''If you project anything, I hope it will be entirely within indoors; and don't let me (when I am gaping into Coleman-street) be directed to the Gentleman's at the ten Pinnacles, or with the Church-porch at his door.''[86]

Gray's approach to the study of gothic architecture was remarkable for the pragmatism of his aesthetic judgment. ''Call this what you will,'' he is reported to have said of a gothic building, ''but you must allow that it is beautiful''.[87] His methods of historical research were equally pragmatic, as William Mason attested: ''He did not so much depend upon written accounts, as upon that internal evidence which the buildings themselves give of

16

their respective antiquity."[88] Such an approach demanded continued and ever-expanding personal observation of the monuments of the gothic style. This was characteristic of Gray's own studies;[89] their influence upon the historical formulations of Wharton in 1763 and Bentham in 1771 is documented by Clark and Frankl.[90]

The influence of Gray can be further documented in the case of an unpublished manuscript by his former pupil at Cambridge, Thomas Pitt (Plate 7), who was to provide designs in the gothic style for Walpole at Strawberry Hill and for his uncle Charles Lyttelton, President of the Society of Antiquaries.[91] Gray had persuaded Pitt to accompany Lord Strathmore on the Grand Tour, beginning in Portugal and Spain, in 1760.[92] The visit was of particular interest to English antiquarians in that it provided the first known opportunity to test pragmatically the validity of Sir Christopher Wren's "Saracenic" theory of the origin of the gothic style,[93] and the manuscript was passed eagerly from hand to hand upon Pitt's return in 1762.[94] "From him I hope to get much information concerning Spain, which no body has seen," Gray wrote to Wharton. "He is no bad observer."[95] The original manuscript has been lost, but fortunately a copy was made in 1772 by William Cole, and it fully justifies the high opinion Gray had of his former pupil.[96]

Pitt was not impressed by classical architecture in the peninsula, but dilated upon what Gray called "remains of Moorish magnificence".[97] The church of Batalha, Portugal, enters into the literature of the gothic revival at this point, and it is possible that James Murphy, who devoted a splendid monograph to that building in 1795, was indebted to the account of Pitt.[98] Pitt's praise certainly was calculated to arouse interest: "This convent is of the most elaborate and exquisite Gothic architecture I ever saw: one part being left imperfect, being so beautiful, that nobody dared to finish it."[99] The interest was considerably increased by the attribution of the building to an English architect, an attribution Murphy was to make his own.[100]. The cathedrals of Segovia, Cordoba, Seville and Granada, and the Cistercian monastery at Alcobaça all receive praise from the young connoisseur, and the phrase "tho' not in the best taste", which occurs frequently, does little to lessen the impact of such serious study of gothic buildings.

Of particular interest are Pitt's comments on the Royal Palace at Granada: "It is impossible to lay down any Plan of the Moorish Palace, as they never seem to have taken more than one apartment into their idea at once, without regarding the communications or symmetry of the whole."[101] This is a more penetrating remark on planning than is to be found in any contemporary or earlier discussions of the gothic style. Pitt is also the first to use the term "Castle Gothic" of English architecture, in the course of his remarks on the cathedral of Lisbon: "The Capitals are Grotesque Gothic, like our Saxon. Over this (western) porch is a kind of list of corbels with masks, like our Castle Gothic."[102] The effectiveness of this manuscript was considerably enhanced by the sketches of plans, elevations, sections and details with which it was accompanied (Plates 8–11).[103] The originals have not been found, and Thomas Pitt was a weak draughtsman. But even in the copies by Cole they retain considerable interest. Pitt, like other amateur architects, was not weaned from the classical style by his love of gothic architecture; indeed, he is responsible for the rebuilding of Stowe House, the largest and most completely realised private neo-classical building in the world. But it is interesting that even in this thoroughly neo-classical building, the library by John Soane is a perfect gem of the gothic revival.[104]

It was partly on the basis of his knowledge of Spanish architecture that Johann Heinrich Müntz felt competent to issue in London on 12 April, 1760, *Proposals for Publishing by Subscription a Course of Gothic Architecture*, another venture not destined to be realised, but one whose scope is worth examination.[105] Its particular interest lies in the

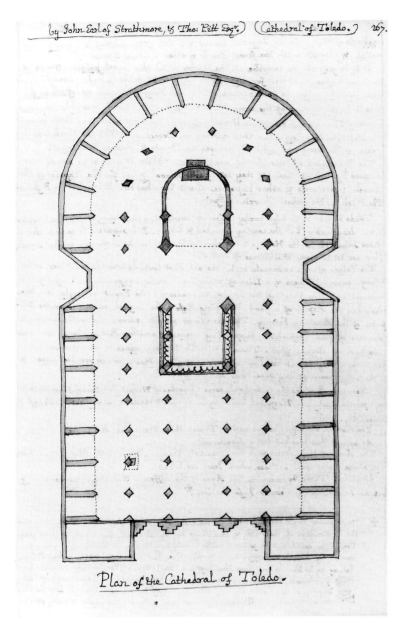

in the Angles, which support an elegant Rib-work, meeting in a Knot in the Centre, as in the Old Sea at Lisbon: which it resembles likewise in having an Isle round it on the Out side, with a Range of 9 Chapels, gilt in the richest & most elegant Taste, dedicated to different Saints, & ornamented with Imagery, Paintings &c. so as to have a very noble Effect.

The Columns which support the Vaulting of this Isle, or Passage, against the Wall of the Capella Mor, are curious. They stand upon a continued Pedestal, about a Foot & ½ high: their Shafts are thick & short, & their Mouldings much resembling the Roman or Grecian. Their Capitals consist of 2 broad Leaves, joined at the Bottom with a Shell, & turning outwards at the Points, in the Manner of a Volute, with another broad pointed flat Leaf between them. The Square over this Capital does not correspond to the Plinth, on which the Column stands, being placed angular, & presenting its Angle & two Sides: whereas the Plinth stands square, in the ordinary Manner.

Pillars round the Outside of the Choir at Alcobaça, in the Isle, placed against the Wall, to support the Arches of the Vaulting: which have the only round Arches in the Building.

"I have represented the Shaft of the Column too thick & clumsy. Wm Cole."

Plan of the Cathedral of Toledo.

8. (*left*) William Cole after Thomas Pitt, *Plan of the Cathedral of Toledo*, ink and wash, 326 × 200 mm, 1772. Courtesy of the British Library.

9. (*right*) William Cole after Thomas Pitt, *Pillars of the Choir at Alcobaça*, ink, 190 × 181 mm, 1772. Courtesy of the British Library.

emphasis given to the structure of the gothic arch and vaulting, which was to be the principal subject-matter of the first part of the work. Müntz had been an engineer with the French army, and his analysis of gothic structure would have been of the greatest importance to the gothic revival had he found enough subscribers to have been able to continue with the project.[106] The application of his theory was to be given in the second part, and the third was to have illustrated the structural principles by designs drawn from gothic buildings in Spain and elsewhere. The final section was to provide measured details of gothic ornaments and designs for internal decoration and garden buildings. A further advantage of the book was that it would have supplied descriptions of the architectural instruments of Müntz's invention for executing any of these designs.

This certainly places Müntz in a far more respectable role than that of contributor to the carpenter's pattern-book of Manwaring.[107] Several of the illustrations for the proposed book fortunately survive, and there are some other drawings by Müntz which can be associated with it.[108] Two prints for trefoil and quatrefoil ornaments (Plates 12 and 13), found among Müntz's drawings, were probably among the engravings for the

Observations on Spain & Portugal made in 1760

A Sè velha di Lisboa.

Arches & Ambulatory in the Nave of the Old See [or Sè velha] in Lisbon.

The modern Ornaments make it difficult what to reject or represent Building. I have left out the large Corinthian Capitals, & marble Pedestal have been added within Memory. The Fire has burnt off most of the Ca

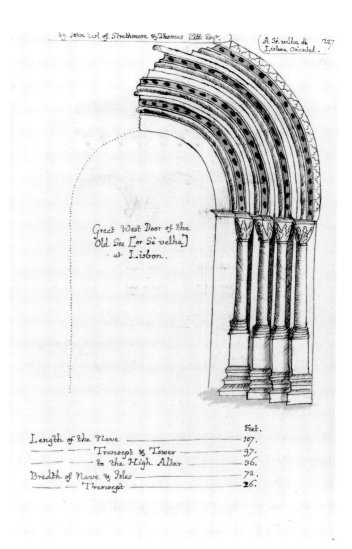

by John Earl of Strathmore & Thomas Pitt Esqr.

A Sè velha di Lisboa Oriental.

Great West Door of the Old See [or Sè velha] at Lisbon.

	Feet.
Length of the Nave	107.
Transept & Tower	97.
to the High Altar	36.
Bredth of Nave & Isles	72.
Transept	26.

work that were available for inspection by prospective subscribers. With them is a drawing signed and dated ''J. H. Müntz. Londini, 1760'', which shows a gothic window intricately ornamented and evidently intended to have accompanying instructions, since there is a rubric *AE* inked on the centre light (Plate 14).[109]

From Horace Walpole's extra-illustrated *Description of Strawberry Hill* (1784) come two drawings of the south door of St Alban's Abbey, signed and dated, one 1759 (Plate 15), the second 1762 (Plate V), which is interesting in that it shows that Walpole collected Müntz drawings after the two men had quarrelled at the end of 1759.[110] These drawings had an immediate impact on the gothic revival, since Walpole used them as models for internal decoration at Strawberry Hill (Plate 116).[111] The second drawing is an elaboration of the lower half of the first, and was probably intended for publication in the third section of the proposed book. With these drawings may be associated the *Tomb of Caducanus* from the De

10. (*left*) William Cole after Thomas Pitt, *Arches of the Cathedral of Lisbon*, ink, 172 × 127 mm, 1772. Courtesy of the British Library.

11. (*right*) William Cole after Thomas Pitt, *Door of the Cathedral of Lisbon*, ink and wash, 198 × 248 mm, 1772. Courtesy of the British Library.

12 and 13. Johann Heinrich Müntz, *Designs for Gothic Ornaments*, 1760. Courtesy of the Lewis Walpole Library, Farmington, Connecticut.

Fig. I

Fig. II

14. Johann Heinrich Müntz, *Design for a Gothic Window*, ink and wash, 203 × 89 mm, 1760. Courtesy of the Lewis Walpole Library, Farmington, Connecticut.

15. Johann Heinrich Müntz, *View in the Abbey of St. Alban's, Herts.*, ink and wash, 457 × 283 mm, 1759. Courtesy of the Lewis Walpole Library, Farmington, Connecticut.

16. Johann Heinrich Müntz, *The Tomb of Caducanus, Bishop of Hereford*, ink and wash, 256 × 175 mm, 1759. Courtesy of the Musées Royaux des Beaux Arts, Brussels.

Grez collection in the Musée Royale of Brussels, signed and dated 1759 (Plate 16).[112] This is one of the most beautiful of Müntz's drawings, taken directly from the monument, which was in Richard Bateman's house at Old Windsor.

Other drawings of Müntz, which will be discussed in a later chapter, are so finished and

17. Johann Heinrich Müntz, *Section of an Egyptian Room for Lord Charlemont*, ink and wash, 267 × 267 mm, 1762. Courtesy of the Lewis Walpole Library, Farmington, Connecticut.

18. Johann Heinrich Müntz, *Design for a Garden Building*, ink and wash, 275 × 200 mm, 1755. Courtesy of the Hampshire County Record Office.

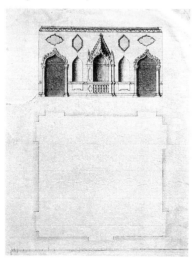

so detailed that they would probably have found their way into his intended publication. The ''Temple for a Garden'' to which he refers in his advertisement, is probably the ''Egyptian Room'' intended to be built for Lord Charlemont at Marino in Dublin, drawings for which survive in the Lewis Walpole Library (Plate 17).[113] An unsigned and undated drawing among the drawings of John Chute, which I ascribe to Müntz, shows alternative elevations and a plan for a garden seat, and this too may have been intended for the final section of his work (Plate 18).[114]

Precision and hardness characterise Müntz's engravings, as one might expect from the sentence of the advertisement written in his characteristically disjointed English: ''Part the first, which as it will be very intricate, and to have every line true, the Author proposes to engrave himself.'' The use of mathematical instruments is evident in all of Müntz's drawings as well as in his engravings, and it is no surprise that he expected ''Descriptions of the Instruments required for that Purpose'' to be a major attraction of his publication. The drawings, however, are very attractive and soft, and Müntz is a master of wash, using it to diffuse light in a way that suggests the poetry and mystery in which the schematised geometry of gothic structure and ornament is softened in reality. No more correct or more faithful interpreter of the gothic style than Müntz was to appear in the eighteenth century, and the failure of his projected publication is to be regretted.[115]

Müntz's designs relate to florid or late gothic architecture, and this may explain the failure of his project to achieve support among English antiquarians.[116] The President of the Society of Antiquaries of London was Charles Lyttelton, who became Dean of Exeter in 1748 and Bishop of Carlisle in 1762.[117] Lyttelton maintained an extensive correspondence on antiquarian matters with Sanderson Miller, who had designed alterations for his house, and with other potential historians of the gothic style.[118] His particular scholarly achievement lay in differentiating between the Norman and Saxon styles, and he read a paper on this subject to the Society in 1742, which is reported by Dr Ducarel in *Anglo-Norman Antiquities considered in a Tour through Part of Normandy* (1767, though the tour was made in 1752). This is dedicated to Lyttelton and supports the findings Lyttelton had communicated to the Society. It seems unlikely that Müntz's predilection for later gothic would have found a sympathetic response in Lyttelton, and, besides, the latter was at this time a close correspondent of Horace Walpole, with whom Müntz had quarrelled.[119] A further reason for the lack of Lyttelton's support may have lain in jealousy for the achievement of his nephew Thomas Pitt, who was currently sending him the first accounts of Moorish architecture, and who was to be engaged on gothic alterations for his uncle and for Walpole immediately upon his return from Europe.

Through contact with Walpole and Thomas Pitt, Lyttelton would undoubtedly have been aware of the researches of Gray, who was the first to propose the pointed arch as the distinguishing feature of gothic style and construction. This was a subject on which Lyttelton had corresponded with Charles Mason in 1753,[120] and five years later, when James Bentham, who learned of Gray's theory from the poet personally, decided to write the history of gothic architecture, it was to Charles Lyttelton that he first confided his intention.[121] Lyttelton had been the chief adviser on the details of the restoration of Ely carried out by James Essex from 1759.[122] There is little doubt, therefore, that Lyttelton was aware of the researches of Essex and of his intention to write the history of gothic architecture. Quite probably, when Müntz's proposal was published in 1760, Lyttelton and the Society of Antiquaries felt that enough English scholars were at work on the subject and there was no point in their encouraging a foreign architect to pursue it.

The failure of Essex to publish his book on gothic architecture may well be related to Lyttelton's decision to back the publication of Bentham. By 1769, when Essex first revealed his intention to Walpole, Lyttelton and Walpole were no longer on terms of easy correspondence, and Walpole had ceased to be an active member of the Society of Antiquaries. He and Essex had a mutual friend in William Cole, who was a firm supporter of the architect and his projected publication.[123] Walpole's letters to Cole reveal that all was in readiness for publication at the end of 1770, but he added ominously: "it will never appear, while I am in being".[124] There is no reason to suppose from this that Walpole was personally averse to the publication by Essex, but it implies his knowledge of factors that would prevent the publication. It is reasonable to suppose that this obstacle was the historical essay by Bentham published in 1771 in *History and Antiquities of Ely*.[125] Essex's letters to Walpole reveal his sensitivity to competition.[126] Had Bentham, and by implication Lyttelton, been in favour of his project, he would have had no need to turn to Walpole for reassurance.

From the Walpole correspondence it is clear that Essex's book would have been technical in nature, and Pevsner's analysis of the Essex Papers confirm this.[127] Walpole proposed that he and Cole should write the historical sections of the volume, however, so he evidently had no faith in Essex's ability to treat the subject-matter historically.[128] His view may well have been shared by Bentham and Lyttelton, and this also would explain their failure to support Essex. The nature of Essex's contribution would have been the same as that of Müntz, and the antiquarians of the eighteenth century showed no appreci-

19. Anonymous, *Portrait of Sanderson Miller*, oil on canvas, 752 × 635 mm, *c*.1755. Courtesy of the Royal Academy and the National Trust.

ation of the advantages of structural analysis to the history of architecture, though Gray's arch theory, given currency by Bentham, pointed obviously in that direction.[129]

A further unpublished history of gothic architecture, one which indeed never got beyond the planning stage, was that of Sanderson Miller (Plate 19), who was vigorously supported by Charles Lyttelton and the members of the Society of Antiquaries.[130] This is first noted in 1750 when Lyttelton approached Smart Lethulieur on the subject and received the enthusiastic response: "He is, I believe, a gentleman every way qualified for it."[131] William Borlase was equally enthusiastic, and it appears from a letter written in 1754 that some progress had been made by Miller in planning the proposed history: "I hope Mr. Miller goes on with his Treatise of Building, of which he was so kind as to show me the Plan; 'tis great pity it should not be pursued."[132] The following year he wrote after a meeting with Miller: "By Mr. Miller's conversation at Oxford I was in hopes that the introduction of the different kinds of architecture into the West should have been fixed e'er this and a sample of the alterations of every age given from proper subjects. Mr Miller, I should think is very able to do this."[133]

The only trace of the proposed treatise that has survived among the Sanderson Miller papers is a note in his Diary under the date 16 August, 1756: "Writing design for the Hist. of Architecture in Britain."[134] However, the high esteem in which Miller was held as an authority on antiquarian matters is witnessed in several other manuscripts. Deane Swift, cousin of the more famous Dean, wrote from Ireland that he imagined Miller to be leading an epicurean life in Warwickshire—"Quantum mutatus ab Antiquario, Metaphysico, Academico."[135] We are justified, therefore, in tracing his antiquarian interests to his Oxford years, when Swift shared his studies. That Miller did not lose his enthusiasm for such pursuits is evident from a passage relating to Conway Castle from George Lyttelton's *Gentleman's Tour through Wales*: "The stonework of the windows is exceeding handsome. Had our friend Miller been with us, he would have fallen down and adored the architect."[136] Nor did his failure to complete the treatise affect the high regard in which other antiquarians held him. Daines Barrington wrote to Charles Lyttelton on 10 January, 1768: "I am infinitely flattered by Mr. Miller's having supposed that Caerphilly was built about the time of Edward the 1st. I know well that he hath a better right to determine this matter than all the architects (and I had almost said antiquaries) of Europe put together."[137]

It must not be supposed that Miller was uncritically enthusiastic about the gothic style, however. Recent gothic improvements at Horton House, Northamptonshire, moved him to heavy sarcasm in a letter of 16 September, 1750, to Charles Lyttelton:

> Mr. Garret is there and is going to make *Gothic* bridges, the which I find are thought very pretty, because there never were any such things seen before. The Temple of Cloacina is of that sort, it should rather be called his castle. I believe it cost more than your Rotunda; it is paved with marble, wainscotted with mahogany, and is really what is commonly called wonderfully fine. I could say with great truth to my Lord when asked my opinion that it was the finest thing, and most extraordinary I ever saw.[138]

One might be reading a diatribe by Morris, Riou or Gwynn against thoughtless novelties in architecture. The passage inevitably recalls the indignation of Walpole upon visiting the gothic temple at Pains Hill in Surrey in 1761:

> The whole is an unmeaning edifice. In all Gothic designs, they should be made to imitate something that was of that time, a part of a Church, a castle, a convent, or a mansion. The Goths never built summer houses or temples in a garden. This at Mr. Hamilton's stands on the brow of a hill—there an imitation of a fort or watch-tower had been properer.[139]

Miller and Walpole never became friends, and their architectural works differed in style considerably, but their theoretical stance did not, and they shared with other antiquarians an interest in the history of gothic architecture.

Before concluding this review of the early literature of the gothic revival, it will be useful to remind ourselves that the subject was of exceptional rather than consuming interest to architects and others in the eighteenth century. Five years after the publication of Bentham's treatise a prize essay was delivered in Oxford by Thomas Lowth on the subject of architecture. It was very severe upon the gothic style; indeed, the only thing it found to say in defence of gothic was that its dimness was suited to religious purposes.[140]

Even a practitioner of the gothic revival could be dispassionate enough on the subject to satirise it publicly. Richard Bentley's play, *The Wishes*,[141] features two antiquarians,

Pantaloon and Doctor. Pantaloon's fortune is sought by Harlequin through Pantaloon's daughter, Isabella, but in order to win her hand and save her from marriage to the Doctor, Harlequin has to become a member of the Society of Antiquaries. The Society's oath reads as follows:

> I, A.B., do from my soul abhor and renounce that Damnable and Detestable Doctrine that Athens and Rome ever had, or now have, or ever ought to have had, any right, claim or pretension whatever, to impose upon these Kingdoms any pretended taste or elegance, either in Architecture, Painting, Statuary or Writing. And I do hereby declare my fixed and determined resolution to defend with my life and fortune the original, lawful and sole title in these realms of Gothic, Chinese, Modern-Antique and their descendants by any mixture whatever, and I do further declare and protest my utter abhorence and dislike of the dangerous and abominable tenets contained in certain books not to be tolerated—entitled the Ruins of Balbek and Palmyra, more particularly a still later performance in Architecture by one Cha—.[142]

II. Garden Buildings in the Gothic Style

Perhaps the earliest appearance of the gothic style in garden buildings in the eighteenth century occurs at the head of the canal in the formal garden at Shotover, Oxfordshire (Plate 20).[1] The architect has not been identified with certainty, but Mavis Batey has argued that the craftsmanship necessary for its erection would have been found among the mason-sculptors of Oxford, and the circumstantial evidence points to William Townesend.[2] The temple might therefore be considered an example of gothic survival rather than of its revival,[3] but I think this is true only in a technical sense. There can be little doubt that the choice of the gothic style was dictated by the political ideology of its owner, James Tyrrell, and this marks it as a new phenomenon in garden architecture, a building which declares its owner's political allegiance by its emphatic separateness from surrounding buildings. No such purpose had been intended or served by gothic buildings in earlier centuries.

The temple is a vaulted arcade of three bays on the ground floor (Plate 22). The first floor is pierced by a rose window and two triangular windows set beneath the battle-mented triangular pitch of the roof, which sports a solid pinnacle at its apex. Hexagonal turrets richly decorated with ogee arches rise to either side in four stages, the upper stages being pierced. Niches are hollowed out of the turrets at the ground level to provide sheltered seating. To quote Mavis Batey: "The Shotover temple is authentic and self-assured and does not anticipate rococo frivolity or romantic feelings for decay; it is not half-hidden like a hermitage but is on the main axis of the house and seen prominently from all the principal rooms".[4] If one accepts it as the first gothic garden building of the revival, built about 1717, then the revival can be said to have sprung full-blown like Athena from the head of Zeus, or perhaps Britannia from the head of Alfred!

Britannia was not to be monopolised by one party, however. The theme next appears in the eminently Tory estate of Lord Bathurst, Cirencester Park in Gloucestershire, at Alfred's Hall, also known as King Arthur's Castle (Plate 21).[5] This was begun in 1721, and was developed over the next decade from a wood structure to a substantial battle-mented two-storeyed lodge with round towers at each end but not aligned to each other. Bathurst was delighted with it, and boasted to Pope: "I will venture to assert that all Europe cannot show such a pretty little plain work in the Brobdingnag style as what I have executed here".[6] Once bitten by the taste for gothic, Bathurst continued to erect buildings in the style, but, like Alfred's Hall, they were well removed from the house and located on the fringes of Oakley Wood rather than in the Home Park.[7]

Whigs like James Tyrrell of Shotover tended to take their gothic more seriously, and

20. The Gothic Temple and Canal at Shotover, Oxon., *c.*1717. Courtesy of *Country Life*.

22. (*facing page*) The Gothic Temple at Shotover, Oxon., *c.*1717. Courtesy of *Country Life*.

21. Alfred's Hall, Cirencester, Glos., *c.*1722. Courtesy of the Royal Commission on the Historic Monuments of England.

23. James Gibbs, The Temple of Liberty, Stowe, Bucks., 1741. Courtesy of the Royal Commission on the Historic Monuments of England.

the most splendid of the political temples in the gothic style is that found in the heart of Whiggery, Stowe, Buckinghamshire. This was the Temple of Liberty designed for Lord Cobham by James Gibbs in 1741 (Plate 23).[8] This triangular temple can be read as an elaboration in depth of the Shotover Temple, and it bore the legend ''I thank God that I am not a Roman''[9]—which is rather ironic, since Gibbs was a Roman Catholic by birth and had a Roman architectural training. Its prominent triangulation constituted a defiance in geometry of the tyranny of the square and circle of classical principles of design associated with Inigo Jones's introduction of Italian renaissance architecture at the Stuart court. By extension it was read as a declaration of Protestant individualism against Catholic uniformity, and of the virtues of constitutional monarchy against the doctrine of the Divine Right of Kings.[10] Lest anybody miss the point, the seven statues of the Saxon deities stood in a solemn ring outside the temple.[11].

A later example of a triangular tower in the gothic style is the most massive of these structures (Plate 24). It was designed by the Burlingtonian architect Henry Flitcroft[12] in 1762 and stands 160 feet high at the edge of the estate of the Tory banker Henry Hoare, at Stourhead in Wiltshire. Henry Hoare's correspondence informs us that its erection was motivated by the accession and recent military victories of "our truely British King George the 3rd". An earlier letter had wished power to the King, "so long as He glorys in the name of Briton & detests the German connections".[13] Clearly the ramifications of the iconography of Alfred and the gothic style grew more confused as the century progressed![14] The political and nationalistic associations of the gothic style were of importance in legitimising its revival in classical landscape gardens; but this was a short-lived impulse, and the style was to continue as a feature of the landscape garden for less ideologically motivated reasons.[15]

24. Henry Flitcroft, Alfred's Tower, Stourhead, Wilts., 1762. Courtesy of the Royal Commission on the Historic Monuments of England.

WILLIAM KENT

William Kent effected the revolution in the design of landscape gardens which was to do away with formal canals such as that at Shotover which lay between the classical house and the gothic temple. He designed an octagonal pavilion and an obelisk for James Tyrrell's son, Colonel Tyrrell, who succeeded to Shotover in 1719.[16] No gothic building was erected by Kent here, but perhaps it is just as significant that he did not demolish the gothic temple. He had such respect for William Townesend, the presumed architect of the gothic temple, that he designed a building in his honour at nearby Rousham, the estate of Colonel Tyrrell's friends, Colonel Robert Dormer and his brother General James Dormer, for whom Townesend had built a raised terrace in 1725.[17]

Kent began to remodel the Rousham landscape about 1737, and in the middle distance of the view from the classical Vale of Venus he dressed up the ends of Cuttle Mill in the gothic style with a pair of buttresses flying in to support the stepped triangle of the roof-line which was pierced by a quatrefoil window and ornamented with crocketed pinnacles (Plate 25). On the hill beyond he focussed the view with a vaguely gothic eyecatcher of

25. William Kent, Cuttle Mill, Rousham, Oxon., c.1740. Courtesy of *Country Life*.

26. William Kent, *View from the Vale of Venus, Rousham, Oxon.,* c. 1740. Courtesy of Rousham House, Oxon.

three arches. These buildings clearly have no symbolic, allegorical or iconographical import; they are sketches in stone, providing points of compositional reference for the viewer and highlighting by contrast the carefully finished classicism of the principal garden features, which have been analysed by Kenneth Woodbridge (Plate 26). This was a function of the gothic style in the landscape garden which was to prove a continuing justification for the erection of buildings in this style throughout the century. They are to be found usually on the boundaries of landscape gardens, designed to be viewed from a distance and pretending neither to accuracy of detail nor depth of structure.[18] Usually they are backed or framed by plantations of wood, since gothic was a ''natural'' style.[19] By extension of association, it was frequently used for entrance gates.

The associations of nature and religion with the gothic style also made it inevitable that it should become the prevalent mode for the building of garden hermitages. But William Kent may be credited with popularising the theme by publishing the section and elevation of Merlin's Cave at Richmond, which he designed for Queen Caroline in 1733 (Plate 27).[20] Its roof was thatched, its columns had the appearance of rugged tree-trunks, and it emerged from a setting of rocks and trees in a suitably primitive manner. Since it was a royal building, it was quickly interpreted as a medium for weighty political

messages, but its influence on the design of garden buildings long outlived any ideological burden inflicted on it by its owner or contemporary political commentators.[21]

PALLADIAN GOTHIC

Among the surviving drawings of William Kent are two for a garden temple at Aske Hall near Richmond, Yorkshire (Plate 28).[22] This was built as a large and richly decorated

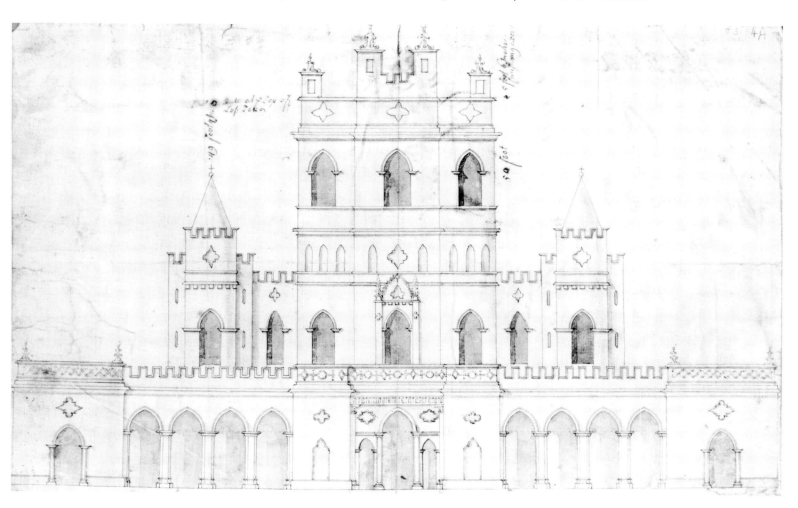

octagonal tower of three storeys, flanked by lower square towers with semicircular bows, all set on a high gothic arcade ending in circular bastions. It was ascribed to Daniel Garrett by Barbara Jones,[23] and Peter Leach's reconstruction of the career of this architect confirms her attribution.[24] To Garrett as executive architect can be attributed also the nearby Oliver's Ducket, a delightful battlemented round tower on a bastion base that recalls his finishing of the Mausoleum at Castle Howard, the best-known of his works, and one at which he again acted as the executive of a design agreed upon by the Burlingtonians, principally Sir Thomas Robinson.[25] Daniel Garrett emerges therefore as the most direct successor of William Kent in the practice of gothic design in garden buildings. Sir Thomas Robinson wrote of him to Lord Carlisle in 1736: "My Lord Burlington has a much better opinion of Mr. Garrett's knowledge and judgement than of Mr. Flitcroft's or any person whatever, except Mr. Kent."[26]

The Aske Hall Temple, with open and blind arcades of pointed arches, round, pointed, trefoil and quatrefoil windows, emphatic horizontal string-courses which sometimes function as labels to the windows, prominent drip-course and battlements on the bows, and its openwork parapet, is a repertoire in stone of the decorative motifs of the early stage of the gothic revival. But this profusion of gothic ornament makes no attempt to disguise the classical symmetry and proportional planning of its varied volumes. In this it is comparable to Kent's Merlin's Cave, and to the other principal garden building attributable to Garrett, the Banqueting House at Gibside, Co. Durham, erected for George Bowes from 1751.[27] A delightfully reticent example of gothic details on a Palladian body—to paraphrase Pugin—is the garden seat of uncertain date at Raby Castle, Co. Durham.[28]

Garrett also provided Raby Castle with a wonderful Vanbrughian eyecatcher, the lack of substance of which is blatantly declared by a painted gothic window of four lights above the central round arch.[29] In function and form it continues the patterns set by Kent's eyecatcher at Rousham, and its more abstract patterns suit its siting at a distance from the observer. For Sir Walter Blackett of Wallington Hall, Northumberland, in 1745, he provided a more extensive eyecatcher of some complexity, which was so oddly decorated that it is probable that Thomas Wright of Durham, who was responsible for the nearby Codger's Fort for the same patron that year, and who is noted for eccentric decoration, succeeded Garrett in this commission.[30]

Garrett died the same year as Lord Burlington, 1753, and the buildings he had in hand were completed by James Paine, who had been nurtured in the Palladian tradition but shared Garrett's evident delight in the decorative elegance of rococo and gothic motifs.[31] The Palladian tradition of design in gothic garden buildings is appropriately concluded by Garrett's constant supporter, Sir Thomas Robinson of Rokeby Hall, who provided architectural designs for Bishop Trevor at Bishop Auckland Palace, Co. Durham, from 1757.[32] They include a large deer-house, with a stately, measured arcade which James Macaulay has characterised as "a set of cloisters turned inside out", and the gatehouse at the town entrance to the castle (Plate 29).[33] This is clearly Palladian in its proportions, and it shares the reticence of the Raby Castle garden seat, with its slightly sunken panels for decoration. The gateway is notable as an instance of a Palladian use of the Batty Langley pattern-book. The clustered columns of the gateway are from Plate 10 of *Ancient Architecture Restored and Improved*, titled "The Fourth Order of the Gothick Architecture."[34] Another instance is by Isaac Ware, who was very closely associated with Sir Thomas Robinson.[35] His gateway at Eythrope House for Sir William Stanhope is shown in two drawings in the British Library (Plates 30–1). It features prominently the strip labels or hoods over the windows and ground-floor buttressing such as Langley had shown.[36]

Another northern set of gothic buildings in a park was that at Stainborough or Wentworth Castle, so vast that Horace Walpole, on visiting his friend Lord Strafford there in 1768, described it as "the ruins of a large imaginary city on an opposite hill, well placed".[37] It marked the site of a Danish encampment, and a statue of Strafford in Roman military dress was set on a high pedestal within the complex of four towers. This has been attributed to James Gibbs, but it is far more likely that it is the design of Lord Strafford himself, another amateur architect with a high reputation for design in the classical manner.[38] The four towers are accounted for in payments recorded in the Strafford Papers from 1727, and it is probable that they started life as lath-and-plaster eyecatchers and were later given more lasting form in stone.[39] Walpole himself contributed to Lord Strafford's garden buildings in suggesting the delightful building in the menagerie that Richard Bentley drew on the model of Chichester Cross in 1756 (Plate

29. Sir Thomas Robinson, Gateway to Bishop Auckland Castle, Co. Durham, *c*.1760. Courtesy of the Royal Commission on the Historic Monuments of England.

35

30. Isaac Ware, *Elevation of a Gateway for Eythrope, M'sex*, ink and wash, 302 × 443 mm, 1751. Courtesy of the British Library.

31. Isaac Ware, *Elevation of a Gateway for Eythrope, M'sex*, ink and wash, 292 × 450 mm, 1751. Courtesy of the British Library.

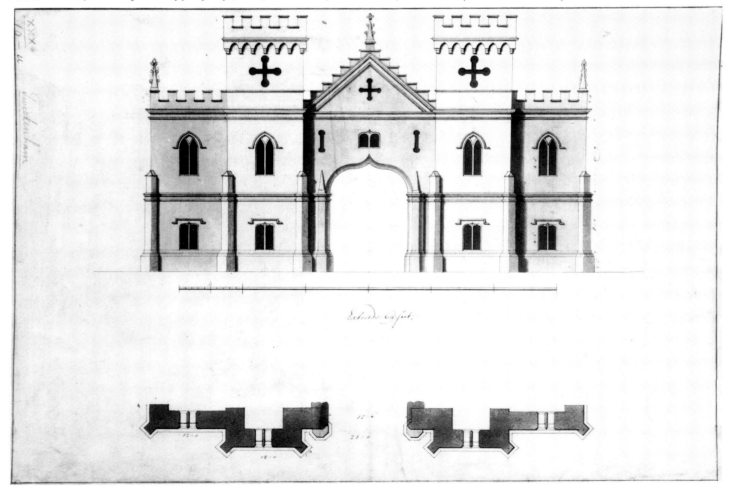

32. Richard Bentley, *Elevation of a Menagery for Wentworth Castle, Yorks.*, ink, 160 × 160 mm, 1756. Courtesy of the Lewis Walpole Library, Farmington, Connecticut.

32). In the work of Bentley it is an instance of evident dependence on an antiquarian source, and the credit for this initiative in the design of garden buildings must be given to Walpole.[40]

RICHARD BENTLEY

More typical of the work of Bentley is the farmhouse built for the Countess of Suffolk at Marble Hill and called the Priory of St Hubert, a pun upon her surname, Hobart (Plate 33). It can be dated by a letter written by Walpole in his inimitable manner to John Chute on 29 June, 1758: "My Lady Suffolk has at last entirely submitted her barn to our ordination. As yet it is only in Deacon's order but will very soon have our last imposition of hands".[41] This was a matter of putting a false front to a building, and is clearly a development of Kent's initiative at Cuttle Mill in the Rousham landscape. Similar in character is the design for a fictitious steeple for Nicholas Hardinge, made to stand on a roof in Kingston-on-Thames to which it bore no structural relationship, though it could claim usefulness in that it bore a clock and a weather-vane (Plate 34). It is a beautiful composition, dated 1753 by Walpole on the verso of the drawing. A hexagonal cone is set on an open decorated "drum" resting on a square base supported by flying buttresses. Perpendicular gothic decoration is used for the panels of the buttresses and for the pinnacles, windows and niches, and the clock-face is shaped into a quatrefoil.

The use of these deceptions was open to the charge of childishness and frivolity, and Walpole had to defend it from an author for whom he had the greatest respect, Thomas

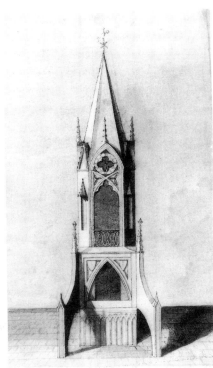

33. Richard Bentley, *Elevation of a Barn for Marble Hill, Twickenham, M'sex*, ink and wash, 333 × 272 mm, 1758. Courtesy of the Lewis Walpole, Library, Farmington, Connecticut.

34. Richard Bentley, *Elevation of a Steeple for Kingston-on-Thames, Surrey*, ink and wash, 382 × 217 mm, 1753. Courtesy of the Lewis Walpole Library, Farmington, Connecticut.

Whately, whose *Observations on Modern Gardening* was published in 1770.[42] Whately's condemnation of deceptions was on the ground that they had been used too often to be effective, and Walpole replied: "If those deceptions, as a feigned steeple of a distant church or an unreal bridge to disguise the termination of water, were intended only to surprise, they were indeed tricks that would not bear repetition; but being intended to improve the landscape, are no more to be condemned because common, than they would be if employed by a painter in the composition of a picture."[43] This defence clearly rests upon an appeal to the practice of Kent, which Walpole had previously analyzed in the following terms: "Where objects were wanting to animate the horizon, his taste as an architect could bestow immediate termination. His buildings, his seats, his temples, were more the work of his pencil than of his compasses".[44]

Richard Bentley also made a design for the gateway to Bishop Auckland Palace for Bishop Richard Trevor (Plate 35), which was rejected in favour of the design by Sir Thomas Robinson described earlier. It provided for flanking lodges and a room above the arch, and these are evident in the Bentley drawing, along with a clock and a crowning decoration of episcopal arms and mitre. It is evident from this drawing that Bentley followed Kent in working method; this building is clearly more the work of his pencils than of his compass. Making all due allowances for the sketchiness of the drawing, however, it remains the most revealing document we have in illustration of Walpole's later rueful reflection upon Strawberry Hill, "Neither Mr. Bentley nor my workmen had *studied* the science".[45] There is an extraordinary confusion of niches with panels, and the intricate decoration proposed is quite irreconcilable with the sturdy arch and the battlements.

Bentley's unexecuted gateway for Strawberry Hill (Plate 36) is a well disguised derivative of the choir-gates from Rouen which had been used for the screen in the Holbein Chamber at Strawberry Hill, and it can therefore be dated to 1758. It has so little

35. Richard Bentley, *Elevation of a Gateway for Bishop Auckland Palace, Co. Durham*, ink and wash, 292 × 185 mm, *c*. 1755. Courtesy of the Lewis Walpole Library, Farmington, Connecticut.

wall-space for a structure that presupposes solidity, that it would hardly pass muster as a stage-prop. This fault was rectified in another version of the theme, the two-storeyed gateway with a central rose window flanked by niches (Plate 37). This does not seem to have been executed. The third variant on the Rouen screen, also unexecuted, is by far the most delightful, a tea-house which incorporated the trunk of an existing tree, designed for Mrs Cavendish's garden at Isleworth (Plate 38).[46] Bentley shared Kent's wit and imagination, as is evident in his marvellous book illustrations, especially those for Gray's poems, which are so close in feeling to Kent's illustrations for Spenser.[47] This should have earned him a large practice as a designer of garden buildings in the fanciful gothic style, but he does not seem to have made any further architectural designs after leaving Strawberry Hill in late 1759.

36. (*above*) Richard Bentley, *Elevation of a Gateway for Strawberry Hill,
Twickenham, M'sex*, ink and pencil, 190 × 268 mm, 1758. Courtesy of the
Lewis Walpole Library, Farmington, Connecticut.

37. (*right*) Richard Bentley, *Elevation of a Gateway, possibly for Strawberry
Hill, Twickenham, M'sex*, ink and wash, 152 × 152 mm, 1758. Courtesy of
the Lewis Walpole Library, Farmington, Connecticut.

38. Richard Bentley, *Elevation and plan of a Tea-house for Isleworth, M'sex*, ink and wash, 267 × 190 mm, 1758. Courtesy of the Lewis Walpole Library, Farmington, Connecticut.

39. Paul Fourdrinier after George Allen, *Portrait of Thomas Wright of Durham*, 1748.

40. Thomas Wright, *Elevation of a Tower for Westerton, Co. Durham*, ink and wash, 260 × 194 mm, *c*.1750. Courtesy of the Avery Architectural and Fine Arts Library, Columbia University, New York.

41. Thomas Wright, *Elevation of a Tower*, ink, 171 × 104 mm, *c*.1750. Courtesy of the Avery Architectural and Fine Arts Library, Columbia University, New York.

THOMAS WRIGHT

Thomas Wright of Durham (Plate 39) was a much more prolific designer and was also, as we have noted, the author of two books of designs which emphasised the use of natural materials in the manner Kent had demonstrated at Merlin's Cave in Richmond.[48] Indeed, George Mason claimed at the end of the century that Wright was the true successor of Kent in landscape gardening.[49] There is considerable truth in this, since Wright worked at Badminton in Gloucestershire and Oatlands in Surrey directly after Kent's death in 1748. One of the most finished of his drawings is for his own observatory, Westerton Tower in County Durham close by the house at Byer's Green to which he retired in 1762. He had been preparing designs for it for many years,[50] but it was incomplete at his death in 1786 and has never been completed to his intentions as shown in the elevation produced here (Plate 40), since it lacks the upper storey and battlements.

This accounts for its recent description as: "A dull, dumpy little tower . . . the dullest, most uninspired and uninspiring curio in the British Isles, its chief claim to the title of folly being that it has never been pulled down."[51] The Avery sketch makes it clear that Wright had hoped to raise it ten feet higher than the existing structure and to crown it with bold battlements at intervals of three feet.

The inspiration for Westerton Tower probably came from a neighbouring landmark erected by another northern astronomer, Archdeacon Thomas Sharpe, at Whitton in Northumberland in the 1720s.[52] Wright's tower is more massive than Sharpe's, with broad buttresses below answering the heavy parapet canted out on vigorous consoles. The doorway is accented with cut-stone surrounds in keeping with the military and masculine air of the composition. The tabernacle window of the first floor was omitted in the execution, probably wisely, since its refined style is entirely at odds with the composition as a whole. Its inclusion in the design demonstrates the eccentricity of Wright's architecture upon which his contemporaries and subsequent commentators have remarked.[53]

Thomas Wright's most delightful essays on the tower theme are those shown in Plates 41–43, proposals for a prospect tower thoughtfully equipped with an umbrello to protect the landscape lovers from summer showers. The fenestration is quite dense in the first example and quite sparse in the second, where all the intricacy is concentrated on the crown of the tower, very richly decorated with a drip-course, corbelling, and little trees set below an open canopy on a central support. Plate 41 seems to be a modified octagon or a square with canted corners in plan, with a square canopy supported at the corners and four prospect kiosks looking to each point of the compass. Neither design seems to have been executed, though it is clear from Plate 43, a measured detail of a circular canopy on a battlemented roof, that serious planning for such a tower was made.

A tower was also projected for Horsebury Hill in Gloucester, both in plan and in elevation in Plate 44. This tower is more complicated and would presumably have been intended primarily as an eyecatcher. The bulky, central round tower is flanked by a smaller round one, one storey in height, and by an equally slim one of two storeys containing a staircase giving access to the first-floor room (12 ft high) and to the battlemented roof of the main tower. The elevation shows an open ground floor, so the structure may have been intended as a gate-lodge as well as an eyecatcher. The plan

42. Thomas Wright, *Elevation of a Tower*, ink, 182 × 112 mm, *c.*1750. Courtesy of the Avery Architectural and Fine Arts Library, Columbia University, New York.

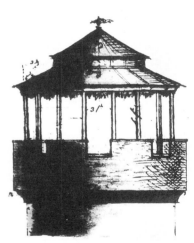

43. Thomas Wright, *Umbrello for a Tower*, ink and wash, 184 × 159 mm, *c.*1750. Courtesy of the Avery Architectural and Fine Arts Library, Columbia University, New York.

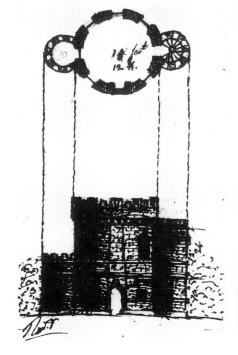

44. Thomas Wright, *Elevation and Plan of a Tower for Horsebury Hill, Glos.*, ink, 197 × 95 mm, *c.*1750. Courtesy of the Avery Architectural and Fine Arts Library, Columbia University, New York.

45. Thomas Wright, *Elevation for a Triangular Tower*, ink, 171 × 137 mm, *c.*1750. Courtesy of the Avery Architectural and Fine Arts Library, Columbia University, New York.

46. Thomas Wright, *Elevation of a Lodge for Selsey Forest, Glos.*, ink and pencil, 155 × 177 mm, *c.*1750. Courtesy of the Avery Architectural and Fine Arts Library, Columbia University, New York.

47. Thomas Wright, *Elevation of a Lodge*, ink, 77 × 156 mm, *c.*1750. Courtesy of the Avery Architectural and Fine Arts Library, Columbia University, New York.

shows no such opening, so it is probably for the first floor. Like the Westerton Tower, this was to have been 30 ft in height; there is no evidence that it was erected.[54]

Plate 45 is the elevation for Wright's most grandiose essay on the tower theme, ''A Caldean(?) Tower 100 feet high.'' It is triangular in plan, rising from a deep rocky base in two levels accented by turrets at the angles to a circular doomed room, again 12 ft high, which is intriguingly described as the ''Rustic House'' in the accompanying legend. One imagines that this monumental structure, had it been erected, would have been sited on an island; and indeed there is no indication in the elevation of a means of access to it.

Forest lodges were usually at a good distance from the house and were screened by plantations, so they too provided a legitimate occasion for indulgence in the gothic style. Wright provides two elevations for such buildings Plates 46 and 47. The first is inscribed ''Extends 105 feet'' and is marked on the back ''Design for a Gothic Lodge for Selsey Forest.'' Selsey is near Woodchester in Gloucestershire, but there is no record of this building having been erected.[54] The high centre piece is a gothic version of the triumphal arch motif, 35 ft in width, and is separated by low walls from square pavilions that are very Vanbrughian in feeling. This composition is framed and backed by a plantation of mature trees, and may perhaps be intended as an eyecatcher or termination point. This is the purpose also of Plate 47, a more tightly-knit and voluminous building, which may have been intended to double as a gate-lodge. This has been associated by Eileen Harris with Holly Bush House in Badminton, Gloucestershire.[55]

There are four elevations for a building that closely resembles the Keeper's Lodge at Badminton, described by Stuart Barton with rather more appreciation that he afforded Westerton Tower: ''this charming little folly . . . A little square rubble castle with one circular turret for the stairs and topped with clumsy-looking stone slabs for castellations (Plates 48–51).''[56] Thomas Wright always seems to be at his best when employing natural materials, practising a kind of architecture of found objects. The small woodland

48 to 51 Thomas Wright, *Elevation for Ragged Castle, Badminton, Glos.*, ink, *c.*1750 (*from left to far right:* 48. 110 × 159 mm; 49. 89 × 159 mm; 50. 115 × 159 mm; 51. 222 × 184 mm). Courtesy of the Avery Architectural and Fine Arts Library, Columbia University, New York.

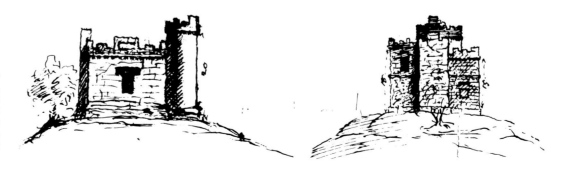

52. Thomas Wright, *Elevation for the Hermit's Cell*, Badminton, Glos., ink, 86 × 137 mm, *c.*1750. Courtesy of the Avery Architectural and Fine Arts Library, Columbia University, New York.

53. Thomas Wright, *Plan of a Temple for Stoke Gifford, Glos.*, ink, 159 × 194 mm, *c.*1750. Courtesy of the Avery Architectural and Fine Arts Library, Columbia University, New York.

cottage of Plate 52, with its thatch and logs is altogether charming. This hut is known as The Hermit's Cell, in Badminton Park, and Dr Harris records a smaller version of it at Berkeley Castle, also in Gloucestershire.[57] Wright was much employed in Gloucestershire, particularly at Stoke Gifford Park, for which he designed a grotto with Druidic overtones, the plan for which is Plate 53, inscribed ''Plan of Bladad's Temple at Storke(?).''[58]

Wright seems to have been particularly fascinated by the management of water-courses, and the Avery Sketchbook contains two slight but attractive pencil sketches inscribed in ink ''a River Head'' (Plate 54) and a ''a Break Water'' (Plate 55). The latter is classical in style, but it bears the same potted ornaments as appear in the immensely complicated sketch, previously published by Alistair Rowan, for a *Concatenation of Cataracts* to be erected at Raby Castle in his native County Durham.[59] He designed the Horn Bridge, possibly for Tollymore Park in County Down, Ireland, and there are two preparatory drawings for it (Plates 56 and 57), the second one inscribed "Gothic Water-gate over a Canal." These drawings show sturdy structures, with tight string-courses binding the round battlemented turrets firmly across the stretch of water. The same taut energy informs a sketch for the Barbican Gate at Tollymore Park, which is inscribed ''Extends 30 ft & the Towers 26½ High Solid'' (Plate 58). Tollymore, a most eccentrically decorated landscape, was laid out by Lord Limerick, who was Wright's host on his visit to Ireland in 1746, so these drawings may date from that year.[60] However, since the estate continued to be developed until the end of the eighteenth century, it is not possible to be specific about the dates of the buildings in the absence of other documentary evidence. None of the buildings at Tollymore bear an exact correspondence with Wright's designs, but they are spiritually his, and some allowance must be made for the fertile inventiveness of local masons, or maybe of Lord Limerick himself, in their execution.

54. Thomas Wright, *Design for a Cascade*, pencil, 178 × 146 mm, *c.*1750. Courtesy of the Avery Architectural and Fine Arts Library, Columbia University, New York.

55. Thomas Wright, *Design for a Break-Water*, pencil, 102 × 165 mm, *c.*1750. Courtesy of the Avery Architectural and Fine Arts Library, Columbia University, New York.

56. Thomas Wright, *Elevation for a Watergate*, ink, 112 × 112 mm, *c*.1750. Courtesy of the Avery Architectural and Fine Arts Library, Columbia University, New York.

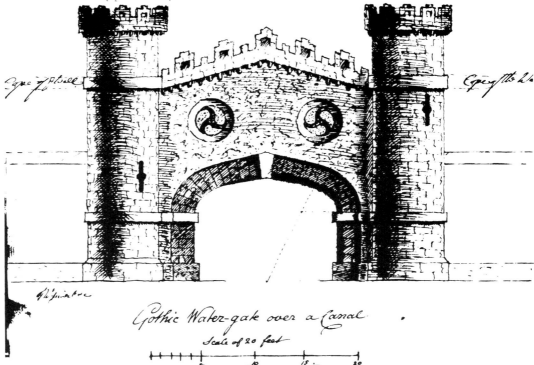

Gothic Water-gate over a Canal
Scale of 20 feet

57. Thomas Wright, *Elevation for a Watergate*, ink, 195 × 262 mm, *c*.1750. Courtesy of the Avery Architectural and Fine Arts Library, Columbia University, New York.

58. Thomas Wright, *Elevation for a Gateway*, ink, 131 × 172 mm, *c*.1750. Courtesy of the Avery Architectural and Fine Arts Library, Columbia University, New York.

The Bryansford Gate, for instance, which is the entrance to Tollymore Park, is clearly dated 1786, the year of Thomas Wright's death and several years after the death of Lord Limerick. But it is so thoroughly Wrightian in feeling that one is convinced of his authorship on stylistic grounds. Some support for this comes from the Avery Sketchbook in the scaled drawing (Plate 59), probably the preparatory drawing for the building. A similarly scaled drawing (Plate 60), the plan and elevation for a round tower 25 ft high and 12 ft in diameter, with flanking gateways and supporting battlemented screen walls,

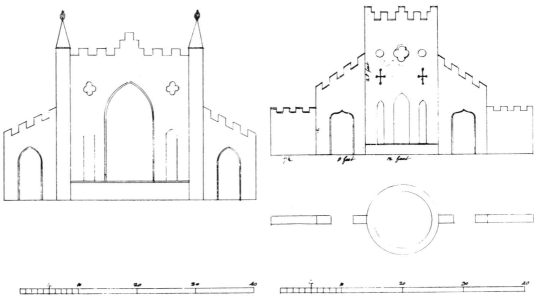

59. Thomas Wright, *Elevation and Plan of an Eyecatcher*, ink, 207 × 226 mm, *c*.1750. Courtesy of the Avery Architectural and Fine Arts Library, Columbia University, New York.

60. Thomas Wright, *Elevation of a Gothic Screen with a Circular Tower*, ink, 207 × 216 mm, *c*.1750. Courtesy of the Avery Architectural and Fine Arts Library, Columbia University, New York.

In Ornamental Gate

in the Saxon Stile of Gothick Architecture ...

61. Thomas Wright after R. Hutchinson, *Elevation of a Gateway*, ink and wash, 235 × 311 mm, *c*.1750. Courtesy of the Avery Architectural and Fine Arts Library, Columbia University, New York.

corresponds sufficiently closely to the gothic house which stood on the shore of Lough Erne in Lord Ross's estate in Bellisle, County Fermanagh, to justify the attribution of the building to Wright, who visited the estate twice in 1746.[61]

We may be on surer ground in dating Plate 61, "An Ornamental Gate in the Saxon Stile of Gothick Architecture", as it is elaborately inscribed. The inspiration for it is credited by Wright to the otherwise unknown Robert Hutchinson. The episcopal coat of arms in the centre may relate it to the gateway for Bishop Auckland Palace in County

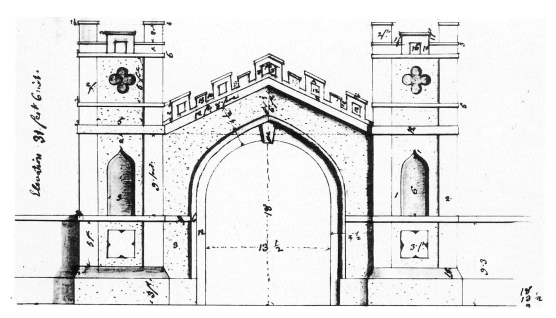

62. Thomas Wright, *Elevation of a Gateway*, ink and wash, 197 × 311 mm, *c*.1750. Courtesy of the Avery Architectural and Fine Arts Library, Columbia University, New York.

Durham, for which Sir Thomas Robinson and Richard Bentley had made designs. Perhaps it is to that commission that we may relate Wright's most detailed elevation for a gothic gateway (Plate 62). It is very sober and rational by comparison with the previous example which is romantically highlighted with deep washes.

In the accepted patterns of development of the gothic revival in garden architecture there is no firm place for Thomas Wright. He is close stylistically to Sir John Vanbrugh in his concern for the massing of volumes and his appreciation of the expressive value of varied surface textures. In scale and in the whimsical wit of much of his work, he recalls rather William Kent. What distinguishes his garden architecture from the works of predecessors and contemporaries can be best characterised as a pronounced instinct for "primitive" values, evident in the attention shown to the settings of his structures and in the frequent use of indigenous materials, local stone, wood and thatch.

No specific iconographic or politically-motivated narrative programme seems applicable to any of his work; nor are there literary or heroic or sentimental associations invoked by inscriptions or figural representations. His buildings are quite self-sufficient, even within a relatively finished scheme, like Badminton. They are not even interdependent. This is rather exceptional in the period. He seems to have been also uninterested in contemporary publications in gothic revival architecture, and one does not find much evidence of interest in real gothic buildings, though there are sketches of contemporary buildings. This distinguishes him sharply from the second generation of the revivalists, especially Walpole. He also never seems to have collaborated with professional architects, other amateurs or patrons. This is quite exceptional in the period, and may also be seen as a further indication of his strong and attractive individuality as a designer for landscape gardens.

LANCELOT BROWN

So far as we know Wright was never consciously in rivalry with "Capability" Brown, whose landscapes in general are distinguished rather by an absence of garden buildings. Another contender for the mantle of Kent in landscape garden design was Sanderson Miller of Radway, to whom Thomas Barrett Lennard had written just before the death of Kent in 1748: "Your fame in architecture grows greater every day, and I hear of nothing else. If you have a mind to set up, you'll soon eclipse Mr. Kent, especially in the Gothick way, in which to my mind he succeeds very ill."[62] Neither Miller not Wright replaced Kent as the arbiter of taste in garden design however; Horace Walpole was quite correct in placing in the succession Lancelot Capability Brown, of whom it was written in 1767:

> At Blenheim, Croome and Caversham we trace,
> Salvator's Wildness, Claude's enlivening grace,
> Cascades and Lakes as fine as Risdale drew,
> While Nature's vary'd in each charming view.
> To paint his works wou'd Poussin's Power require,
> Milton's Sublimity and Dryden's fire . . .
> To him each Muse enwreathes the Lawrel Crown,
> And consecrates to Fame immortal Brown.[63]

Not every author was so ecstatic, however, and the revolution affected by Capability Brown could be seen as destructive of the inheritance of Kent, as is witnessed by the following verses, admittedly satirical, by Walpole's friend and Brown's champion, William Mason:

63. Lancelot Brown, High Lodge, Blenheim, Oxon., 1765. Courtesy of the Royal Commission on the Historic Monuments of England.

There was a time 'in Esher's peaceful grove,
Where Kent and Nature vied for Pelham's love',
That Pope beheld them with auspicious smile,
And own'd that Beauty blest their mutual toil.
Mistaken Bard . . .
To Richmond come, for see, untutor'd Brown,
Destroy's those wonders that were once thy own.
Lo, from his melon-ground the peasant slave
Has rudely rush'd, and levell'd Merlin's cave;
Knock'd down the waxen Wizzard, seiz'd his wand,
Transformed to lawn what late was Fairy land.[64]

Mason's verses make a good point in indicating that Brown's emphasis on unbroken stretches of lawn did not lend itself to the kind of profusion of garden buildings that had characterised earlier landscape gardens. But there was some room for buildings, and Brown proved himself a competent if unexciting practitioner of the gothic style. "Not bad", was Walpole's verdict on the stables and greenhouse at Burghley, Northamptonshire, in 1763.[65] In the latter building Dorothy Stroud has noted the influence of Gibbs's Temple of Liberty at Stowe, where Brown had made his reputation.[66] One can also readily detect the influence of Isaac Ware's stables at Eythrope, also in Buckinghamshire, upon Brown's designs for the Park Farm Granary at Blenheim, Oxfordshire, in 1765, a plainer version of which he was to propose for Burton Constable, Yorkshire, eight years later.[67] For the garden house by the lake at Burghley, he turned to a Jacobethan precedent in topping it with a lace-work parapet, and Daniel Garrett, as we have seen, had used an open-work parapet at the Aske Hall Temple in Yorkshire about 1750. So Brown's designs look back to those of his immediate predecessors, and in general his gothic is of the simplest sort. The High Lodge at Blenheim (Plate 63) and an unexecuted design for a lodge at Rothley, Northumberland, both of 1765, show symmetrical facades with semi-hexagonal projections at the centre, pierced by pointed windows of two lights and crowned with regularly-spaced battlements.[68] More

attractive is a pavilion of three bays articulated by columns and pointed arches and pierced by quatrefoil windows, set on a base that featured deeply receding ogee openings. This was proposed for both Blenheim and Rothley, but was not executed in either place.[69] His richest composition is the Bath House at Corsham Court in Wiltshire, designed in 1761, which has canopied niches on either side of the familiar two-light window set beneath an athletic-looking ogee arch (Plate 64). Every other battlement is pinnacled, and a final crocketed pinnacle tops the peak of the square, stone-tiled roof.[70]

There is very little here of the spirit of William Kent's gothic garden buildings. Primitivism, or a sense of the "natural" affiliations of the style, is absent, and the buildings all serve a thoroughly useful function rather than a solely aesthetic one, so that—to paraphrase Walpole on Kent—one feels that Brown's buildings are more the work of his compasses than of his pencil. For this reason, Richard Bentley, Thomas Wright or Sanderson Miller could more justly claim to be Kent's successors in the gothic revival in garden buildings.

Sanderson Miller and Capability Brown were good friends, and on 10 August, 1750, Brown came to visit Miller at his house, Radway Grange in Warwickshire, and they dined at the gothic castle Miller had built there from 1745 to 1747 (Plate 65).[71] This was a complex consisting of the small but primitive and thatched Egge Cottage, which nestled against the base of the tower proper, which was octagonal like the famous Guy's Tower of nearby Warwick Castle. They were sited at the top of Edge Hill, overlooking Radway Grange, and in 1749 Miller had extended the composition with a ruinated wall, a smaller square tower, and a realistic but non-functional drawbridge. Brown had come too early for the opening ceremony, which was held with some fanfare on 3 September, 1750. Lady Luxborough, with characteristic tartness, asked Miller's jealous neighbour, William Shenstone: "Were you at Mr. Miller's Ball in his Gothic room? He is sending to Birmingham for cannon-balls and such-like military store, to defend his castle."[72]

The Radway complex is, as Pevsner has pointed out, an amazingly prescient invention on the part of Miller, and in its lack of symmetry and growth by accretion it is as gothic in plan (or lack of apparent plan), as it is in decoration. He sees it therefore as the first complete realisation of the picturesque in architecture, a system of building that had been adumbrated in Sir John Vanbrugh's alterations of 1721 to his own house at Greenwich,

65. Sanderson Miller, Tower at Radway, Warwicks., 1747. Courtesy of the Royal Commission on the Historic Monuments of England.

66. Sanderson Miller, Tower at Hagley, Worcs., 1748. Courtesy of the Royal Commission on the Historic Monuments of England.

and one that was to be revivified in domestic architecture by Richard Payne Knight's design of Downton Castle in Herefordshire in 1771.[73] It is worth quoting Payne Knight's cousin and guardian, Edward Knight, who took careful note of Radway when he visited it on 28 August, 1768, and wrote the following remarks in his travel diary:

> Mr. Miller's tower at Radway is octagon, the sides about 10 feet and the whole is about 70 ft. high. The parapet is divided into 4 parts by as many openings, each of which is supported by a block. The blocks are egg-shaped. The spaces between them very wide, they project about as much as the distance between them. The point of the roof appears above the parapet and has a bad appearance.[74]

What distinguishes Miller's castle at Radway from the castellated buildings of Vanbrugh and subsequent practitioners of the gothic style in garden building is that his tower was modelled on a genuine example of gothic architecture, and its erection was inspired by his antiquarian interests as much as by the aesthetic interest he shared with his contemporaries in the design of landscape gardens and garden buildings. When he succeeded to the Radway estate upon his father's death in 1737, he found himself possessed of the land upon which King Charles the First had raised his standard before the fateful battle of Edge Hill, considered by many to be the turning-point of the Civil War, and this was the justification for his deviating from the classical style to the gothic style, which had more war-like associations.[75] Shenstone was to remark of later improvements that Miller intended for Radway but never executed: "Surely Edge-Hill fight was never more unfortunate for the nation than it was lucky for Mr. Miller! He prints, together with his plan, another sheet of Radway Castle. I approve his design. He will, by this means, turn every bank and hillock of his estate there, if not into *classical*, as least into historical ground".[76]

Evidently, a new category of garden building had been born, and if it won the guarded approval of William Shenstone, it was thoroughly endorsed by Miller's many influential friends. He began to provide designs for neighbouring and more distant estates,

67. James Essex, Tower at Wimpole, Cambs., 1768. Courtesy of the Royal Commission on the Historic Monuments of England.

beginning with considerable *éclat* by building a ruined gothic castle for George Lyttelton in Hagley Park, Worcestershire (Plate 66), which was already a famous landscape garden because of its associations with James Thomson, the poet of *The Seasons*. This was erected in 1748, while the Radway complex was still in the making. Horace Walpole visited it in 1753 and paid Miller his highest compliment in writing to Bentley that Miller's castle at Hagley "would get him his freedom of Strawberry; it has the true rust of the Barons' Wars". With a proper regard, however, for the susceptibilities of his correspondent he tempered his praise of Miller with the remark: "in his castle he is almost Bentley!"[77]

Sanderson Miller was always a ready collaborator with his patrons and with professional architects in designing architectural works other than those for his own property, and there is considerable difficulty in determining the degree of his responsibility for the many gothic castles in landscaped gardens that claim descent from those of Radway and Hagley. Their creation justifies his title to the fatherhood of the genre, but certainly too many later follies have been attributed to his direct invention. A case in point which deserves clarification because of its fame, in the literature of the landscape garden as well as that of the gothic revival, is the eyecatcher at Lord Hardwicke's estate, Wimpole Hall, Cambridgeshire (Plate 67). George Lyttelton of Hagley certainly secured the interest of the Lord Chancellor, Hardwicke, in a design Miller made for a gothic castle for the park at Wimpole in 1753. However, that castle was not to be erected until 1768, and as executed it has nothing to do with Miller's design of twenty years earlier. A letter addressed by the Steward of Wimpole, Richard Bartons, to the Cambridge architect James Essex, makes it clear that the castle was designed by Essex.[78] In style too, the castle is not at all like the Miller castles. It allows far too many apertures in relation to the wall-space, its machicolations are slender by comparison to those of Radway and Hagley, and it lacks altogether the solid, defensive air of Miller's early work. It differs in function also, since it never served as a prospect tower and never had a room for convivial meetings. It was given a useful twist in having a keeper's lodge attached to it, but that was a later alteration by Humphrey Repton.

68. Sanderson Miller, Gateway to Lacock Abbey, Wilts., 1754. Courtesy of the Royal Commission on the Historic Monuments of England.

The Wimpole castle is also devoid of historical associations, and in this respect it is more typical than Radway of the garden buildings of the period. It is solely an ornamental building in the park, situated on a hillock, and backed and framed by judiciously planted clumps of trees, to terminate the vista from the drawing-room of the house. But of course Shenstone was right in remarking on the luck of Miller in having historic ground to build on. Rather quickly, Miller found himself supplying designs that were purely Kentian in their inspiration. An example is a request from Sir Edward Turner for a gothic design for a stable-block for his friend, the poet Richard Owen Cambridge: ''I was not to omit that the tower of a church will be seen over one end of the stable, which is the reason for confining the length of the building.''[79] Compositional considerations such as this, that is, the position of buildings relative to each other in a prospect, remained the most frequent factor determining the style as well as the dimension in the design of garden buildings.

Sanderson Miller is not often like Kent in his detailing, which tends to be heavy, but a notable exception must be made of the gateway to Lacock Abbey in Wiltshire, built in 1754 (Plate 68). This is a simple but deep open arch of ogee shape, with remarkably fine cutting in the stone, and with an elaborately carved cusp.[80] More typical is the castellated gateway at Enville in Staffordshire, of the following year. The Enville garden buildings demonstrate also the difficulty of making a positive attribution to Sanderson Miller. The most elaborate of them was the billiard room or museum, which Timothy Mowl has recently argued should rather be attributed to Henry Keene on stylistic grounds.[81] This change in attribution should cause no surprise, since it has long been established that Miller and Keene were close collaborators from the start of Miller's gothic career at Hagley Castle.[82] Miller even collaborated with Walpole in the making of the grotto for the new Hagley Hall in 1754,[83] though this happy state of affairs did not survive the shock Walpole received when John Chute's designs for the new building were passed over in favour of those of Sanderson Miller.[84]

In the middle decade of the century, Sanderson Miller was undoubtedly the designer of garden buildings in the gothic style with the highest reputation among his contemporaries. His wide correspondence testifies to this, and one can also sense it in the envy which inspired the criticism of his neighbour Shenstone at The Leasowes, who told Lady Luxborough that he was about to erect, ''a piece of Gothic Architecture, at sight of which, all the Pitts and Millers Castles in the world shall bow their heads abashed—like the other sheaves to Joseph's—I send you the plan. The said Hermit's Seat will amount, on a moderate computation, to the sum of fifteen shillings and six pence three farthings''[85] Lady Luxborough faithfully reassured Shenstone: ''As to myself, I am not ashamed to own that I like even a root-house at the Leasowes better than I do his *modern ruin* of an *ancient castle.''*[86]

The influence of Sanderson Miller has however been overrated. Few garden buildings are attributable to him with certainty,[87] and these buildings were not widely known through prints. Far better known than Radway were the smaller *fermes ornées* of Charles Hamilton at Painshill in Surrey, and of William Shenstone at The Leasowes, literary descriptions of which were widely circulated.[88] No such description of Radway was available and the estate, although it sported such a remarkable castle complex, could not be classified as *ferme ornée*, park, or landscape garden, since Miller did not have the money to develop the land or the house in pace with his wealthier friends. He recognised this, and wrote of it in 1750:

> My study holds three thousand volumes,
> And yet I sigh for Gothic columns,
> Such as Sir Roger, learned Knight of Taste
> At Arbury as well has placed
> Or such as Dacre, Gothic master
> Has introduced instead of Plaister . . .
> The Squire still said 'Get ground in front'
> By dint of Parliament I've don't—
> But still they say, 'No piece of water,
> No duckery for Wife and Daughter!'
> Should that be done, they'd still cry out
> And hourly put me in a pout.[89]

Miller's health also prevented his making a continuing impact on the design of garden buildings or on the progress of the gothic revival, just as it had made his writing the history of the gothic style impossible. The first of recurring bouts of insanity occurred in 1759, and he did not have much connection with architecture after that date.[90]

69. Johann Heinrich Müntz, *The Cathedral at Kew, Surrey*, ink and wash, 470 × 330 mm, 1759. Courtesy of the Metropolitan Museum of Art, New York (Harris Brisbane Dick Fund).

THE ANTIQUARIAN IMPULSE

By then the demand for antiquarian fidelity had taken a hold on the practitioners of the gothic revival and its impact was felt in the design of garden buildings. As we have seen, Lord Strafford erected at Walpole's suggestion a menagerie building, drawn by Richard Bentley on the model of the Chichester market cross, in 1758. Walpole rejected Bentley's designs for the Strawberry Hill gateway of the same year, even though they were allied to a historical precedent, and he erected instead the gateway by James Essex which was a faithful replica of a tomb in Ely Cathedral.[91] One must admit that it was a far more attractive gateway than those proposed by Bentley.

At Stowe, which was traditionally in the forefront of design in gardens and garden buildings, major developments took place in landscaping and in architecture during the 1760s, and the principal designer was Thomas Pitt, who had briefly been a member of the Strawberry Hill Committee of Taste, and who succeeded Sanderson Miller as the arbiter of architecture at Hagley. No gothic buildings were erected on either estate, however.[92]

When William Chambers decided to turn Kew Gardens into an encyclopedia of architectural styles, he commissioned the gothic cathedral from Johann Heinrich Müntz in 1759, and got one of the richest, and most delicately ornamented, of the gothic garden buildings of the century (Plate 69).[93] This became well known because it was published in elevation and plan in 1763.[94] But this was only a temporary structure, as a German visitor discovered to his surprise in 1762: "All these buildings consist of wood only, but are so cleverly covered with plaster, and painted in oil colours, that you would swear they were solid buildings of quarry stone, unless by knocking them you discovered the truth from sound."[95]

The gothic revival continued to influence the design of garden buildings after 1760 of course, but not in the most fashionable gardens, where the Greek revival temporarily supplanted it. Ironically, the first Greek revival garden building was that designed by James "Athenian" Stuart in 1758 and erected the following year in Hagley by Sanderson Miller, who was better informed on the subject of recent research into Greek architecture at Paestum than most professional architects.[96] The temporary eclipse of the gothic style in garden buildings in favour of the more fashionable Greek style was given vivid expression in the Shepherd's Monument at Shugborough in Staffordshire (Plate 70). This

70. Thomas Wright and James Stuart, The Shepherd's Monument, Shugborough, Staffs., c.1765. Courtesy of the Royal Commission on the Historic Monuments of England.

71. Samuel Grimm, *View of Roche Abbey, Sandbeck, Yorks.*, watercolour, 358 × 523 mm, 1780. Courtesy of the Royal Commission on the Historic Monuments of England.

consists of a rustic arch derived from Thomas Wright's *Book of Grottoes* (1758), framing a carved relief by Peter Scheemakers after Poussin. But two primitive Doric columns with an entablature were superimposed on Wright's arch by Athenian Stuart in the 1760s.[97]

All this emphasis on antiquity, gothic or Greek, led to a wonderful development in the fortunes of gothic buildings and in the design of landscape gardens. The true native antique buildings of England, the gothic monastic buildings, began to be prized precisely for their antiquity, and their ruins began to be cherished even in the most classical gardens. An early instance occurred with the building of the terrace above Rievaulx Abbey at Duncombe Park in Yorkshire in 1758, and ten years later Fountains Abbey was brought into the landscape garden at Studley Royal, also in Yorkshire.[98] In 1774 Capability Brown contrived to incorporate the ruins of Roche Abbey into his design for Sandbeck, Yorkshire (Plate 71), ''according to the ideas fixed on with Lord Scarborough (With Poet's Feeling and with Painter's Eye)'', in the words of the contract, the phrase in parenthesis being a quotation from William Mason's poem of 1772, *The English Garden*.[99] Even at the time, there were people who complained of the artificiality of this contrived preservation of ruins. But it was an immense improvement upon the vandalism exhibited for instance by Shenstone, who in 1758 had sought permission to rip out the windows of Hagley Abbey in order to decorate a gothic screen in his garden.[100] It certainly marked a turning-point in the appreciation of gothic monuments, and in that sense, the Greek revival did untold good for the gothic revival. In 1776 an appeal, *The Groans of the Abbeys*, was addressed to the Society of Antiquaries, seeking the promotion of an Act of

Parliament for the preservation of ancient monuments from the depredations of what was rather nicely described as "a selfish race of unfeeling Goths!"[101] Any effective legislation was to be far in the future, but it should be better appreciated that the revival of the gothic ensured the survival of the gothic, and in doing so made a larger contribution to architectural heritage than any tally of its monuments can suggest.

One instance on a smaller scale of the preservation of monuments in preference to the erection of new gothic monuments, was that which occurred at Nuneham Courtney, Oxfordshire, the home of Horace Walpole's great friends, Lord and Lady Harcourt. This was landscaped by Capability Brown in collaboration with William Mason, who undertook to design a gothic tower for which Walpole had promised to supply stained glass.[102] The whole project was cheerfully abandoned, however, when Lord Harcourt got the opportunity to re-erect the Carfax Conduit from Oxford in place of the tower.[103] Henry Hoare had given the lead in this respect by erecting the High Cross in 1765 (Plate 72) and St Peter's pump in 1768 at Stourhead in Wiltshire. Both were medieval monuments from Bristol, which he had rescued from possible destruction by the city authorities, who saw nothing more in them than traffic hazards.[104] At Ampthill in Bedfordshire, Horace Walpole contributed to the stone crosses of England by having James Essex design and erect one in memory of Catherine of Aragon.[105] This is very beautiful in its simplicity, with three short arms of equal length atop a tapering clustered column of four colonnettes, set on a high octagonal base.

HORACE WALPOLE

It is only fitting that Walpole should be responsible for the most sophisticated of the garden buildings in the gothic style, the Chapel-in-the-Woods at Strawberry Hill (Plate IV). This was begun in May 1772[106] and was completed by September 1773.[107] Four stone pedestals were placed in front of it ten years later.[108] Its principal feature was the front elevation, "taken from a tomb of Edmund Audley bishop of Salisbury, in that cathedral".[109] This was to become a favourite of later gothic revivalists, beginning with Lewis N. Cottingham, who in 1823 used the working drawing for it by Thomas Gayfere as the frontispiece to *Working Drawings for Gothic Ornaments* (Plates 73 and 74).[110]

72. The Bristol High Cross, Stourhead, Wilts., re-erected 1765. Courtesy of the Royal Commission on the Historic Monuments of England.

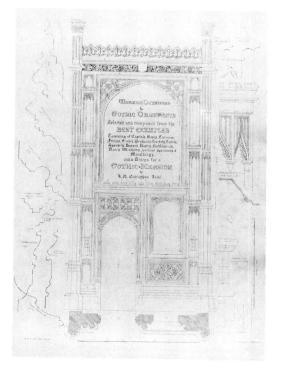

73. Lewis Nockalls Cottingham, Title-Page to *Working Drawings for Gothic Ornaments*, 1823. Courtesy of the British Library.

74. Thomas Gayfere, *Elevation for the Chapel-in-the-Woods, Strawberry Hill, M'sex*, ink and wash, 532 × 365 mm, 1772. Courtesy of the Lewis Walpole Library, Farmington, Connecticut.

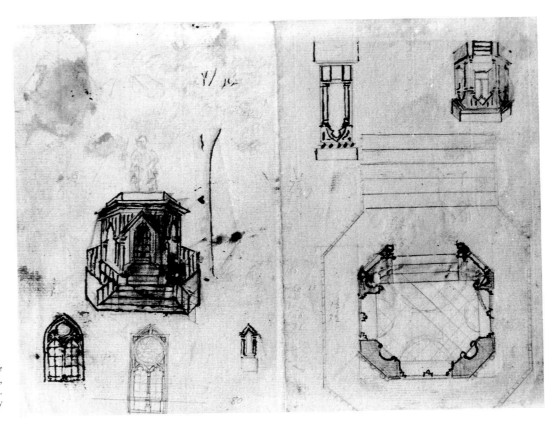

75. John Chute, *Elevation and Plan for the Chapel-in-the-Woods, Strawberry Hill, M'sex*, ink, 176 × 228 mm, 1768. Courtesy of the Hampshire County Record Office.

It would seem that this is an instance in which Walpole at first intended to erect a building to a new design of John Chute, but later decided on the use of an antique frontispiece in its place. Among the Chute papers in the Hampshire County record Office there are several drawings which are likely to be preliminary studies for the building, since they certainly refer to a chapel in some woods, and there was no intention of erecting such a structure at Chute's own house, The Vyne.[111]

Probably the earliest sketch is a folded sheet, which shows in plan and elevation a modified octagon raised on five steps and surmounted by a statue (Plate 75). A square pier is lightly inscribed in the centre of the plan of this building, and we may suppose that this was to act as a support for the large statue. Details of fenestration surround this

76. (*this page*) John Chute, *Plan and Part-Elevation for the Chapel-in-the-Woods, Strawberry Hill, M'sex*, ink, 228 × 367 mm, 1768. Courtesy of the Hampshire County Record Office.

77. (*facing page, left*) John Chute, *Section of proposed Chapel-in-the-Woods, Strawberry Hill, M'sex*, pencil, 139 × 63 mm, 1768. Courtesy of the Hampshire County Record Office.

78. (*facing page, middle*) John Chute, *View of proposed Chapel-in-the-Woods, Strawberry Hill, M'sex*, pencil, 86 × 54 mm, 1768. Courtesy of the Hampshire County Record Office.

79. (*facing page, right*) John Chute, *Door and Window for proposed Chapel-in-the-Woods, Strawberry Hill, M'sex*, pencil, 187 × 145 mm, 1768. Courtesy of the Lewis Walpole Library, Farmington, Connecticut.

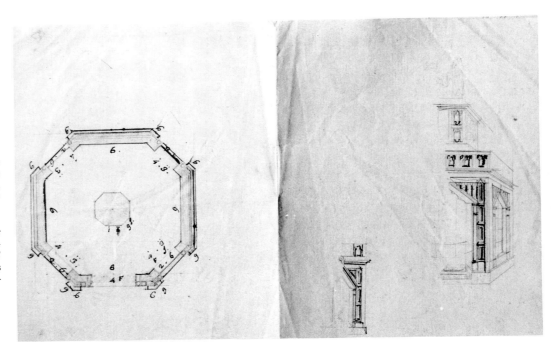

elevation and plan, and some calculations are also inscribed on the sheet. Plate 76 represents a refinement upon this early scheme. The octagon is less irregular, the dimensions are given fully, and the central pier has now become a smaller octagon. The simple stone balustrade has been adorned with gothic openings, and an attic storey has been added to give visible external support to the statue, still inscribed in a tantalisingly faint manner on the half-elevation which is shown with a detail on the second part of this folded sheet.

Three drawings show the interior of this proposed building in perspective, with alternate schemes of decoration for the central pier and the windows (Plate 77). The building was to be lighted on four of the eight walls, and the pier was to contain four corresponding niches. The entrance was to run the full height of the building almost, and the statue was to rise from a rather bulky stand on the roof. The third of these sketches shows the statue as a well-draped figure bearing a rod of office and set at an angle of 45 degrees to the entrance, a device which gives the composition a sense of movement which enlivens it considerably. In a final view (Plate 78), the building is placed securely in its sylvan setting. The small balustrade has been restored above the building and the plinth for the statue has been raised, but otherwise the building is seen as it had been originally designed. One other drawing that can be associated with this set is of a gated entrance and a window (Plate 79).[112]

The Chapel-in-the-Woods, in its final form, looks so very different from that proposed by Chute in these drawings that it may seem unwise to associate them with that building. But it looks more different than it is. The striking facade obscures the fact that Walpole's chapel is, like the one designed by Chute, a modified octagon in shape. A more serious objection is that the chapel was used to house the tomb of Capoccio which Walpole had received from Sir William Hamilton in 1768.[113] This tomb was a large structure for such a small building, and it certainly could not have been fitted easily into a building with a pier in the centre such as John Chute proposed. But Walpole at first had no intention of providing a separate building for this tomb. He wanted to break it up to convert it into a chimney-piece.[114]

A consideration of the chimney-piece in the north bed chamber indicates the decisiveness of Walpole's own contribution to the architecture of Strawberry Hill. Along with the facade and details of the Chapel-in-the-Woods, it was illustrated in Cottingham's *Working Drawings for Gothic Ornaments* (Plate 80). Like the facade, it was of Portland stone,

80. Lewis Nockalls Cottingham, detail of Plate 34 of *Working Drawings for Gothic Ornaments*, 1823. Courtesy of the British Library.

and was built by Thomas Gayfere, payment for it being included in the bill for the Chapel. Yet we know that it was designed by Walpole himself on the model of the tomb of Bishop Dudley of Durham, illustrated in Dart's *Westminster*.[115]

In view of Walpole's role in selecting the models that were to serve for the design of the principal features of the Round Room by Adam, and the Great North Bedchamber by Gayfere, it is reasonable to credit him with the choice of the tomb of Bishop Audley in Salisbury Cathedral for the facade of the Chapel-in-the-Woods. The building can therefore be seen as the culmination of a trend in the design of garden buildings that Walpole had initiated in 1756, when he had Lord Strafford erect the building in the menagerie at Stainborough, based upon the Market Cross at Chichester and drawn out by Richard Bentley. This was an independent strain of design that is seen particularly in the work of Walpole and his circle, though it occurs also in the internal decoration of Henry Keene. Walpole however applied it to entire buildings, and the happy outcome was the Chapel-in-the-Woods, the finest garden building of the period in the gothic style. Its excellence lay entirely in the fidelity with which the original was copied. Walpole's principles of design are stated clearly in a letter of advice on the design of a tomb addressed to Lord Harcourt in 1778: "... it is quite in the *esprit du gothique*. The person however who drew it, is not correct, especially in his trefoils. He ought to copy the pattern exactly, of which there are many in Dart's *Westminster or Canterbury*."[116]

It is appropriate that the principal historian of the landscape garden in England in the eighteenth century should be the creator of the finest garden building of the century in the gothic style. Even Eastlake, who was not generous in his assessment of Walpole, was forced to admit that the Chapel-in-the-Woods was, "a very creditable performance if we consider the time at which it was erected". Indeed, it was because of the garden building rather than the house itself that Eastlake allowed that Strawberry Hill—or "Walpole's Gothic", as he likes to call it—"holds a position in the history of English art which commands our respect".[117]

III. Horace Walpole and Strawberry Hill

THE FIRST PHASE

"I am going to build a little Gothic castle", Horace Walpole wrote from Twickenham on 10 January, 1750, to his friend Horace Mann[1] (Plates I–IV): Mann's reaction to this news was probably typical of the reaction of all of Walpole's friends. "Why will you make it Gothic? I know it is the taste at present, but I really am sorry for it."[2]

Walpole's reply to Mann is important to observe, since it demonstrates that from the start of his building operations at Strawberry Hill he intended that it should be an asymmetrical house, and that the idea for this extraordinary arrangement was one that had been suggested to him by changes in garden design that William Kent had initiated. He wrote on 25 February, 1750: "Columns and all their beautiful ornaments look ridiculous when crowded into a closet or a cheese-cake house. The variety is little, and admits no charming irregularities. I am as fond of the Sharawaggi, or Chinese lack of symmetry, in buildings as in grounds or gardens."[3] It is worth remarking in this respect that Twickenham was hallowed for him by the ghost of Alexander Pope, "just now skimming under my window by a most poetical moonlight",[4] and that in the essay *On Modern Gardening*, he remarked of the poet's garden, which he credited with having influenced Kent in revolutionising garden design, "it was a singular effort of art and taste to impress so much variety of scenery on a spot of five acres."[5] It is not at all inconceivable that Walpole should have set himself to emulate in architecture the achievement of Pope in gardening. By 1753 he had determined to emulate the architectural hero of Pope's *Moral Essays*, Lord Burlington, and he wrote to Mann on 4 March of that year, "As my castle is so diminutive, I give myself a Burlington-air, and say, that as Chiswick is a model of Grecian architecture, Strawberry Hill is to be so of Gothic"[6] At this date the first gothic alterations to the interior of the house were being completed, to the entrance hall and gothic staircase, "which is so pretty and small", he told Mann, "that I am inclined to wrap it up and send it to you in my letter"[7] (Plate IX). The larger rooms of this phase of building were the dining-room and the library above it, which was not completed until November 1754.[8]

The external appearance of Strawberry Hill at this date is shown in a "before and after" sketch by Walpole as well as in a painting by Johann Heinrich Müntz of 1756, and in some prints (Plates 81–3). These are all faithful renderings of the features evident in two preparatory drawings, which are among John Chute's papers (Plates 84–5). They confirm that Chute was, in Walpole's words, "the genius that presided over poor

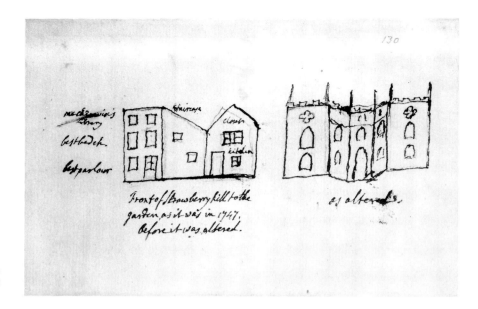

81. Horace Walpole, *Strawberry Hill before and after the alterations of 1753*, ink, 109 × 167 mm. Courtesy of the Lewis Walpole Library, Farmington, Connecticut.

82. Johann Heinrich Müntz, *View of Strawberry Hill*, oil on canvas, 619 × 743 mm, 1756. Courtesy of the Lewis Walpole Library, Farmington, Connecticut.

83. J. Woolston, *View of Strawberry Hill*, 1754. Courtesy of the Lewis Walpole Library, Farmington, Connecticut.

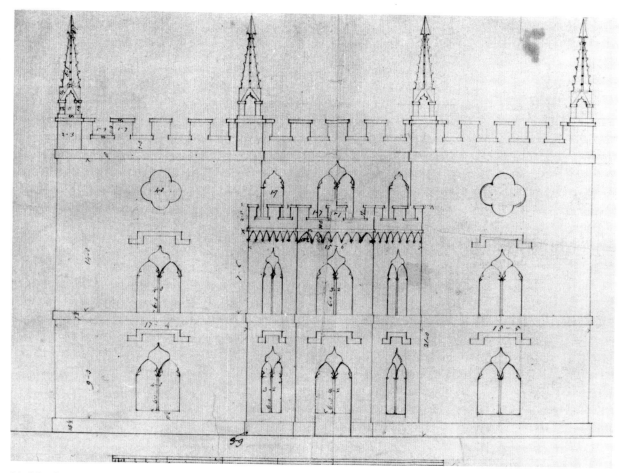

84. John Chute, *Elevation for Strawberry Hill*, ink, 288 × 406 mm, 1753. Courtesy of the Hampshire County Record Office.

85. John Chute, *Elevation for Strawberry Hill*, pencil, 180 × 169 mm, 1753. Courtesy of the Hampshire County Record Office.

86. John Chute, *Part-Elevation for Straw-berry Hill*, pencil, 226 × 288 mm, 1753. Courtesy of the Lewis Walpole Library, Farmington, Connecticut.

Strawberry''.[9] The three-storeyed facade is symmetrically disposed, with side bays framing a semi-hexagonal bay window of two storeys. Quatrefoil windows light the third floor, and flat horizontal labels over the pointed windows of the first and second floors accentuate the planar or two-dimensional quality of the design. The elevation lacks depth, and the linearity of its articulation seems to be summarised in the thin crocketed pinnacles of the roof-line.

The gothic features of this composition strike us now as being thoroughly tame and derivative. The quatrefoils and the window-labelling have their nearest printed source in Batty Langley's *Ancient Architecture Restored and Improved* of 1742.[10] This may appear unlikely, in view of Walpole's denunciations of Batty Langley, but that it was indeed the source is confirmed by Walpole's own copy of the book, now in the Lewis Walpole Library. On the endpapers it bears a third preparatory drawing for this first section of the south elevation (Plate 86), which corresponds to the two drawings from the Chute Papers.[11]

Besides this printed source, however, Chute and Walpole had close at hand across the river in Surrey, the most famous instance of William Kent's use of the gothic style in domestic architecture—Esher Place (Plate 87). Here, Kent had not only added gothic wings symmetrically to either side of old Waynflete Tower, but had taken out the original windows of the tower and replaced them with pointed windows of two lights topped by flat labels, and with quatrefoil windows on the top floor, to make the old building harmonise with the decoration of his new wings.[12] Given his enthusiasm for Kent's garden design, it is understandable that Walpole should have gone first to William Kent's Esher for archi-tectural inspiration. ''Esher I have seen again twice'', he wrote in August 1748, ''and I prefer it to all villas, even to Southcote's; Kent is Kentissime there''.[13] This sentiment would have had the approbation of his friend Thomas Gray, who wrote six years later to Wharton, ''You do not say enough of Esher; it is my favourite place.''[14]

As we have seen in the first chapter, Gray is, to apply his own memorable phrase,

87. Luke Sullivan, *View of Esher, Surrey,*
c. 1750. Courtesy of the Lewis Walpole
Library, Farmington, Connecticut.

''some mute inglorious Milton'' in the development of scholarship in the history of gothic architecture.[15] Walpole and he had made the Grand Tour together, and though their comments on gothic monuments at the time are not enlightening, it is probable that some of the close attention that Gray gave to gothic architecture made an impression on his travelling companion. In 1753 Gray was probably the most important person in Walpole's life and was no longer mute as a poet. ''This year I published a fine edition of six poems by Mr. T. Gray, with prints from designs of Mr. R. Bentley,'' is Walpole's laconic entry under 1753 for the most momentous event of his life.[16] It is not too much to say that this publication alone would have assured Walpole an honourable niche in the history of art as well as of literature, for Bentley's illustrations to Gray's poems are masterpieces of the rococo style in the graphic arts, and it is difficult to say whether the success of the publication was due in greater part to its visual or its literary content.[17] Bentley's success in this publication explains the unwavering trust Walpole reposed in him as a designer of gothic architecture, though he was to reject most of Bentley's proposals for Strawberry Hill once he had determined on an antiquarian rather than an imaginative process of design for his gothic castle.[18]

Besides the illustrations to the poems of Gray, Richard Bentley also designed in 1753 the frontispiece to Walpole's manuscript history, *Memoirs of the Reign of George II* (Plate 88). The author is seen between Heraclitus and Democritus, and in the background is a view of Strawberry Hill from the south-east. The symmetry of the south facade is in contrast to the east facade, where the two new large rooms, the dining-room and the library above it on the north-east, are broader and higher than the bay on the other side of the bow window. The library had not been completed by this date, and Bentley shows it without the quatrefoil windows that were to go on either side above the three-light pointed window.[19] Three drawings by John Chute must also be of this date, since they show the library with a pair of pointed windows (Plates 89–91). These drawings make it clear that at this date the entrance was on the east front, where simple

88. Richard Bentley, *Frontispiece to Horace*
Walpole, Memoirs of the Reign of George II,
ink, 288 × 173 mm, 1753. Courtesy of the
Lewis Walpole Library, Farmington,
Connecticut.

supports on the ground met the overhanging bay window of the Blue Bedchamber on the first floor. Walpole proposed to fill this in for a columbarium designed by Bentley in 1757.[20] But this was never realised and the space was built in simply to serve as a waiting-room after 1764.[21] In 1759 the principal entrance was made on the north side, directly behind the dining-room and library of 1754.[22]

The internal fittings of the rooms of the first phase of the building are due to Richard Bentley. He designed the nervous fretwork of the staircase, the pattern of the wallpaper (painted in perspective by him after it had been hung), and the octagonal lantern with the stained glass. This entire scheme is based upon historical precedent. The lantern was supposed to be a genuine antique from Hedingham Castle,[23] and the staircase is a faithful rendering in wood of the pattern of the upper flight of the stone staircase to the library of the cathedral of Rouen, which is appropriate since it led to the new library of Strawberry Hill.[24] The paper pattern was taken from a print in Frances Sandford's *History of the Kings of England* (1677) of the tomb of Prince Arthur in Worcester Cathedral (Plate 92).[25]

It is a measure of the naiveté of Walpole's approach to historicism in architecture at this date that he was completely taken aback on visiting Worcester Cathedral for the first time in September 1753, to find that gothic architecture in reality differed in scale and material from the idea he had derived from the print in Sandford. He wrote to Bentley: "Prince Arthur's tomb, from whence we took the paper for the hall and the staircase, to my great surprise, is on a scale less than the paper, and is not of brass but stone, and that wretchedly whitewashed. The niches are very small, and the long slips in the middle are divided every now and then with the trefoil."[26] Those who berated Walpole and his contemporaries for structural dishonesty in converting gothic tombs to chimney-pieces have obviously never taken into consideration the absence of any scale and any consistent application of perspective in the primitive prints that were the only sources of visual information available.

From the passage quoted above, it is clear that Walpole realised that he had a great deal to learn about the gothic style, and it is significant that he proceeds to berate his former mentor Kent, for the design of tombs. He does this by way of favourable comment on the tomb in Worcester Cathedral of Bishop Hough, which is by Roubiliac. This, he says, is "in the Westminster Abbey style".[27] He is not referring to the gothic style, as the modern reader at first assumes, but to the baroque style in English sculpture. There could be no better demonstration of how thoroughly confused and confusing the subject of stylistic evolution must have been for Walpole. The available prints were unreliable, as he now realised, and the only alternative was first-hand acquaintance with gothic monuments by travel to their sites. He and John Chute had actually made a field trip into

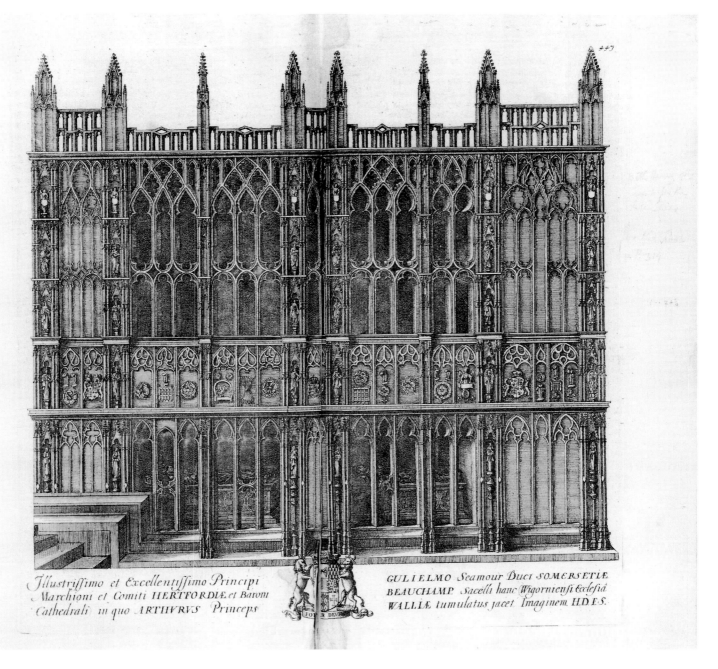

92. Page 477 of Francis Sandford, *A Genealogical History of the Kings of England*, 1677. Courtesy of the Lewis Walpole Library, Farmington, Connecticut.

Kent to study gothic ruins the previous year, and had experienced the physical hazards of travel at the period. Nevertheless, that journey may have been the turning-point in his realisation of the necessity for personal knowledge of gothic architecture, since he wrote to Bentley of Battle Abbey, "Mr. Chute says, 'What charming things we should have done if Battel Abbey had been to be sold at Mrs. Chevenix's as Strawberry was'."[28] The closeness of the study he and Chute made of this gothic building is evidenced by the "thousand sketches" that he promised to show Bentley on his return.

In his journey to Worcester, Hagley, Gloucester and Oxford the following year he was more critical of the monuments that he saw and particularly of William Kent's gothic design for the screen in Gloucester Cathedral. He declared flatly that Kent "knew no more there than he did anywhere else how to enter into the true gothic taste".[29] That dismissal of Kent left the problem of defining the true gothic taste open, but Walpole did not take long to find an instance of perfection, and wrote enthusiastically, "but of all

93. Edward Edwards, *The Cloister and North Entrance of Strawberry Hill*, 1774.

delight is what they call the abbot's cloister. It is the very thing that you would build, when you had extracted all the quintessence of trefoils, arches and lightness."[30]

THE EXTERIOR: THE SECOND PHASE

Five years later, in 1758, when the second phase of building at Strawberry Hill began, Walpole had not changed his opinion and he made a three-bay cloister the principal feature of the addition of two storeys behind the dining-room and library on the north side

I. Paul Sandby, *View of Strawberry Hill from the South-East*, watercolour, 136 × 190 mm, *c.* 1783. Courtesy of the Lewis Walpole Library, Farmington, Connecticut.

II. Anonymous, *View of Strawberry Hill from the South*, watercolour, 299 × 442 mm, n.d. Courtesy of the Lewis Walpole Library, Farmington, Connecticut.

III. Edward Edwards, *View of the Pior's Garden and North front of Strawberry Hill*, watercolour, 333 × 298 mm, 1781. Courtesy of the Lewis Walpole Library, Farmington, Connecticut.

IV. Thomas Rowlandson, *View of the Chapel-in-the-Woods at Strawberry Hill*, watercolour, 142 × 218 mm, 1822. Courtesy of the Lewis Walpole Library, Farmington, Connecticut.

(Plate 93 and III). A pantry on the ground floor was cased externally with the cloister of three bays, and above this was a bedroom decorated with drawings after Holbein and consequently called the Holbein Chamber. This at first had a bay window overhanging the ground, like the Blue Bedchamber on the east side.[31] Strawberry Hill now had its cloister, but what was a cloister without an oratory? In 1762 Walpole filled in the area below the bay window to create an oratory housing a saint in bronze. The statue has recently found its way into the Victoria and Albert Museum.[32]

There are no designs by Richard Bentley for this two-storeyed addition, and none by John Chute that date from 1758. However, the design of the oratory of 1762 is Chute's, as three drawings attest (Plates 94–6), and this later addition is so closely tied to the cloister and north entrance that there is no reason to doubt his having designed the exterior of this two-storeyed addition. The drawing for the north entrance, erected in 1759, is a drawing by Richard Bentley at base, but an examination of the original shows that the additions made to it, namely the quatrefoil window below the battlements, and the labels inserted over the door and the windows, are not only in John Chute's style, but are pentimenti in his hand (Plates 93 and 97).[33]

94. (*left*) John Chute, *Elevation of the Oratory at Strawberry Hill*, ink, 83 × 83 mm, 1762. Courtesy of the Lewis Walpole Library, Farmington, Connecticut.

95. (*middle*) John Chute, *Section of the Oratory at Strawberry Hill*, ink, 98 × 114 mm, 1762. Courtesy of the Lewis Walpole Library, Farmington, Connecticut.

96. (*right*) John Chute, *Section and Plan of the Oratory at Strawberry Hill*, ink, 156 × 204 mm, 1762. Courtesy of the Lewis Walpole Library, Farmington, Connecticut.

97. John Chute and Richard Bentley, *Elevation of the North Entrance of Strawberry Hill*, ink and wash and pencil, 307 × 195 mm, 1758. Courtesy of the Lewis Walpole Library, Farmington, Connecticut.

98. Johann Heinrich Müntz, *View of Strawberry Hill from the East*, ink and wash, 152 × 292 mm, 1758. Courtesy of the Lewis Walpole Library, Farmington, Connecticut.

99. (*facing page, above*) John Chute, *First Design for the Cloister and Gallery of Strawberry Hill*, ink, 215 × 312 mm, 1759. Courtesy of the Lewis Walpole Library, Farmington, Connecticut.

100. (*facing page, below*) John Chute, *Second Design for the Cloister and Gallery of Strawberry Hill*, ink, 248 × 388 mm, 1759. Courtesy of the Lewis Walpole Library, Farmington, Connecticut.

Strawberry Hill was now thoroughly knocked off symmetry (Plate 98) and before these alterations were completed Walpole had determined that its eventual shape would be even more asymmetrical. He wrote to Horace Mann on 9 September, 1758, "a day may come that will produce a gallery, a round tower, a larger cloister, and a cabinet".[34] He evidently decided to hasten the day, because the first of John Chute's three designs for this extension must have been made soon afterwards. In this drawing all the elements prescribed in Walpole's letter to Mann are present in plan and in elevation (Plate 99), though changes were to be made in every area, and the alternative windowing, described by John Chute on the flap attached to the drawing, indicates that it was of a tentative character. In many respects this is the most attractive of the schemes, besides being the fullest. The piers of the four-bay cloister are convincingly solid, and their plan in the upper right of the sheet shows them to be richly decorated with eight clustered colonnettes alternating in girth. The same solidity and volumetric feeling informs the round tower and its emphastic machicolations, all set off to good effect by the light conical cap and the slender staircase turret. These were not erected at this time, but they eventually took shape in 1776 when the Beauclerk Tower, moved round to the north to nestle between the tower and the tribune, was erected.[35]

Walpole evidently found this composition erred on the side of heaviness, if we can judge by his praise of the lightness of the second version, the cloister and gallery only, a drawing which displays Chute's attenuated draughtsmanship at its most anorexic (Plate 100). Walpole's letter is worth quoting in full, not merely for its charm, diplomacy and wit, but to demonstrate how very closely his prescriptions, practical and aesthetic, determined the compositions of his architects. The letter has poignancy too, because it is the last occasion of co-operation among the members of the original Committee of Taste, and unfortunately the quarrel that alienated Bentley and Müntz from each other and from Walpole and Chute was soon to sunder the harmony celebrated here.

Well, how delightful! How the deuce did you contrive to get such proportion? You will certainly have all the women with short legs come to you to design high-heeled shoes for them. The cloister, instead of a wine-cellar, has the air of a college. It has already passed the Seals. Mr. Müntz had commended it in a piece of every language, and Mr.

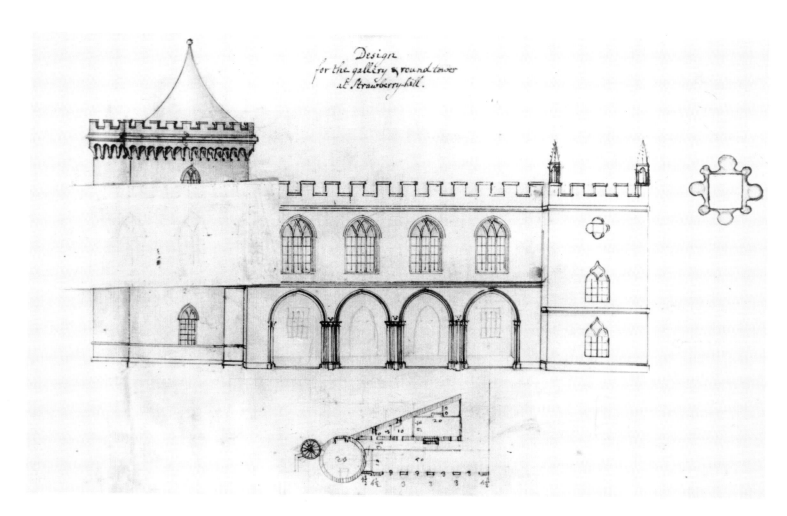

Design
for the gallery & round tower
at Strawberry-hill.

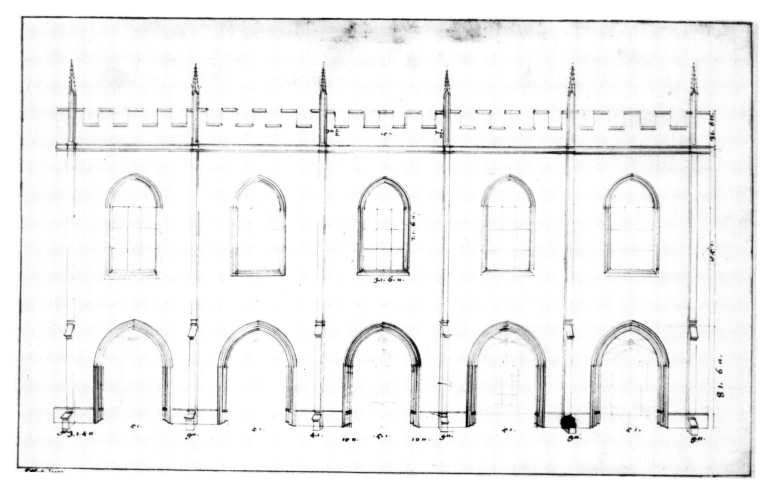

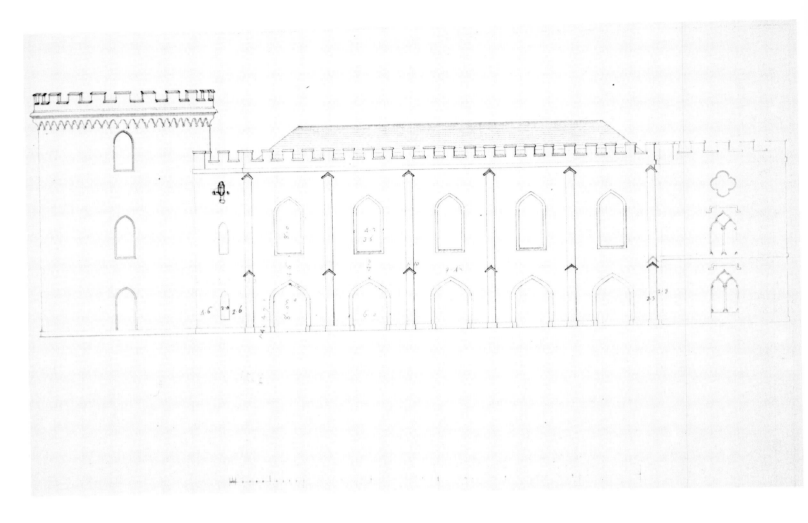

101. John Chute, *Third Design for the Cloister and Gallery of Strawberry Hill*, pencil, 255 × 385 mm, 1759. Courtesy of the Lewis Walpole Library, Farmington, Connecticut.

Bentley is at this moment turning it outside inwards.—I assure you, Mr. Chute, you shall always have my custom. You shall design every scrap of the ornaments: and if ever I build a palace or found a city, I will employ nobody but you. In short, you have found a proportion and given a simplicity and lightness to it that I never expected. I have but one fault to find, and that is no bigger that my little finger: I think the buttresses too slight; and yet I fear, widening them would destroy the beauty of the space around the windows. There is another thing which is more than a fear, for it seems an impossibility, that is, of setting pictures over the windows within; and if I can't, what shall I do with the spaces?[36]

In the final design the criticisms of Walpole were taken into account, as can be seen in Plate 101. The arches were further simplified and the buttresses were widened and brought to a halt below the battlements, which increased their strength, at least to the beholder's eye. A greater depth of wall-space was left between the tops of the windows and the line of the battlements, and Walpole was able to hang portraits of his relatives and ancestors above the windows of the gallery as a result.

THE PLAN

To turn to the plan of the extension as executed, a corridor running the length of the cloister on the ground floor gave access to the service rooms (Plate 102). On the first floor (Plate 103), the gallery took up the width consumed by the cloister and corridor below,

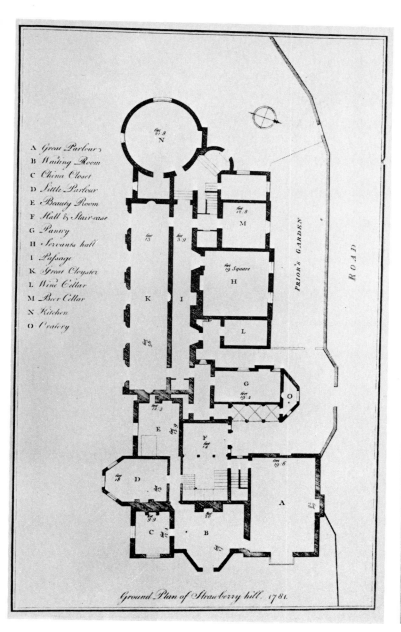

A Great Parlour
B Waiting Room
C China Closet
D Little Parlour
E Beauty Room
F Hall & Stair-case
G Pantry
H Servants hall
I Passage
K Great Cloyster
L Wine Cellar
M Beer Cellar
N Kitchen
O Oratory

PRIOR'S GARDEN

ROAD

Ground Plan of Strawberry hill. 1781.

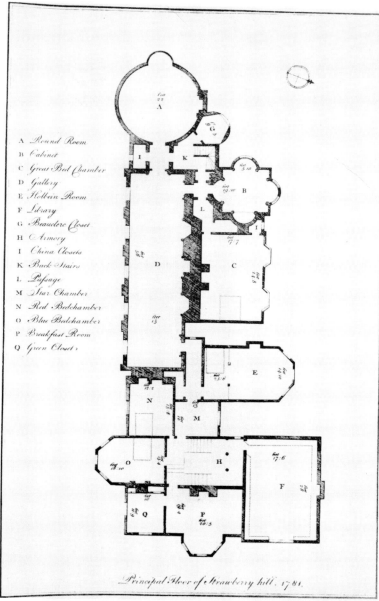

A Round Room
B Cabinet
C Great Bed Chamber
D Gallery
E Holbein Room
F Library
G Beauclerc Closet
H Armory
I China Closets
K Back Stairs
L Passage
M Star Chamber
N Red Bedchamber
O Blue Bedchamber
P Breakfast Room
Q Green Closet

Principal Floor of Strawberry hill. 1781.

and led through a door at the west or tower end to the room which was most adventurous in shape, the tribune. From the tribune a private passage led to the north bedchamber, which took up the rest of the first floor and was not finished until 1773.[37] Walpole had not lost his love of projecting bay windows. There were two semi-hexagonal ones in his bedchamber, and an ornate round one relieved the bulk of the tower at the western end when that was made into a bedroom in 1771.[38] Walpole had only two storeys to the tower and turret; the third was added a hundred years after their erection.[39]

To the modern observer, the greatest absurdity of Strawberry Hill has nothing at all to do with its gothic decoration but with its lack of convenience in planning. This is most noticeable in Walpole's having placed the kitchen on the ground floor of the tower, so that dishes had to be brought by a tortuous route, too complex to describe, but evident in the plan, to the dining-room at the far end of the building. The very good practical explanation of this arrangement is that in the days of open-fire roasting, people were only too happy to sacrifice piping-hot meals for the benefit of having eating, living and reception rooms free from inevitable kitchen smells. In Palladian houses too the kitchen

102. Plan of the ground floor of Strawberry Hill.

103. Plan of the first floor of Strawberry Hill.

77

104. Edward Edwards. *The Tribune of Strawberry Hill*, 1774.

was removed far from the living areas of the main block, frequently at the end of a colonnade.[40]

To appreciate the more purposeful reasoning behind Walpole's planning of Strawberry Hill, however, one has to consider the importance to him of his activities as a collector of art and antiquities and his desire to share his collections with the public. Clive Wainwright has recently pointed out that Walpole had formulated his ideas on this subject long before buying Strawberry Hill, and it should be remembered that his first book had been a catalogue of the collection of his father at Houghton Hall, Norfolk.[41] His career as a collector and art historian took a major leap forward with his acquisition of the manuscripts and works of art of George Vertue in 1758. As we have seen, the Holbein Chamber of that year owes its name to that event. I believe we can go further and say that the building programme of Strawberry Hill from that time found its logic in Walpole's desire to show his collection. He began to issue tickets to the public in 1774, but crowds came to view the collections as soon as the gallery and tribune were completed in 1763.[42]

Walpole's collection and the need for its appropriate display explains his fixing the name "tribune" upon the room off the gallery which, prior to 1774, he had called the "cabinet" or the "Chapel" (Plate 104).[43] It was the room for display of the rarest objects of his collection, and was therefore analogous to the most famous instance of the public display of a private collection, namely the Uffizi in Florence, where the octagonal tribune held the major works of art in the Medici collection.

A close reading of the plan of Strawberry Hill will show the path that viewers of the collection followed. Entering at the north door, they went immediately up the staircase to the armoury and library on the first floor. Passing through the Star Chamber, they went into the Holbein Chamber. From there the perambulation through the gallery led them to the climax of interest of the collection, housed in the tribune. This was an acceptable arrangement from a planning point of view, since it ensured that Walpole's guests and staff need not be inconvenienced by the viewing public. The library and each of the private rooms could be closed against intrusion if they were in use. Our study of the interior decoration of these rooms will show that the viewing sequence also ensured a progressive intensification of the architectural experience for the viewer.

THE INTERIOR

Unlike the architecture of the exterior of the house by John Chute, the decoration of the interior was derived from the start from historical sources, as we noted in discussing the contribution of Richard Bentley to the first phase of the building programme. Bentley also designed the chimney-pieces of most of the rooms up to the time of his departure from Strawberry Hill for Jersey late in 1753.[44] After he had returned in the middle of 1756, Walpole accepted from him the designs for the screen and chimney-piece of the Holbein Chamber, and the description of that room by Thomas Gray shows how thorough-going were Walpole's efforts to achieve antiquity by that date. Gray wrote to Wharton on 8 September, 1759:

Mr. W. has lately made a new Bedchamber, which as it is the best of anything he has yet done, and in your own Gothic way, I must describe a little. You enter by a peaked door at one corner of the room (out of a narrow winding passage, you may be sure) into an Alcove, in which the bed is to stand, formed by a screen of pierced work opening by one large arch in the middle to the rest of the chamber (Plate 105), which is lighted at the other end by a window of three bays, whose tops are of rich painted glass in mosaic.

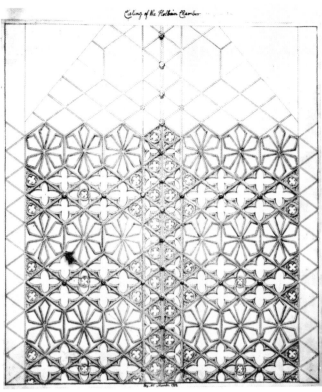

The ceiling is coved and fretted in star and quatrefoil compartments, with roses at the intersections, all in papier-mâché. The chimney on your left is the high-altar in the cathedral of Rouen (from whence the Screen is also taken) consisting of a low surbased Arch beneath two octagonal Towers, whose pinnacles almost reach the ceiling, all of nich-work. The chairs and dressing-table are real carved ebony, picked up at auctions. The hangings uniform purple paper, hung all over with the court of Henry ye 8th, copied after the Holbein's in the Queen's Closet at Kensington, in black and gold frames. The bed is to be either from Burghleigh (for Lord Exeter is new furnishing it, and means to sell some of his original household-stuff) of the rich old tarnish'd embroidery; or if that is not to be had, and it must be new, it is to be a cut velvet with a dark purple pattern on a stone-coloured ground, and deep-mixt fringes and tassels.[45]

Gray is mistaken in the derivation of the chimney-piece, which is based on the tomb of Archbishop Warham in Canterbury Cathedral, but he was clearly pleased with Walpole's striving for historical authenticity. In the event, the bed from Burghley House was not available, and Walpole had a new one made by William Vile. Gray must have been shown Richard Bentley's design for this bed, he describes it so closely, so the fact that he does not credit Bentley with designing the room's interior decoration indicates that Walpole directed Bentley to the historical sources. The ceiling of this chamber had been drawn out in detail by Johann Heinrich Müntz (Plate 106).[46] Bentley also made designs for the columbarium, the gallery and the tribune after his return from Jersey in 1756, but none of these designs were executed. In 1754, while Bentley was away, Walpole and John Chute had found in designing the library interior, that, with the help of their printed sources, they could manage the interior decoration of Strawberry Hill without the aid of Bentley.

The library was clearly a room of great importance to Walpole, and the pride he took in it can be gauged by the delightful portrait he commissioned from Johann Heinrich

107. G. R. Harding after Johann Heinrich Müntz, *Portrait of Horace Walpole*, ink and wash, 178 × 121 mm, date unknown. Courtesy of the Lewis Walpole Library, Farmington, Connecticut.

Müntz in 1756, which shows him seated against the window, with the Thames in the background and his spaniel Rosette in attendance (Plate 107). Müntz had painted the gothic script on the ceiling of the library which was designed by Walpole himself.[47]

The designing of the library was first placed in the hands of Richard Bentley, who executed a series of highly finished and detailed drawings. These show doubled arches intersecting with single arches to form the bays of bookshelves which were to line the walls completely except at the east end, where the window of three lights with quatrefoils above

108. Richard Bentley, *First Design for the Library of Strawberry Hill*, ink and wash, 185 × 308 mm, 1753. Courtesy of the Lewis Walpole Library, Farmington, Connecticut.

was placed, and at the fireplace and door. This is seen in elevations and in plan (Plates 108–9), but all Bentley's labour was lost even before he left Strawberry Hill for Jersey as Walpole had him design a second scheme, seen in a lively elevation showing a figure (presumably, since it is so slight, that of Walpole himself), reaching for a volume from bays where gothic arches no longer intersect but come together and dangle perilously unsupported, in a very mannerist way (Plate VII). Walpole's letters to Bentley show that

109. Richard Bentley, *First Plan for the Library of Strawberry Hill*, ink and wash, 167 × 235 mm, 1753. Courtesy of the Lewis Walpole Library, Farmington, Connecticut.

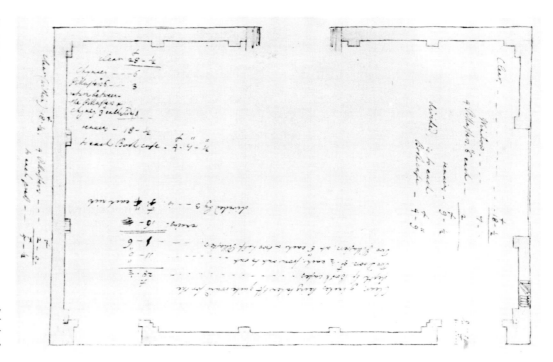

112. (*facing page, bottom*) John Chute, *Elevation for the wall of the Library of Strawberry Hill*, ink, 156 × 273 mm, 1753. Courtesy of the Lewis Walpole Library, Farmington, Connecticut.

110. John Chute, *Sheet of Sketches, one for the Library of Strawberry Hill*, ink and pencil, 325 × 228 mm, 1753. Courtesy of The National Trust.

111. Wenceslaus Hollar, *Screen in Old St Paul's Cathedral* (detail), 1716.

he rejected this second scheme on 19 December, 1753.[48] But he had not rejected its source, a print by Wenceslaus Hollar of the screen which had separated nave from choir in old St Paul's Cathedral (Plate 111).[49] By 2 March, 1754, he had decided to execute a scheme for the library by John Chute which was based on the same source, so one may fairly assume that the choice of the Hollar print was made by Walpole rather than by either of his draughtsmen. John Chute simply developed the motif to a scale commensurate with the room, and he can be seen doing this in a very slight sketch among a sheet of classical sketches, and also in a fully detailed pencil drawing of one of the bays (Plates 110, 112–13), both of which are inscribed on the end pages of his copy of Vincenzo

113. John Chute, *Design for a Bay of the Library of Strawberry Hill*, pencil, 325 × 228 mm, 1753. Courtesy of The National Trust.

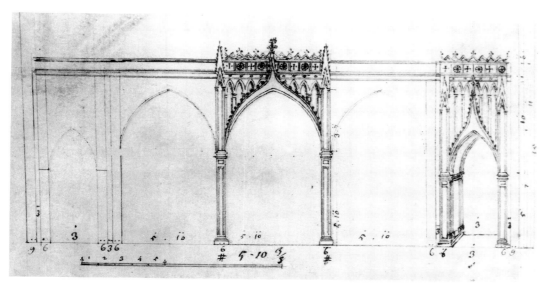

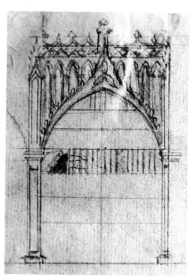

Scamozzi, *Les Cinq ordres d'architecture* (Paris 1585), which is still in the library of The Vyne. Walpole was able to tell Bentley on 3 November, "The Library is delightful", and he installed his books on the shelves over the Christmas holidays (Plate 114).[50]

From this point on, the internal decoration of Strawberry Hill was determined by Walpole and simply adapted to the site by his several architects. In most cases he used printed sources. For example, he sent the following note to Robert Adam when he had determined on the design of the round room at the end of the gallery in 1766: "Mr. Walpole has sent Mr. Adam the two books and hopes at his leisure he will think of the ceiling and the chimney-piece. The ceiling is to be taken from the plate 165 of St. Paul's, the circular window. The chimney is from the shrine of Edward the Confessor at Westminster. The diameter of the room is 22 feet."[51] For the doorway to the gallery and the niches of the tribune he used an original drawing by Johann Heinrich Müntz of a true gothic monument, the Abbot's door of St Alban's Abbey (Plate V).[52] Only when Thomas Pitt rented "the Palazzo Pitti" in Twickenham in 1762 does some invention in design seem to have been endorsed. Pitt designed the grated door to the tribune, and, with the help of John Chute, the chimney-piece of the gallery, of which a half-elevation has survived in a pencil sketch by Chute (Plate 115).[53] Isolated, this seems a little out of place in the decorative scheme of that room, which is dominated by the rich groin vaulting of the ceiling, derived from the chapel of King Henry the Seventh in Westminster Abbey. Walpole described his ceiling as being "richer than the roof of Paradise".[54] But in

execution, the lack of antiquity of the chimney-piece was disguised by its being encased in one of the five niches (designed on the model of the tomb of Archbishop Bourchier in Canterbury Cathedral) which projected from the north wall of the gallery and served to break the monotony of its length (Plate 116).[55]

The tribune was known originally as the cabinet, and was intended "to have all the air of a Catholic chapel—bar consecration".[56] The fittings for this room were certainly made-to-measure in London, since Walpole wrote to Montagu on 20 August, 1761, "I am expecting Mr. Chute to hold a chapter on the cabinet—a barge-load of niches, window-frames and ribs is arrived".[57] Since the digging of the foundations for the building had only been begun on 30 June of that year, Walpole certainly believed in having everything to hand before committing himself to the execution of his buildings. It is not possible from Toynbee's publication of the *Strawberry Hill Accounts* to determine the names of the craftsmen but with the exception of William Peckitt, the stained-glass artist from York, they can be assumed to have been London craftsmen; and even Peckitt was in London in 1761 exhibiting his designs.[58] He supplied the skylight of yellow glass in an eight-pointed star which gave an ecclesiastical glow to the interior of this room and was perfectly in keeping with the scheme of decoration since it simulated the stone star which

116. Edward Edwards, *View of the Gallery of Strawberry Hill*, 1774.

114. (*facing page, above*) Edward Edwards *View of the Library of Strawberry Hill*.

115. (*facing page, below*) John Chute, *First Design for the Chimney in the Gallery of Strawberry Hill*, ink, 198 × 106 mm, 1762. Courtesy of the Lewis Walpole Library, Farmington, Connecticut.

knits together the vaulting of the ceiling of the Chapter House at York Minster. The pattern of the vaulting itself however, is not from that ceiling, as is frequently asserted, but from a design by Chute executed in London and brought to the site by barge. The design is based on the flowing tracery of the stained-glass windows of York Minster.

The experience of gothic architecture is at its most intense in the tribune, because of the closed nature of its plan, which is felt with great effect after the openness and relative gaiety of the gallery, "all Gothicism and gold and crimson, and looking-glass", as Gray described it.[59] It is a square, but with large absidal projections on each side, and the hollowing out of the walls in niches, the fluting of the columns, and the weaving pattern of the ribs give an effect of insubstantiality, or what Walpole would probably have referred to as "lightness". The viewer's perception of this spatial complexity was considerably enhanced by the carpet specially woven for the room at Moorefields, which repeated at its centre the shape of the golden skylight.[60].

Walpole considered the building complete once the tribune was finished and began admitting visitors at least from 3 September, 1763, when he wrote to Montagu, "I keep an inn; the sign "The Gothic Castle"—Since my gallery was finished I have not been in it a quarter of an hour altogether; my whole life is passed in giving tickets for seeing it, and hiding myself when it is seen."[61]

THE STYLE

The archaeological element in the composition of Strawberry Hill has long been recognised as the factor which was to bear most directly upon the theory and practice of later advocates of the gothic revival. Although John Chute enjoyed an enviable reputation as a genealogist, his drawings for Strawberry Hill are dependent upon archaeological examples only where the evidence indicates that Walpole played a leading role in determining the design. Richard Bentley, whose visual imagination was completely unfettered by precedent, was just as subject to Walpole's historical bent when designing for Strawberry Hill. Mr Lewis has demonstrated how Walpole and Bentley set about amalgamating the elements that appealed particularly to them from the limited visual resources at their disposal. They decided upon Prince Arthur's tomb in Worcester Cathedral for the decoration of the paper hanging in the hall and staircase, and the print showing this tomb in Francis Sandford's *History of the Kings of England* (London, 1677) (Plate 92) bears several manuscript notes, "With Henry V's tomb for the interstices", is one of the directions, perhaps intended for Mr Tudor, who took over the painting of the paper when Bentley had gone to Jersey.[62] A note on the endpapers of Walpole's copy reads, "for an architrave 329", and on turning to page 329 we find a print of the railing of the tomb of the Earl and Duchess of Somerset in Windsor. In deriving ornaments for Strawberry Hill from these printed sources Walpole would have felt himself on secure ground methodologically, since neo-classical architects turned to prints of classical buildings to provide sources for decoration for their houses in the eighteenth century. In fact, in these very years Walpole and Chute were using the treatise of Sebastian Serlio in this manner to design very beautiful classical facades for Hagley Hall, Worcestershire.[63]

By comparison with the interior of the house, the exterior of Strawberry Hill is tame and without character in the details (Plate 117). As the drawings demonstrate, John Chute was not deeply versed in gothic architecture of longer lineage than that of Batty Langley and William Kent at the time of the creation of Strawberry Hill, though as we shall see in a later chapter he was to become quite archaeological when designing the changes to the chapel at The Vyne. His first design for the cloister, sacrificed to Walpole's

117. Anonymous, *View of Strawberry Hill from the south-east in 1763*.

desire for lightness, also shows a grasp of the muscular and volumetric qualities of gothic architecture which appears very rarely in his drawings. These are mainly in a thin and dry technique, conditioned by the use of rulers, set-squares and compasses, with little shading and no wash, and nourished only on the meagre fare to be gleaned from the current textbooks on perspective. This astringency of draughtsmanship carries over into the buildings themselves, making them appear far more frail than they actually are; nothing in the history of the gothic revival has proved more durable than the architecture of John Chute.

Strawberry Hill shares with the work of William Kent the misfortune of being frequently classed in the stylistic category of "the rococo", and even in the nonsense category of "rococo gothic".[64] This is sometimes done in the mistaken belief that its principal designer was Richard Bentley, famed for his rococo book illustrations.[65] It is an indefensible descriptive term for the architecture of the building, however. John Chute's exterior has none of the exuberance of linear patterning that characterises the rococo style; and by definition the rococo style is free from historical association, whereas the interior of Strawberry Hill is characterised by faithful adherence to historical precedent. The plan of Strawberry Hill features asymmetry as its main characteristic, and admittedly asymmetry is typical of rococo design. There is a very important difference, however, in that rococo asymmetry is linear and confined to two dimensions and does not express itself in plan even in the most rococo buildings. The asymmetry of Strawberry Hill is a matter of planning and it expresses itself in a variety of volumes clearly perceived to be three-dimensional in elevation. This is a difference in kind from the asymmetry of the rococo and there is no reason to confuse the two.

John Chute, however, used rococo designs for two of his ceilings at The Vyne, and it is possible that he was linked with the circle of artists associated with the St Martin's Lane Academy, which was the centre of rococo design in England at that date.[66] Apart from an uninstructive geometrical drawing of a gate, signed and dated on the verso 'John Chute 1732',[67] there are no drawings from Chute's hand earlier than those for Strawberry Hill and Hagley Hall. This is the more surprising because of his many years of residence in Italy, from which he would, in the normal course of events, have brought back many sketches, had he been a proficient draughtsman when he was there. He certainly had a keen interest in architecture at the time, and in one of his rare letters expressed particular appreciation of the buildings of Raphael.[68] It is possible therefore, that John Chute only began to learn to make sketches in architecture after his return from Italy to England.

If that were the case, he would have gone to the most fashionable drawing-master of the day, John Joshua Kirby, who was to become perspective-master to the Prince of Wales and who in 1752 gave lessons in the St Martin's Lane Academy.[69] Since Kirby's treatise *The Perspective of Architecture* (1761) is listed in an inventory of the books of John Chute at The Vyne, this possibility is strengthened. Chute also acquired Isaac Ware's *Complete Body of Architecture* (1756), and a third work, listed simply as *Perspective*, could be either Kirby's *Perspective Made Easy* of 1754 or Ware's *The Practice of Perspective*, of 1756.[70] Isaac Ware was also a prominent member of the St Martin's Lane Academy, so John Chute's architectural training may have been in the centre of the rococo movement in England. The evidence is inconclusive but, such as it is, it points in that direction.

In so far as the rococo of the St Martin's Lane group had an impact, beyond the decorative and graphic arts, on the practice of architecture in England at the mid-century, Mark Girouard has described its effects as follows:

> The Palladianism of Lord Burlington's generation was not abandoned, but it was liberalised; experiment and eclecticism took the place of the search for the ideal; it became possible once more to admire Wren, Vanbrugh and even the Gothic; imagination (or 'fancy' as they called it then) was stressed at the expense of authority. Approval of what Isaac Ware termed ''variety of figures'' led to the prolific reintroduction of the bay window.[71]

This clearly has relevance to some architectural features of Strawberry Hill, and in that sense a connection can be made between the rococo movement and the creation of Strawberry Hill by Horace Walpole, John Chute and Richard Bentley. But it should not be pushed too far; bay windows, after all, were a common feature of gothic domestic architecture, and Walpole did not need the licence of Isaac Ware to indulge in them since they were sanctioned by antique precedent. For the reasons stated earlier, rococo is a most unhappy label to attach to Strawberry Hill, whether in terms of its plan or its elevations or its decoration.

The major innovation in architecture effected by Walpole at Strawberry Hill was the asymmetry of its plan. A similar asymmetry with castellations had been the outcome of Sir John Vanbrugh's additions to his house in Greenwich, but there is no evidence that Walpole was conscious of this precedent and he is remarkably blind to the virtues of Vanbrugh's architecture in his writings.[72] This idea of asymmetry, as we have seen, was one that he imported from Kent's practice of design in landscape gardening, and it is entirely appropriate that the historian of the picturesque in gardening should, in the words of Sir John Summerson, have ''opened the door to the architecture of the picturesque''.[73] However reticently realised in the elevations of John Chute, Walpole very purposefully gave his house the variety of volumes and indeterminacy of outline that were to characterise villa architecture from that time forward. That he, rather than his

Gothick Door, standing in the South Wall within ye old Abby-Church of St. Alban, at St. Albans, in Hertfordshire.
J. H. Müntz 1762.

V. Johann Heinrich Müntz, *Internal elevation of a Door in St Alban's Abbey*, ink and wash, 215 × 260 mm, 1762. Courtesy of the Lewis Walpole Library, Farmington, Connecticut.

VI. Johann Heinrich Müntz, *Section of the Octagonal Room for Mr. Bateman's House at Old Windsor*, ink and wash, 215 × 370 mm, 1761. Courtesy of the Lewis Walpole Library, Farmington, Connecticut.

VII. Richard Bentley, *Internal elevation of the Library proposed for Strawberry Hill*, ink and wash, 141 × 305 mm, 1753. Courtesy of the Lewis Walpole Library, Farmington, Connecticut.

draughtsmen John Chute and Richard Bentley, was responsive to, and responsible for, the picturesque in architecture can be demonstrated by analysis of their designs for other houses, which are totally lacking in picturesque feeling. Walpole, however, wrote in 1776, when the Beauclerk Tower was finished, ''it has an exceedingly pretty effect, breaking the long line of the house picturesquely and looking very ancient''.[74]

IV. The Domestic Architecture of the Strawberry Hill Architects

JOHN CHUTE

It is a measure of how completely John Chute had replaced Richard Bentley in the confidence of Horace Walpole that in 1755 he was entrusted with the design of Chalfont House, Buckinghamshire, acquired for Walpole's newly-wed niece, Lady Maria Walpole, and her husband Charles Churchill. Walpole wrote in that year that the building of a new house would prove very expensive, but that "Mr. Chute has designed the prettiest house in the world for them".[1] Bentley designed the stable block, but the house itself was by Chute.[2]

None of Chute's drawings can be associated positively with this commission, but there is one elevation which, simply because it cannot be connected with other known building projects by Chute, may represent his intentions for Chalfont (Plate 118). It shows a rectangular building of five bay windows by three, two storeys high, battlemented, and with bow windows of pointed lights surmounted by the flat labels that had been used in the first designs for Strawberry Hill. But even if this could be identified as the elevation for Chalfont, it would not help very much with a reconstruction of the house, since in 1760 Walpole wrote that the Churchills were too busy making babies to put into effect any of the suggestions for alterations that he provided for them.[3] Rebuildings and expansions of the house in the nineteenth century have obliterated any evidence of Chute's work on the site.[4]

Time has been more kind to John Chute's work at Donnington Grove, Berkshire, which he designed in 1763 for the antiquarian James Pettit Andrews (Plate 119).[5] The house was subsequently owned by Beau Brummell's parents, who added the porch to the entrance front and the large saloon of one storey to the north of the main block, but they did not alter Chute's building structurally or decoratively.[6] Some preliminary elevations are in the Chute Album in the Lewis Walpole Library (Plates 120–1), and at The Vyne there are four elevations in wash drawings prepared for engraving, which were formerly in Walpole's collection at Strawberry Hill (Plates 122–4).[7] These are by the London carpenter John Hobcraft, who appears regularly in building documents of the eighteenth century as the craftsman responsible for some of the most attractive and surprising features in the architecture of the period.[8]

Donnington Grove has been analysed in detail by Christopher Hussey, who pointed to it as the outstanding example of gothic revival architecture "handled with a classical purist's sense of style and proportion".[9] This is borne out by the evidence of the elevation drawings. 1763, the year of its design, is also the date of completion of the principal buildings at Strawberry Hill designed by John Chute, but one would never

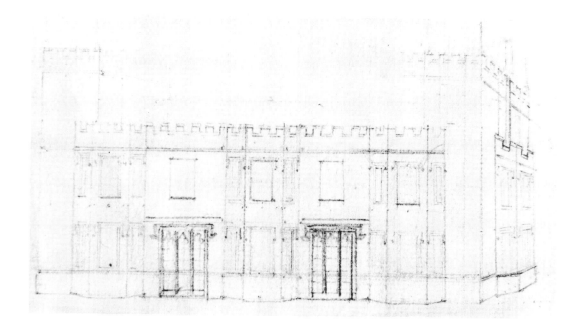

guess this from a study of the drawings or of the house. It is a rectangular building of five bays by three, three storeys high, with battlements and pinnacles. There is not the slightest suspicion of the asymmetry that had given distinction to the planning of Strawberry Hill.

As Hussey has pointed out, there is, however, a close similarity between the elevations of Donnington (Plate 125) and those that Chute had made for the south and east fronts in the first phase of building at Strawberry Hill ten years earlier. There is larger and more frequent fenestration in the Donnington elevations, but all the principal features of Strawberry Hill are present. A three-bay cloister acted as entrance on the west front and there was a projecting oriel window on the south front and a bay window of three storeys on the east. The windows were pointed, and Chute extended the flat labels above the windows, so that they acted as string courses between the storeys. But otherwise the elevations are different only in being the richer for the introduction of attractive niches, with sculpted figures on gothic bases, at the first floor level on the south front.

The internal decoration of Donnington Grove differs completely from that of Strawberry Hill in that Chute depends for his effects entirely upon a clarity and symmetry

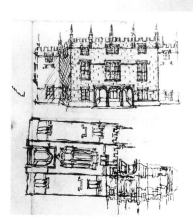

120. (*a and b*) John Chute, *Elevations for Donnington Grove, Berks.*, ink, 114 × 190 mm, 1763. Courtesy of the Lewis Walpole Library, Farmington, Connecticut.

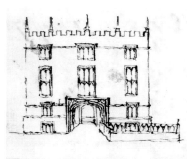

121. John Chute, *Elevation for Donnington Grove, Berks.*, ink, 75 × 128 mm, 1763. Courtesy of the Lewis Walpole Library, Farmington, Connecticut.

119. James Pettit Andrews, *View of Donnington Grove, Berks.* Courtesy of the Lewis Walpole Library, Farmington, Connecticut.

122. John Hobcraft after John Chute, *Elevation for Donnington Grove, Berks.*, ink and wash, 305 × 610 mm, 1763. Courtesy of The National Trust.

123. John Hobcraft after John Chute, *Elevation for Donnington Grove, Berks.*, ink and wash, 507 × 507 mm, 1763. Courtesy of The National Trust.

124. John Hobcraft after John Chute, *Elevation for Donnington Grove, Berks.*, ink and wash, 507 × 507 mm, 1763. Courtesy of The National Trust.

of disposition of the architectural elements (Plate 127). This is particularly striking in the centre of the house, which is occupied by the sparsely decorated staircase, cantilevered out over the ground floor and lit from the top by a clerestorey of intersecting pointed arches (Plate 128). Thin clustered colonnettes, like those of the door-casings, rest on a cast-iron balustrade that simulates gothic panelling: but otherwise, decoration is confined to a series of quatrefoils running below the stair platform, and above the arches of the first-floor walkway. The antiquarian interests of James Andrews played a minimal part in the decoration of his house by comparison to that of Horace Walpole. There is some gothic plasterwork comparable to that in the first-floor ceiling of the round tower at Strawberry Hill, and several chimney-pieces are lightly touched with gothic decoration. But the dining-room is decorated in chinoiserie, and Chute supplied the design for a gothic and chinoiserie bed (Plate 126), so he certainly did not follow Walpole in the latter's predilection for historical correctness in the choice of motifs for interior decoration.

The importance of Donnington Grove within the *oeuvre* of Chute is that its decoration reflects a flexibility of attitude towards style that one would not suspect from seeing his work at Strawberry Hill. It also confirms, in the adventurousness of the staircase, a feeling for structure in architecture that only rarely appears in his drawings, for instance in the first design for the long cloister at Strawberry Hill. Hussey has remarked that Chute's staircase is exceptional, "in assimilating Perpendicular Gothic forms to an essentially Georgian conception with an easy elegance that Wyatt sometimes achieved but later architects rarely".[10] Staircases were a subject of intense study on the part of John Chute, and at The Vyne, he built an example in the classical style with a virtuosity

125. John Chute, Donnington Grove, Berks., *c*.1765. Courtesy of the Royal Commission on Historic Monuments of England.

126. John Chute, *Designs for a Gothic Bed for Donnington Grove, Berks.*, ink, 228 × 188 mm, 1763. Courtesy of the Hampshire County Record Office.

127. John Chute, The Hall of Donnington Grove, Berks., *c.* 1765. Courtesy of *Country Life*.

128. (*facing page*) John Chute, The Staircase at Donnington Grove, Berks., *c.* 1765. Courtesy of *Country Life*.

parallel to that he displayed in the gothic style at Donnington Grove, as though to prove Walpole's claims that Chute was "an able geometrician and was an exquisite architect and of the purest taste both in the Grecian and Gothic styles".[11]

On the death of his brother Anthony in 1754, John Chute inherited The Vyne, the family house and estate, near Basingstoke in Hampshire (Plate 129).[12] There is only one reference to it in his letters to Horace Walpole before this date. On the death of his brother Francis in 1745 he wrote from Rome: "my loss is inexpressible on all accounts, nor am I able to find the least comfort in being one horrid step nearer to a mouldering estate, which has lost the only chance of ever being repaired".[13] This unenthusiastic account of The Vyne does not seem to have been warranted for it had been so well cared for by Anthony Chute during his 32 years of ownership, that John was spared problems of major renovation, except to the hall and staircase.[14] The estate was reported to be worth £4,000 annually, and even the zeal of Horace Walpole could not predict an expenditure of much

129. Johann Heinrich Müntz, *View of The Vyne, Hants., from the north*, ink and wash, 393 × 545 mm, 1756. Courtesy of The National Trust and The Paul Mellon Centre, London.

above £5,000 for the alterations which he proposed in the "Inventionary" he drew up for The Vyne on 1 July, 1755.[15]

That was not the first time Walpole had proposed alterations for his friend's house. He started to make suggestions on his first visit there the previous October when he drew a sketch of the chapel, which he then sent to Richard Bentley "to draw out better" on 3 November, 1754.[16] John Chute, however, was not to be rushed into alterations, and three years later Walpole wrote dejectedly to George Montagu: "I have done advising, as I see Mr. Chute will never execute anything. The very altarpiece that I sent for to Italy is not placed yet.[17] But when he could refrain from making the little Gothic Columbarium for his family which I proposed and Mr. Bentley had drawn so divinely, it is not probable he should do anything else."[18]

As we shall see in the chapter dealing with ecclesiastical architecture, John Chute provided a very fine memorial to his family, even if he had rejected Walpole's prescription for a "Gothic Columbarium". He also renovated the hall and staircase of The Vyne, but not until 1770, and then in the classical rather than the gothic style.

More than 70 drawings for the staircase survive,[19] but unfortunately there are no building accounts, so we cannot identify the craftsmen who translated Chute's splendid conception into the richly detailed masterpiece that survives (Plate 130). Chute himself guided every part of the work, as detailed drawings for even the roof coffering

130. (*above*) John Chute, The Staircase of The Vyne, Hants., *c*.1770. Courtesy of The Royal Commission on the Historic Monuments of England.

131. (*left*) John Chute, *Design for the Staircase of The Vyne, Hants.*, pencil and ink, 274 × 176 mm, *c*.1770. Courtesy of the Hampshire County Record Office.

132. (*below*) John Chute, *Design for the Staircase of The Vyne, Hants.*, ink, 292 × 329 mm, *c*.1770. Courtesy of the Hampshire County Record Office.

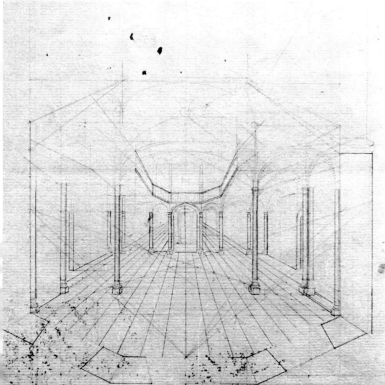

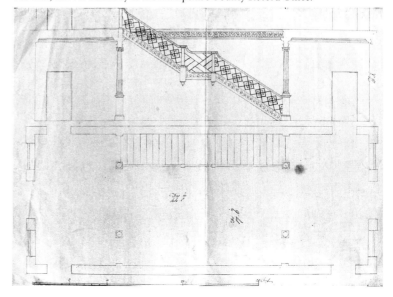

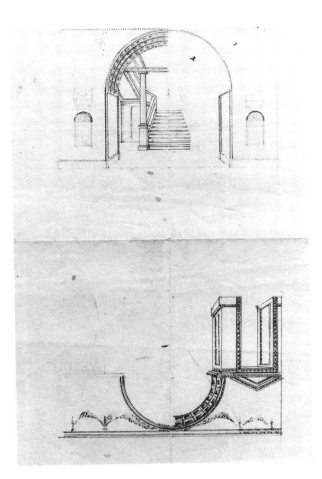

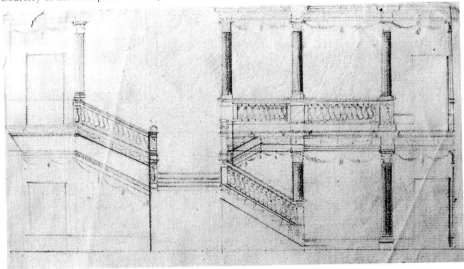

133. (*left*) John Chute, *Design for the Staircase of The Vyne, Hants.*, ink, 228 × 180 mm, *c.*1770. Courtesy of the Hampshire County Record Office.

134. (*below*) John Chute, *Design for the Staircase of The Vyne, Hants.*, pencil, 184 × 225 mm, *c.*1770. Courtesy of the Hampshire County Record Office.

demonstrate.[20] It was not an easy design to bring to realisation, for the hall was a quite narrow rectangle, 44 ft by 17½. Chute's skill in perspective drawing came into good service on this occasion, and the drawings reflect the obsessive industry and precision with which he calculated the visual effects he sought to achieve (Plate 131).[21] The result still surprises and delights, partly because of the vigorously modelled details of ceilings, doors, walls and banisters, but principally because of the extensive space evoked by the assured placing of the fluted Corinthian columns in a manner that produces an illusory lengthening and broadening of the area.

The successful scheme was arrived at only after many alternatives had been drawn out by Chute. A gothic hallway is envisaged in Plate 131 with a three-arched entrance to the stairway. Then there is a columned entrance to the stairway, slenderly Ionic and mixed with a Chinese-gothic banister in Plate 132 and this must have been seriously considered, since it is accompanied by a floor-plan of the hall. There are two schemes on one sheet that are more thoroughly classical and they propose a coffered arch for entrance, and, in the upper drawing, a Doric column for support (Plate 133). Plate 134 shows the staircase as executed, with the exception of the columns on the ground floor, shown here as Corinthian, but in fact Doric. The order changes to Corinthian on the first floor, a change which is consistent with the order of the portico which gives access to the staircase.

It is not surprising that Chute should have considered classical elevations for The Vyne. The principal feature of the house is the Corinthian portico built on to the north entrance by John Webb and so classical alterations to the south front would have had the virtue of consistency.[22] The present battlements of the north front and the blind gothic windows of the chapel wing on that front destroy its consistency; but these are alterations of the mid-nineteenth century, and John Chute had nothing to do with them.[23] He made

135. Gabriel Mathias, *Portrait of John Chute*, oil on canvas, 1270 × 1055 mm, 1758. Courtesy of The National Trust and The Paul Mellon Centre, London.

no drawings for alterations to the north front, and his designs for gothicising The Vyne refer to the interior and to the south and west fronts.

In the long run, Chute was not to make any alterations to these fronts either. A tower was built by one of his successors in the centre of the south front, but this was removed by Wiggett Chute, who gave the elevations their present character in the nineteenth century.[24]

Nevertheless, it is clear that John Chute had resolved to apply gothic architecture to the south front of The Vyne. He must have felt rather defiant about this decision because the large portrait which he had painted by Gabriel Mathias in 1758 shows him holding a sheet of paper bearing the proposed gothic elevation (Plates 135–6). His pose is that of a Grand Tourist, in richly embroidered vestcoat and in a relaxed stance typical of Batoni

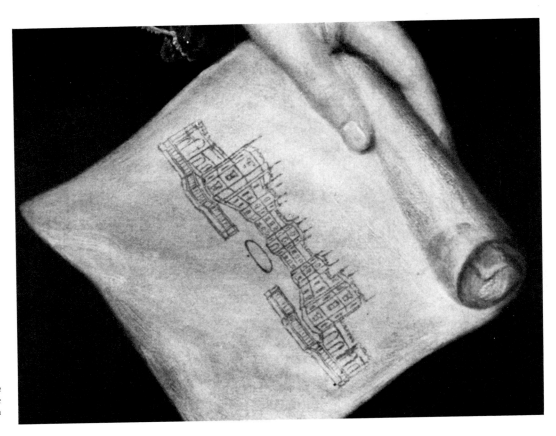

136. Gabriel Mathias, *Portrait of John Chute* (detail), 1758. Courtesy of The National Trust and The Paul Mellon Centre, London.

portraits, but against John Webb's classical portico rather than against Roman temple ruins. The elevation so uncompromisingly displayed corresponds to many sheets of designs for The Vyne among Chute's papers. The most finished are two framed drawings at The Vyne (Plates 137–8). These are certainly based on drawings by John Chute, but the foliage and staffage are the work of a second artist, Johann Heinrich Müntz.[25]

The most interesting feature of these designs for gothicising The Vyne is that they differ so little from the drawings Chute had made for the building of Strawberry Hill. The rectangular windows of The Vyne are retained without alteration, but the flat stone labels over the windows, the semi-hexagonal bays, and the thin pinnacles of the west front of Strawberry Hill reappear here and are applied to the existing structure without in any way affecting its balanced and ungothic form.

Other alterations by John Chute to The Vyne consisted of plasterwork to the ceilings of the chapel parlour, the further drawing-room and its ante-room, and the large drawing-room. These are in a very thin rococo manner, and the drawings for them, though among the Chute Papers, are probably not by John Chute.[26] But this use of the rococo, classical and gothic styles in the one building in which he had total freedom of choice in design demonstrates how wrong it is to think of John Chute simply as the architectural amanuensis of Horace Walpole. As at Donnington Grove, Chute showed no inclination to follow Walpole in his love of asymmetry, and was not as single-minded as his younger friend in the revival of the gothic style in decoration.

137. (*facing page, above*) Johann Heinrich Müntz after John Chute, *View of the proposed South Front of The Vyne, Hants.*, pencil and ink, 95 × 146 mm, *c.* 1758. Courtesy of The National Trust.

138. (*facing page, below*) Johann Heinrich Müntz after John Chute, *View of the proposed West Front of The Vyne, Hants.*, pencil and ink, 95 × 146 mm, *c.*1758. Courtesy of The National Trust.

RICHARD BENTLEY

Richard Bentley designed the elevations and plan of an unexecuted farm-house for Sir Thomas Seabright of Beechwood, Herefordshire, as Walpole's inscription on one of the drawings informs us (Plate 139 and Plate VIII).[27] It consists of four of John Chute's

139. Richard Bentley, *Elevation of a Farm for Beechwood, Herefs.*, ink and wash, 254 × 191 mm, 1759. Courtesy of the Lewis Walpole Library, Farmington, Connecticut.

towers for Strawberry Hill squashed together, so its date must be 1759. Only the fenestration of the third floor is changed. In a very mannerist way, Bentley runs the three-light windows through the drip-course into the corbels of the battlements. This is a unique design, however, in that the plan of the house resembles a quatrefoil opening and may have been intended therefore to demonstrate the applicability of gothic decorative motifs to domestic planning.

An elevation and plan for a gothic cloister were made by Bentley and have been associated with Strawberry Hill (Plate 140).[28] Since there is no provision in the drawings for either a gallery or a tower, it is more probable that they were designed for Richard Bateman's cloister at Old Windsor, for which there are designs by Johann Heinrich Müntz, to be discussed below. There is also a drawing of the elevation of a small house of three bays in the gothic style by Bentley, but there is no indication of its having been executed, and it is of little interest by comparison with his other gothic revival designs.[29]

140. Richard Bentley, *Elevation of a Cloister for The Grove, Old Windsor, Berks.*, ink and wash, 230 × 382 mm, 1759. Courtesy of the Lewis Walpole Library, Farmington, Connecticut.

Bentley (Plate 141) did not design any other houses in the gothic style. This was no fault of Walpole, who never seems to have lost faith in the architectural abilities of Bentley, though, as we have seen, his designs for Strawberry Hill were rejected more often than not. Walpole suggested that Bentley should make alterations to Ragley in 1751, Roel in 1752, Cassiobury in 1754, Greatworth and The Vyne in 1757, Hinchinbrooke in 1759

141. John Giles Eccardt,
Portrait of Richard Bentley,
1754. Courtesy of the Lewis
Walpole Library, Farmngton,
Connecticut.

and Aston in 1760. Bentley could not have had a friend more anxious to forward his talents, such as they were.[30]

JOHANN HEINRICH MÜNTZ

It is difficult to understand why Walpole made no significant use of the architectural abilities of Johann Heinrich Müntz, who lived in Strawberry Hill during much of its construction from 1756 to 1759. Müntz drew the decorative plan for the ceiling of the Holbein Chamber and we have seen that motifs for the gallery and tribune were derived from his study of St Alban's Abbey. But there is no indication of his having played a part in the planning of Strawberry Hill. While he was there he was busy with experiments in encaustic painting and took an interest in the establishment of the Strawberry Hill Press, besides painting topographical landscapes.[31] He must have discussed gothic architecture with Walpole and Bentley and Chute, but his participation in the building of the house seems to have been confined to laudatory endorsements of the drawings of Chute.

The most complete set of drawings by Müntz are for the house of Richard Bateman at Old Windsor, and possibly it was due to misunderstandings about this project that the quarrel between Müntz and Bentley, which led to Müntz leaving Strawberry Hill, occurred.[32] As we have seen, there are two drawings by Bentley for the cloister at Old Windsor, and in a letter of 24 September 1762 to George Montagu, Walpole attributes that building to Bentley: "I did not doubt but you would approve of Mr. Bateman's, since it changed its religion; I converted it from Chinese to Gothic. His cloister of founders, which by the way is Mr. Bentley's, is delightful. I envy him his old chairs, and

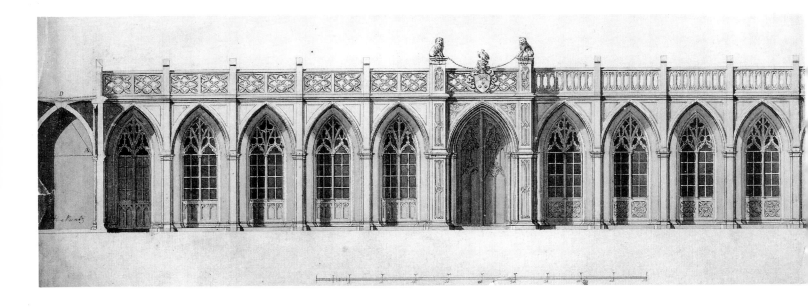

142. Johann Heinrich Müntz, *Elevation of a Cloister for The Grove, Old Windsor, Berks.*, ink, 203 × 392 mm, 1759. Courtesy of the Lewis Walpole Library, Farmington, Connecticut.

the tomb of Caducanus.''[33] That would seem to settle the issue, were it not that all the visual evidence surviving points rather to Müntz as the architect of the cloister and octagonal dining-room that were built at Old Windsor, and his too is the drawing in Brussels of the Tomb of Caducanus, Bishop of Hereford, which Bateman seems to have removed from Dore Abbey, Herefordshire. Walpole, however, never mentions Müntz in connection with Richard Bateman, and in his ''Account of Richard Bentley'', he wrote, ''The Hon. Rich. Bateman at Old Windsor has altered his offices in 1758 according to a plan given by Mr. Bentley'', and says nothing of the additions of cloister and dining-room of 1761.[34] Walpole's falling-out with Müntz was certainly occasioned by a conviction that Müntz had offered a slight to Bentley, and if Bateman passed over Bentley's designs in favour of those of Müntz, Walpole's angry reaction would have been predictable. He had been outraged when the Lytteltons rejected John Chute's designs for Hagley Hall in favour of those of Sanderson Miller.[35]

Whatever the truth about this sad disagreement, Richard Bateman cannot be faulted in his choice, because Müntz provided him with the most sophisticated of any designs for gothic revival architecture in the century (Plate 142). His drawings are marked by a richness and intricacy which neither the earlier architects, nor Chute and Bentley, could reach, because their designs were based on geometrical determinants of form which were foreign in their simplicity to the complex nature of gothic structure and ornament. His traceries for doors, panelling and windows are rich and flowing, with a vitality heightened by the restraints of buttresses and horizontal elements. Müntz was able in linear terms, heightened by even but effective washes, to convey an intensity inherent in the gothic style, which no other architect of the revival was able to express.

Richard Bateman had been able to judge all these qualities in the drawing of the Tomb of Caducanus.[36] But he must have been impressed also by the technical superiority of Müntz's drawings, meticulously scaled and measured in plan and elevation, and with precise correspondence between the sections and the details. Nor did Müntz fail to flatter. One section of the dining-room shows a portrait of the patron, and the other provides a view through the window to the garden which brought the house its fame (Plate 143 and Plate VI).[37] But it was probably the technical assurance displayed in the drawings that had most effect in winning the commission for Müntz. Richard Bateman was no stranger to the gothic revival style by this date, for he had been responsible for the rebuilding of the Church of St John the Evangelist in Shobdon, Herefordshire, in the style associated with William Kent. This will be discussed in detail in the final chapter,

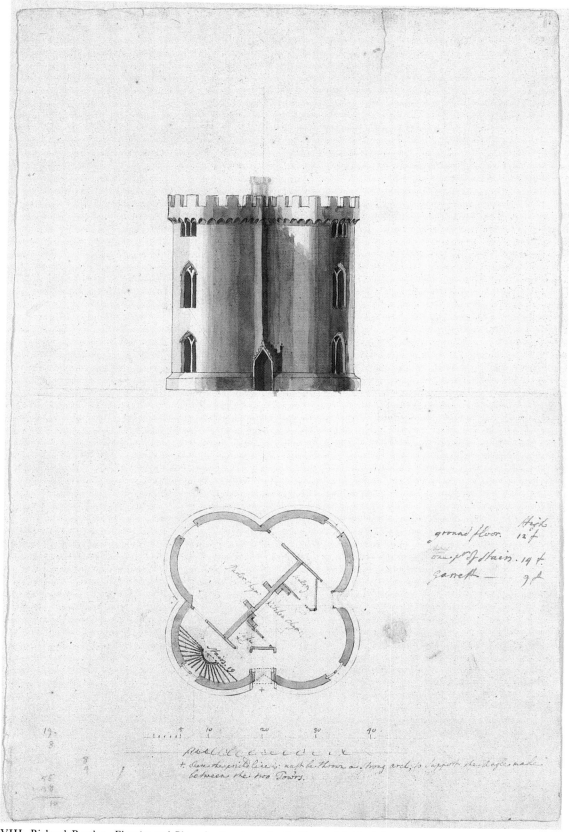

VIII. Richard Bentley, *Elevation and Plan of a Farmhouse for Sir Thomas Sebright*, ink and wash, 382 × 254 mm, *c.* 1758. Courtesy of the Lewis Walpole Library, Farmington, Connecticut.

IX. Richard Bentley, *View of the Hall and Staircase at Strawberry Hill*, ink and wash, 288 × 178 mm, *c.* 1753. Courtesy of the Lewis Walpole Library, Farmington, Connecticut.

143. Johann Heinrich Müntz, *Section of the octagonal room for The Grove, Old Windsor, Berks.*, ink and wash, 254 × 229 mm, 1761. Courtesy of the Lewis Walpole Library, Farmington, Connecticut.

144. Johann Heinrich Müntz, *Elevation of the octagonal room for The Grove, Old Windsor, Berks.*, ink and wash, 229 × 292 mm, 1761. Courtesy of the Lewis Walpole Library, Farmington, Connecticut.

145. Johann Heinrich Müntz, *Design for the Porch and Door for The Grove, Old Windsor, Berks.*, ink and wash, 370 × 150 mm, 1761. Courtesy of the Lewis Walpole Library, Farmington, Connecticut.

but it is sufficient to remark here that he had had the embarrassment and expense of three separate building campaigns before that structure achieved stability.

To judge from the tracery of the double doors of the centre bay of the cloister, Müntz's inspiration for this design is properly antiquarian in its dependence on his study of the St Alban's Abbey doorway. But there is no exact copying, and he demonstrates considerable versatility in gothic ornament. His cloister design suggests alternative decoration at the parapet level as well as at the base panel level, but the discipline of the structure is firmly stated in the emphatic horizontals that respond to the two-stepped stylobate.

The richness of the exterior of the cloister is repeated in the panelling of the octagon dining-room, but the porch and the exterior of the room are by comparison Spartan in their simplicity (Plate 144). The contrast may have been intended to be piquant, but a more probable explanation is that Müntz was simply proposing alternatives from which Bateman could choose. With these drawings can be associated others in the Lewis Walpole Library, one of which is inscribed on top of the sheet, "This half for Porch/this half for Door" (Plate 145). Most of Müntz's detailed drawings suggest alternative schemes. Plate 146, which was probably prepared for Bateman, is an example. An unsigned drawing inscribed "Flat Arch of 4 Centers" provides an alternative to the porch connecting the dining-room to the cloisters. A third elevation and plan for the

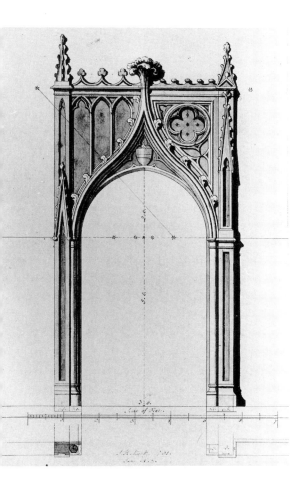

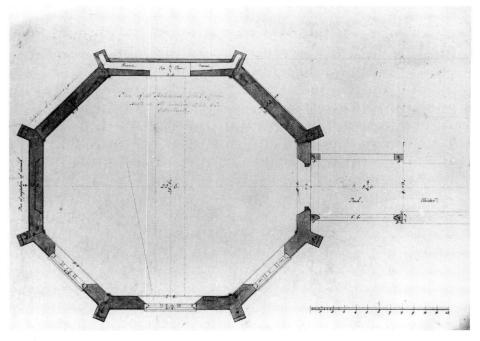

146. Johann Heinrich Müntz, *Door for the octagonal room for The Grove, Old Windsor, Berks.*, ink and wash, 342 × 210 mm, 1761. Courtesy of the Lewis Walpole Library, Farmington, Connecticut.

147. Johann Heinrich Müntz, *Plan for the octagonal room for The Grove, Old Windsor, Berks.*, ink and wash, 254 × 342 mm, 1761. Courtesy of the Lewis Walpole Library, Farmington, Connecticut.

porch can be identified from the correspondence of the dimensions with those shown on the ground-plan of Plate 147, and this too is the justification for associating a drawing for a gothic fireplace, unsigned and undated but similar in markings and technique, with the building scheme at Old Windsor. The plan of the octagon room provides the dates of building, 1761–2.

Müntz's "Egyptian" room for Lord Charlemont, of which a section and plan survive (but no exterior elevation) was oval in shape (Plate 148). It is not certain that the building was ever erected, though the inscription on the back of the plan claims that it was "to be executed in Ireland". These are probably the drawings Müntz refers to in his printed *Proposals* of 1760 as "a Temple in a garden, in the Moresque Stile, of the Author's Composition, and which is going to be executed at a Nobleman's Country Seat".[38] The "Egyptian" of the title refers to the antiquities the room was designed to house rather than to the style of its decoration. Müntz had made a thorough study of Egyptian and other ancient urns during his student years in Rome (1749–53), and he prepared an elaborate publication of these studies in 1772.[39] We find him associating urns with gothic decoration once more in the elevation and plan of a chimney-piece (Plate 149). This unsigned and undated drawing bears an inscription on the back, "Executed for H. Bearns, Esq.", but the whereabouts of Bearn's house and the extent of Müntz's work for him is not known. The mixing of classical urns with gothic niches was quite a familiar feature of gothic revival architecture at this period, so it is no surprise to find Müntz adopting this practice in his drawings for Lord Charlemont; its prevalence and the reasoning that lay behind it will be discussed in the chapter on ecclesiastical architecture.

What is more remarkable by far is Müntz's use of the oval form for the plan of the room, since there is no precedent for this in contemporary practice and no historical example in gothic architecture. The explanation lies in the theories of beauty which

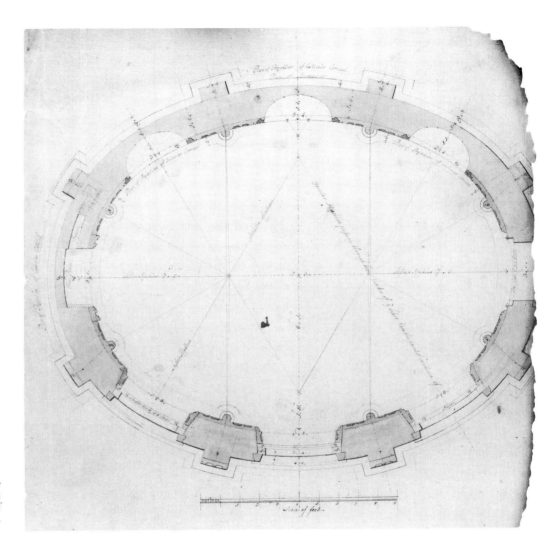

148. Johann Heinrich Müntz, *Plan for the Egyptian room at Marino, Dublin*, ink and wash, 267 × 267 mm, 1762. Courtesy of the Lewis Walpole Library, Farmington, Connecticut.

Müntz had formulated under the influence of Winkelmann in Rome and Hogarth in London, and which he was to articulate in his unpublished treatise on ancient vases. In this work he developed the proposal of Hogarth that the principle of beauty was to be found in the serpentine line. By painstaking geometrical analysis of the vases of antiquity, following the example of Winkelmann, he sought to establish that the higher manifestation of this principle lay, as Hogarth had maintained, in the oval form, or as Müntz adhering to Hogarth preferred to term it, the egg-shaped form.[40] Since Lord Charlemont's room was for the display of the collection of vases he had acquired in his extensive travels in the east and in Italy, Müntz expressed this purpose in its plan. Thus, by a logic that found its structure in aesthetic reasoning, this Egyptian Room in the gothic style became as much a manifesto of the architectural theories of neo-classicism as the very beautiful neighbouring Casino designed for Lord Charlemont by Müntz's friend and fellow-student in Rome, William Chambers. It should be classed among the earliest examples of the *architecture parlante* that was to be the focus of endeavour for the second generation of neo-classical architects in Europe.

Another building at Lord Charlemont's estate at Marino may possibly have been designed by Johann Heinrich Müntz, and it too was in the gothic style; indeed it may

149. Johann Heinrich Müntz, *Design for a Chimney*, ink and wash, 215 × 178 mm, *c*.1760. Courtesy of the Lewis Walpole Library, Farmington, Connecticut.

have been the same building as the one shown in the drawing. So frustratingly scanty is the documentary and visual evidence relating to Marino, that one cannot be certain. Later records, however, show that one of the most admired of the Marino buildings was ''Rosamund's Bower'', which was in the gothic style. No certain visual evidence of it remains, but it may have been connected with drawings that Chambers obtained from Müntz for an unspecified building for Lord Charlemont in 1768.[41] Müntz returned to London for a visit in that year, probably to arrange for the sale of his encaustic paintings which took place in January 1769.[42] He had been living in Holland since leaving Strawberry Hill in 1763.

From Müntz's years in Holland there survives one elevation of a one-storeyed house in Amsterdam, signed and dated 1764 (Plate 150).[43] There is no evidence of its having been

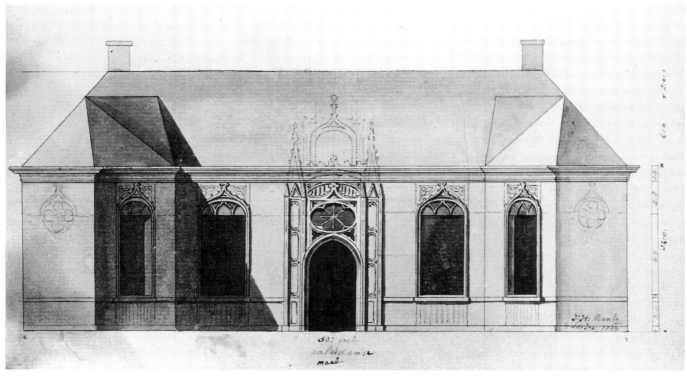

150. Johann Heinrich Müntz, *Elevation for a House in Amsterdam*, ink, pencil and wash, 127 × 254 mm, 1764. Courtesy of the Lewis Walpole Library, Farmington, Connecticut.

151. Johann Heinrich Müntz (attributed), *Elevation of a House for Thomas Hudson in Twickenham, M'sex*, ink and wash, 294 × 369 mm, *c.* 1760. Courtesy of The Richmond Public Libraries and The Paul Mellon Centre, London.

erected, and it is not of great interest, except that it displays the versatility in the handling of gothic ornament that characterised his work in England, but has not got the slightest trace of gothic asymmetry in plan and was clearly intended to be classical in its proportions. Versatility of ornament and symmetry and proportion also marked the small gothic house which the portrait painter Thomas Hudson erected in Twickenham, sometime in the late 1750s, and which is known from a watercolour by J. C. Barrow and an unsigned drawing which may well be by Müntz himself (Plate 151).[44] One would like to have confirmation of this attribution from the correspondence of Horace Walpole, who surely knew it well. But his silence on the subject of the dining-room and cloister for Richard Bateman seems to imply a studied avoidance of notice of the works of Müntz.[45] It should be attributed to him on stylistic grounds and the circumstantial evidence of his activity in architectural design in that locality from 1758 to 1763.

Müntz's career as an architect of the gothic revival in England was more brief than that of any other practitioner, and this should be borne in mind when assessing the importance of his contribution to the style. The slimness of the volume of his output should not be allowed to obscure its excellence in technical terms and visual impact. His patrons were tastemakers, and the fact that he worked for Horace Walpole, Richard Bateman, William Chambers and Lord Charlemont may well have given his work a more pronounced impact upon contemporaries than we can now assess, particularly because of Walpole's later coldness towards him. This did not prevent Walpole from having recourse to the drawings of Müntz in devising architectural features for Strawberry Hill long after his departure from the building, as we have seen. Müntz's other buildings have perished, with the exception of the octagonal room for Richard Bateman, but even if we did not have the drawings to justify admiration for his work, the inspiration he provided at Strawberry Hill would earn him a place of high distinction in the gothic revival. He brought professionalism to a movement in architecture that had previously been amateur in character.

V. The Domestic Architecture of Sanderson Miller and Sir Roger Newdigate

"The Graces droop—am I in Greece or Gothland?", was the despairing cry of William Shenstone after he had seen the proposal drawn up by Sanderson Miller for building Hagley Hall in the gothic style in 1752.[1] Nor was he alone in his disapproval. The prospective builder, Sir George Lyttelton, was faced with the concerted opposition of his wife, his brother Charles, who was the President of the Society of Antiquaries, and his friend and political mentor, William Pitt.[2] As we have noted, even Horace Walpole and John Chute, though busy with designing the first phase of the gothic rebuilding of Strawberry Hill at this date, provided plans and elevations for Hagley Hall that were uncompromisingly classical.[3] "The Grecian is proper only for magnificient and public building", Walpole had explained to Mann,[4] and Hagley Hall could properly be classed as a public building because of the fame of the Lyttelton family, distinguished for its role in public life, and of Hagley Park, hallowed by association with James Thomson, author of *The Seasons*.[5] After much consultation and frequent changes of plan, Hagley Hall arose as a Palladian mansion, and Sanderson Miller, though thus losing his greatest opportunity to design a house in his beloved gothic style, collaborated with Thomas Prowse and John Sanderson, to erect the building which in the end bore their signatures rather than his.[6]

An examination of the contribution of Sanderson Miller to the gothic revival in domestic architecture is therefore limited to alterations and additions to existing buildings, and in all cases the results must be seen as the outcome of a collaboration of Miller with other amateurs and occasionally also with professional architects. He was properly modest about his design abilities, writing to Thomas Prowse, "I can always see more faults in my own performance than I love to think on, and I would never draw a line more if I did not see much worse in the shocking designs of common workmen."[7] By this date, his fame as the architect of the ruined castles at Radway and Hagley had spread far and wide, and he had recently won accolades for the design of the Shire Hall at Warwick in the classical style.[8] Here he had used the technical expertise of the principal Warwick architects, the brothers William and David Hiorne, who were at the same time working for him in effecting the first gothic alterations to Arbury Hall.[9] The most important outcome of Miller's use of the gothic style in house architecture was the eventual development of Arbury Hall into a showcase of antiquarian gothic, a process which was completed many years after Miller's death.[10] The owner of Arbury, Sir Roger Newdigate, whom Miller had called the "learned Knight of Taste", is to be credited with this development, rather than Sanderson Miller. But Miller's example at Radway Grange was certainly the most important influence upon Newdigate in the first stage of the transformation of Arbury Hall.

RADWAY GRANGE

Sanderson Miller's father had acquired Radway in 1716, and the house was given to Sanderson by his mother upon his marriage to Susannah Trotman in 1746. Two years earlier, he had made the first alterations, in extending the house by one bay on the south-east front. This is remarkable in that the centre three bays of five are pierced by pointed windows in all three storeys, and at the ground level the three windows take up the entire height of the floor and are deeply recessed, suggesting that the arches of a cloister may have inspired the design. Polygonal turrets, formerly topped by crotcheted and domed caps, framed this centre section, which was crowned with a triangular pediment. Upon his marriage in 1746, Miller extended the rooms on the adjoining south-west front by adding bay windows of two storeys, with quatrefoil panels between the floors (Plate 152). Six years later, he added the doorway to this front between the bay windows, and the rather lame petal-shaped ornament above; the porch over the doorway is a nineteenth-century addition.[11] Nobody has been found to praise Miller's work at Radway Grange, and the chorus of laudatory comments from his friends on his design of the castle at Radway was never extended to include his alterations to the house.[12]

ARBURY HALL: THE FIRST PHASE

However, while the south-east front of Radway was ignored, the bay windows of the south-west front received the highest form of commendation, that of imitation, in the design of alterations to other houses, beginning with Arbury Hall in 1748 (Plate 153).[13]

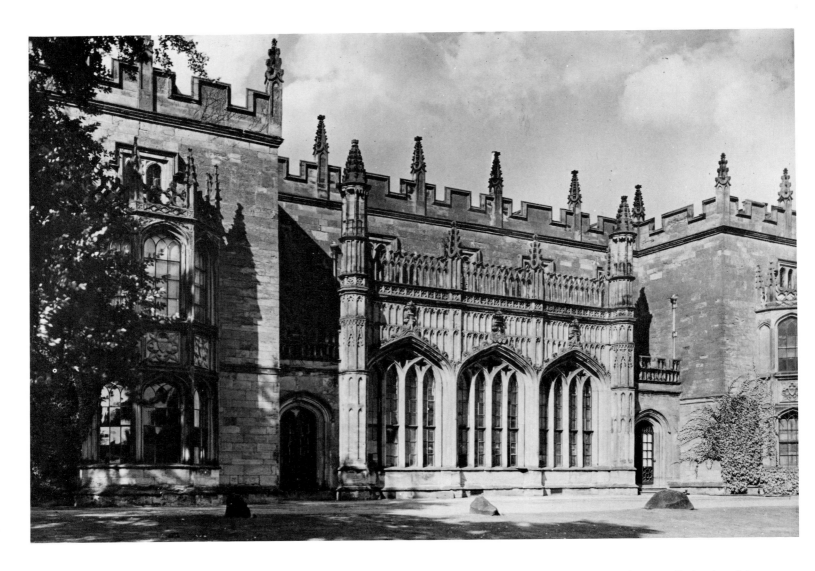

153. Sanderson Miller and Sir Roger Newdigate, The South front of Arbury Hall, Warwicks., 1748–70. Courtesy of the Royal Commission on the Historic Monuments of England.

There the bow window of two storeys, differing from those at Radway only in the rich brattishing that crowns it, was added on the south front to the library, in 1751; a matching bow was added to the drawing-room ten years later. It is typical of Sir Roger Newdigate's slow and careful approach to his alterations that the library walls were not completed until 1755.[14] He would not have to utter Walpole's self-reproach: ''I was always too desultory and impatient to consider that I should please myself more by allowing time, than by hurrying my plans into execution before they were ripe.''[15]

In the intervening years, the friendship of Sir Roger Newdigate and Sanderson Miller had been irreparably damaged by their political differences, as we learn from a letter of Lord Dacre of Belhus, Essex, to Miller, of 1754: "I t'other day saw Sir Roger Newdigate who is extreamly jolly and in good spirits, but says he never sets eyes on you now, tho' he has told you he is willing to waive all party topics when you are together.''[16] Earlier their friendship had been close, since Miller records in his diary a week-long visit to Arbury in December 1749, during which he applied himself to learning perspective drawing from Sir Roger, while his host in turn took lessons from him in the drawing of gothic arches.[17] In his will, Miller mentioned ''my proportional compasses, which were given me by Sir Roger Newdigate'', and these were probably a gift in recognition of his advice on the first alterations to Arbury Hall.[18] Miller's mason, William Hitchcox, was paid £50 for erecting the bow window to the library in 1752, so we may assume that the friendship was intact at that date. By the time the library was fitted up internally by William Hiorne in

1755, however, Newdigate was looking beyond his Warwickshire neighbourhood to London and to the new Strawberry Hill for design inspiration.[19]

Just as Walpole recorded his pride in his new library by commissioning his portrait in the room from Johann Heinrich Müntz, Sir Roger Newdigate commissioned his portrait in his new library from Arthur Devis in 1755 (Plate 154). It is clear from a perspective drawing in his own hand (Plate 155) that he dictated to Devis the compositional structure of the portrait, with a view to including as much of the library as possible. But both the drawing and the painting leave the ceiling of the room deliberately undefined. This ceiling is remarkable for having a neo-classical decoration based upon prints of the ceiling of the bath of the Empress Livia in Rome but this was not added until 1791.[20] The bays of the library bookshelves are clearly shown, however, and though not so ornate, they are dependent upon those designed in 1754 by John Chute for Strawberry Hill, as Hussey has remarked. [21] This must have seemed unacceptably ironic to Walpole, who was diametrically opposed to Newdigate in political allegiance. He refers to Newdigate only in political contexts and always in derogatory terms, since he suspected him of covert support of the Stuart claim to the monarchy.[22] This is the most probable reason why we find that Walpole excludes from his histories and notebooks any mention of the gothic revival work of Sir Roger Newdigate. He exercised the same censorship on him that he inflicted on Johann Heinrich Müntz after their quarrel in 1759, and with the same devastating effect. Arbury Hall has been omitted from the histories of the movement published by Eastlake in 1872, Clark in 1928, Germann in 1972, and Macaulay in 1975.[23] Needless to say, it was also ignored by the professed followers of Walpole, James Dallaway and Ralph Wornum.[24] The same fate attended the critical fortunes of the executive architect of the building, Henry Keene, even in respect of buildings in the gothic style executed for patrons other than Sir Roger Newdigate, such as the church for Sir Thomas Lee at Hartwell in Buckinghamshire.[25] Yet Newdigate and Keene brought Walpole's antiquarian ideal of design in gothic revival architecture to the most complete stage of realisation in domestic and ecclesiastical architecture. It is fair to say that just as the library at Arbury Hall is unthinkable without the precedent of the library at

154. Arthur Devis, *Portrait of Sir Roger Newdigate*, oil on canvas, 890 × 762 mm, *c*.1755. Courtesy of Lord Daventry and The Royal Academy, London.

155. Sir Roger Newdigate, *Perspective of the Library of Arbury Hall*, pencil, 150 × 225 mm, *c*. 1755. Courtesy of Lord Daventry and the Warwick County Record Office.

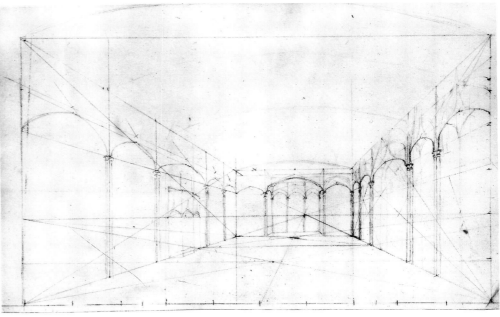

156. Sanderson Miller, Adlestrop Park, Glos., 1750–60. Courtesy of the Royal Commission on the Historic Monuments of England.

Strawberry Hill, the ceiling of the gallery at Strawberry Hill and of the chapel at The Vyne are unthinkable without the precedent of the work of Henry Keene and Sir Roger Newdigate.

ADLESTROP PARK AND OTHER BUILDINGS

Before examining this antiquarian trend in the gothic revival, however, the further impact of the architecture of Sanderson Miller should be considered. The bay windows with quatrefoil panels between the floors, and the turrets with domed and crotcheted caps, reappeared at Adlestrop Park in Gloucestershire (Plate 156), built for Sir William Leigh in two stages.[26] In 1750 Miller's mason, William Hitchcox, undertook to erect two bay windows, "built with Barington face stone with three sashes in each window and nine feet in the front and to be erected to the design given by Mr. Miller".[27] A second agreement, dated 2 March, 1759, provided for the building of further rooms at Adlestrop by Samuel and Thomas Collett, conforming to the design of the bay-window rooms, and following plans given by Sanderson Miller. At Thomas Collett's suggestion, Leigh added octagonal turrets to the corners of the house, so that substantially Adlestrop is, to adapt a phrase of Walpole, "a child of Radway": it is also "prettier than the parent".[28]

Closer to Radway in distance was Rockingham Hall in the village of Hagley. This was bought for Admiral Smith, half-brother to Sir Thomas Lyttelton, and renovated in 1751.[29] It has now been destroyed, and the building accounts have not come to light, but the photographs surviving show it to have been fronted by bay windows with quatrefoil panels.[30] This hall-mark of Sanderson Miller reappears at Siston Court in

157. (*facing page, top left*) Sanderson Miller (attributed), Siston Court, Glos. – the West wing, *c.* 1750. Courtesy of the Royal Commission on the Historic Monuments of England.

158. (*facing page, top right*) Sanderson Miller (attributed), Siston Court, Glos., the Entrance, *c.* 1750. Courtesy of the Royal Commission on the Historic Monuments of England.

Gloucestershire (Plates 157–8), which was owned by Miller's father-in-law. At an uncertain date its south wings had a variation of the Radway bows attached; they are shallow and the windows are square-headed rather than pointed, but it is possible that they owe their form to the Radway windows. A matching entrance-porch built at the same date may also be by Miller.[31] Finally, at Ecton Hall, Northamptonshire, owned by Ambrose Isted, we find bay windows closer to the Radway originals, though again with square rather than pointed windows (Plates 159–60).[32] Here a pointed drip-course is added by way of decoration beneath the battlements, which are much lighter than those surmounting the main block. A similar fragility is evident in the entrance-porch, a semi-hexagon with ogee arches. This might lead us to doubt Miller's authorship, were it not

159. Sanderson Miller (attributed), Ecton Hall, Northants. – the South front, 1756. Courtesy of the Royal Commission on the Historic Monuments of England.

160. Sanderson Miller (attributed), Ecton Hall, Northants. – the Entrance, 1756. Courtesy of the Royal Commission on the Historic Monuments of England.

161. Sanderson Miller, Lacock Abbey, Wilts. – exterior of the Hall, 1754. Courtesy of the Royal Commission on the Historic Monuments of England.

that the drip-course with ogee arches appears in the west front of Lacock Abbey, Wiltshire, built to designs by Miller from 1754 to 1756.[33]

LACOCK ABBEY

At Lacock, Miller was concerned with building a new hall to replace the existing hall of a genuine medieval building which had been inherited by John Ivory Talbot (Plate 161). He was suggested as the designer precisely because of the antique quality of the fabric, which is a testimony to the extreme scarcity of competent gothic designers among professional architects in the middle of the century. Richard Goddard, a neighbour of Talbot, wrote to Miller in 1753: "As his house consists of the Remains of an Old Nunnery it was agreed on all hands that it would be most proper to fit it up in the Gothick Taste. **Mr.** Talbot was entirely of that opinion, but doubtful whether he shou'd be able to meet with the assistance requisite for such an Undertaking. You will not be surprised that I mentioned your name on the occasion."[34] The subsequent correspondence shows that Miller efficiently provided designs for the intentions expressed by Talbot, with the notable difference that, though Talbot first wanted bay windows, he later agreed to have windows flush to the wall and professed to recognise an antique precedent for them in a building in the north of England.[35] Shallow ogee arches surmount these windows and are connected with the string-course that runs along the front, emphasising the linearity of the composition. Their source is Plate 38 of Batty Langley's *Ancient Architecture Restored*, though the Lacock version is not as elaborate as the print.

In one other matter of importance the owner and the architect of Lacock Abbey differed. John Ivory Talbot proposed to treat the external chimney of the kitchen, which adjoined the hall, with sufficient elaboration in the gothic style to throw off-balance the symmetry of the composition. He wrote: "The Chimney being converted into an ornament, will have a pretty effect: and as I would by no means have my Front regular

will fully answer that intent: since the Beauty of Gothic Architecture (in my opinion) consists, like that of Pindarick Ode, in the boldness and Irregularity of its Members''.[36] This is a very original statement on the subject of planning in gothic architecture for its date. The argument by analogy with poetry was to become commonplace after the publication in 1762 of Richard Hurd's *Letters on Chivalry and Romance*, but Talbot's insight is paralleled only by that of Horace Walpole, who argued by analogy with design in landscape gardening. Unfortunately, Sanderson Miller's appreciation of the picturesque in the design of garden buildings did not extend to his notions of design in domestic architecture. Talbot's firmly expressed wishes notwithstanding, the hall of Lacock was as *retardataire* in plan as in fenestration, and it must count as a lost opportunity in the development of the gothic revival. Internally the decoration of the doorways is taken from Radway Grange, but the most enterprising features of the interior, the niches with statuary by Sederbach, and the chimney-piece with monastic iconography (Plate 162), are due to Talbot rather than to Sanderson Miller.[37]

162. Sanderson Miller and John Ivory Talbot, Lacock Abbey, Wilts. – interior of the Hall, 1754. Courtesy of the Royal Commission on the Historic Monuments of England.

In the same years, Sanderson Miller was involved in alterations for Lord Dacre at Belhus, Essex (Plate 163). He had been in correspondence with him often on the subject of their common inclination to nervous depression, since 1744.[38] Thomas Barrett-Lennard, Lord Dacre, was an active member of the Society of Antiquaries of London, and he made the acquaintance of Sanderson Miller through Charles Lyttelton, President of the Society. He was also related to John Chute, and though Walpole's attitude towards him was guarded at times, Dacre has the remarkable distinction of having maintained friendship with Horace Walpole and Sir Roger Newdigate and Sanderson Miller simultaneously, though the alterations to Belhus put a very severe strain on his friendship with Miller in the long run. Walpole and Chute visited Belhus together in 1754, and on a second visit in 1761 Walpole noted the "new front and hall, gothic, built by this Lord, under the direction of Mr. Sanderson Miller".[39] In 1777 Walpole was asked by Lord Dacre to give advice on the decoration of the house, but he declined with customary grace: "You have not only done everything there with taste, my Lord, but to my taste."[40]

The extent of the alterations at Belhus is discussed by Dickins and Stanton, who conveniently published a sketch of the old house along with a photograph of the new.[41] Here a summary, taken from a manuscript *Short Account* written by T. Barrett-Lennard in 1917 before the demolition of Belhus, may be quoted:

Lord Dacre's chief alterations were doing away with the entrance-door under the

163. Lord Dacre, Belhus, Essex – the exterior, 1745–77. Courtesy of the Royal Commission on the Historic Monuments of England.

X. Anonymous, *View of Arbury Hall, Warwickshire from the South*, from F. O. Morris, "A Series of Picturesque Views of Seats", Vol. 3, *c.* 1870. Courtesy of The Royal Commission on the Historic Monuments of England.

XI. Anonymous, *The Interior of the Chapel at Audley End, Essex, designed by John Hobcraft in 1768.* Courtesy of English Heritage.

tower, putting up an entirely new front to the west of the house where he placed his entrance door, adding a new wing to the east side of the south front, dividing the old great hall into two rooms by putting a floor across it thus making a dining-room and an upstairs sitting-room, and constructing an imposing front staircase. When the alteration of the old hall was in progress the large bay window must have been pulled down and rebuilt a few feet to the east of where it was originally.[42]

These alterations took forty years to complete, and Sanderson Miller was involved in only part of them. He and his mason Hitchcox went to Belhus in 1745, the year in which the new hall and staircase were finished, but not until the end of that year, so their involvement in the planning of these changes cannot have been deep.[43] The following year the vestibule and upstairs sitting-room were finished, and the tone of Lord Dacre's letters to Miller in that year do not suggest that Miller was responsible for the new rooms.[44] No building occurred at Belhus during the years 1747–51, in which Dacre's only legitimate child died and he made the Grand Tour with Lady Dacre.[45] On 17 December 1751 he wrote to Miller, "I would have fitted up my great eating-room, formerly Hall, if my architect had not made me what in my opinion was too dear an estimate, which has caused me to demur for the present."[46] However, he stated his intention to carry out this phase of the reconstruction in the spring of the following year, and asked for Miller's advice. This is the first indication of the active participation of Miller in the rebuilding of Belhus, and Dacre's reference to "my architect" suggests that the plans had already been made by someone other than Miller.

Miller went to Belhus in March 1752, but he seems on that occasion to have advised only on the making of shields for the decoration of the dining-room.[47] Letters later in the year show that he also designed two chimney-pieces, though the carver, Carter, did not execute the dining-room chimney-piece exactly in accordance with the design (Plate 164).[48] 1753 seems to have been a slack year, but the drawing-room above the dining-room was decorated in 1754. On 31 January Dacre sent Miller a plan of the room, along with decorative designs made by James Lovell in imitation of decoration Miller had used at Radway and Wroxton.[49] This room was finished in the summer of 1754.[50]

Miller was next consulted on the decoration of Lady Dacre's bedroom in September 1757, and the model here chosen was his earlier work at Arbury Hall.[51] He was asked to supply a stucco-man to execute this, but the man was late in coming and Miller was slow in providing the designs. When the plans did come, Lord and Lady Dacre decided against using any of them except those for the ceiling.[52] By December the stuccoist still had not arrived, and when he came early in 1758 the Dacres were not at Belhus. On their return in mid-February they found he had done everything wrong,[53] and that was the beginning of the end of Miller's involvement with alterations at Belhus. Later letters reveal misunderstandings about the purchase of chimneys, dissatisfaction with shields made by Robert Moore, and indignation at the amount of the bill Moore had sent.[54] In 1759 Lord Dacre told Miller, "I am new fitting up and somewhat enlarging my Breakfast room", but he did not invite Miller to contribute designs or suggestions for that alteration.[55]

It does not seem probable that Miller was involved in the changes to the exterior of the house, in spite of Walpole's statement of 1761; Lord Dacre's letters are so detailed that this would certainly have been mentioned had it been the case. Nor was he involved in the further changes recorded in a letter of 1763 from Lord Dacre to Charles Lyttelton, "My dressing-room is finished (I should rather call it my Library) and an excellent room it is; being 24 feet long in the clear."[56] The east wing was not built until 1778, and the estimate for building was by an otherwise unrecorded builder, named Watson.[57]

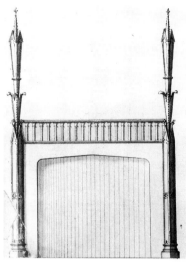

164. Sanderson Miller, *Design of a Chimney for Belhus, Essex*, ink and wash, 220 × 147 mm, 1752. Courtesy of The British Architectural Library.

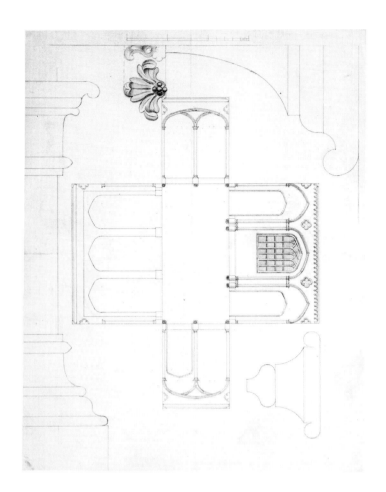

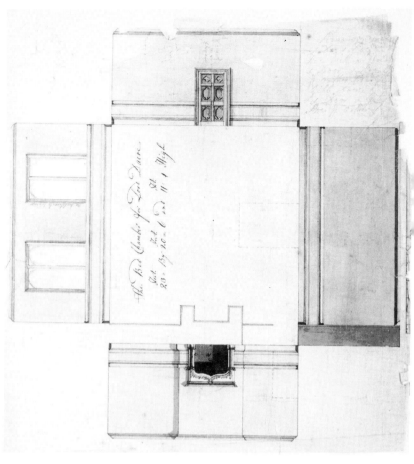

165. Sanderson Miller (attributed), *Design of a room for Belhus, Essex*, ink, 270 × 378 mm, 1754. Courtesy of the Lewis Walpole Library, Farmington, Connecticut.

166. Sanderson Miller (attributed), *Design of a room for Belhus, Essex*, ink and wash, 285 × 325 mm, 1754. Courtesy of the Lewis Walpole Library, Farmington, Connecticut.

The exterior of the house was not of any great interest, and the same must be said of the drawings, possibly by Sanderson Miller, for the interiors (Plates 165–6). It is the nature of its decoration, however, which gives it a place of distinction in the gothic revival and this was duly noted by Eastlake.[58] Heraldic glass was placed in the windows, and heraldic shields formed the principal decoration of the interiors. This feature appealed to Horace Walpole particularly, as his letter of 1777 attests.[59] It is evident from the amount of imitation of Miller's work at Radway, Wroxton and Arbury Hall that went into the remaking of Belhus, that he as well as Lord Dacre must be credited with the spirit of the internal decoration and sometimes with its design.

ARBURY HALL AFTER 1760

As has been mentioned earlier, Sir Roger Newdigate took lessons in drawing gothic arches from Sanderson Miller during the latter's week-long visit to Arbury Hall in December 1749. Perhaps it was Miller who drew his attention to Batty Langley's *Ancient Architecture Restored and Improved* and thus occasioned the carefully scaled drawing of the moulding of a cornice, titled "Langley from Westm. Abbey" (Plate 167), which is among his surviving drawings. Early exercises such as these led to his ability to make the drawings "at large" for the workmen responsible for the later stages of the architecture at Arbury Hall which contains the most elaborate gothic interiors of the period. Detailed

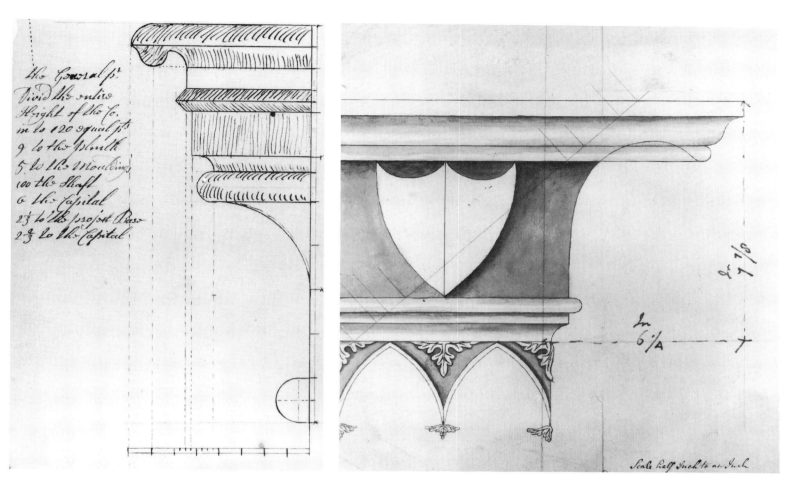

The General [?]
Divid the entire
Hight of the Co.
in to 120 equal pts
9 to the [Plinth]
5 to the Moulding
100 the Shaft
6 the Capital
2⅓ to the project Base
2⅓ to the Capital

Scale Half Inch to an Inch

drawings in ink and in wash for the profiles of an architrave and a cornice, the latter with an intricate half-column sketched in pencil below, demonstrate how close was his direction of the plasterers and carpenters (Plate 168).[60] Sir Roger was careful to have experienced builders as consultants to the alterations at Arbury Hall, Henry Keene from 1761 to his death in 1776, and subsequently Henry Couchman.[61] But drawings which survive for every stage of the rebuilding programme but the earliest are from the hand of Sir Roger himself, and they are among the most exciting drawings of the early gothic revival. A set of relatively staid examples of plans and elevations was published in 1973, and these can be supplemented here by examples from three folios which have more recently come to light in the Newdegate Papers.[62]

Their range in graphic terms may be suggested by comparing the quick impressions in pencil of fan-vaulted ceilings seen in plan, section and perspective with the sheet of precisely figured drawings in ink of mouldings, capitals, bases and vaulting from the Chapel of King Henry the Seventh in Westminster Abbey (Plates 169–70).[63] As we have noted, Sir Roger was alert to all strands of influence in the revival of the gothic style and had learned from Batty Langley and Sanderson Miller in the earliest phase of the reconstruction. When he rebuilt the library internally in 1755 he had learned from the work of Walpole and Chute at Strawberry Hill the previous year and it was most likely their example which alerted him to the virtues of archaeologically-based design. Certainly the rich and intricate architecture of the Chapel of King Henry the Seventh was his ideal from the 1760s and his choice of Henry Keene as consultant was logical since Keene was

167. Sir Roger Newdigate after Batty Langley, *Drawing of a Cornice*, ink, 221 × 121 mm, *c*.1750. Courtesy of Lord Daventry and the Warwick County Record Office.

168. Sir Roger Newdigate, *Profile of a Cornice*, ink and wash, 188 × 210 mm, *c*.1750. Courtesy of Lord Daventry and the Warwick County Record Office.

171. (*facing page, above*) Sanderson Miller, *Design of a room for Arbury Hall, Warwicks.*, pencil, 211 × 296 mm, 1750. Courtesy of Lord Daventry and the Warwick County Record Office.

172. (*facing page, below*) Sanderson Miller, *Design of a room for Arbury Hall, Warwicks.*, ink and pencil, 309 × 382 mm, 1750. Courtesy of Lord Daventry and the Warwick County Record Office.

169. Sir Roger Newdigate, *Sketches for Gothic Architecture*, pencil, 200 × 310 mm, *c.*1750. Courtesy of Lord Daventry and the Warwick County Record Office.

170. Sir Roger Newdigate, *Details from King Henry the Seventh's Chapel, Westminster Abbey*, ink and pencil, 187 × 307 mm, *c.*1750. Courtesy of Lord Daventry and the Warwick County Record Office.

Surveyor to the Fabric of Westminster Abbey. The impetus that this new source of design gave to his imaginative and graphic understanding of the style may be gauged by comparing the drawings noted above with an elevation in pencil and a part-elevation in ink by Sanderson Miller of the interior of Lady Newdigate's dressing-room, which was above the library and was fitted up five years earlier, in 1750 (Plates 171–2).[64]

These drawings by Miller are rich in their detail of ornament and cresting but are

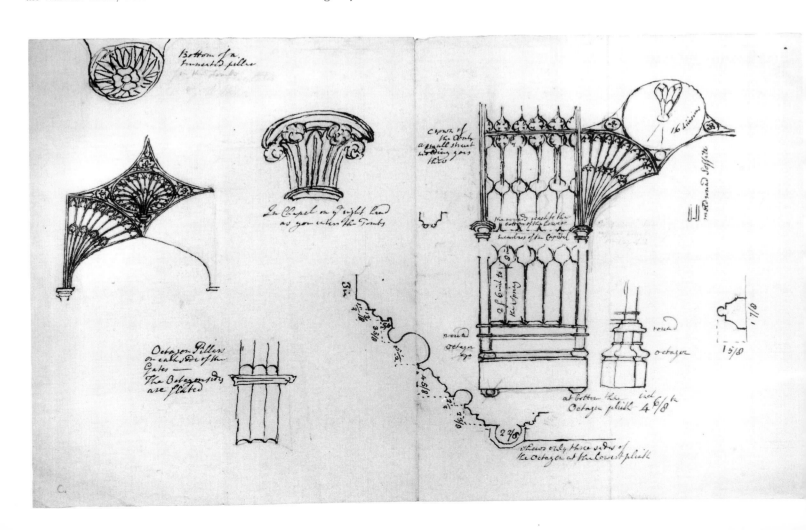

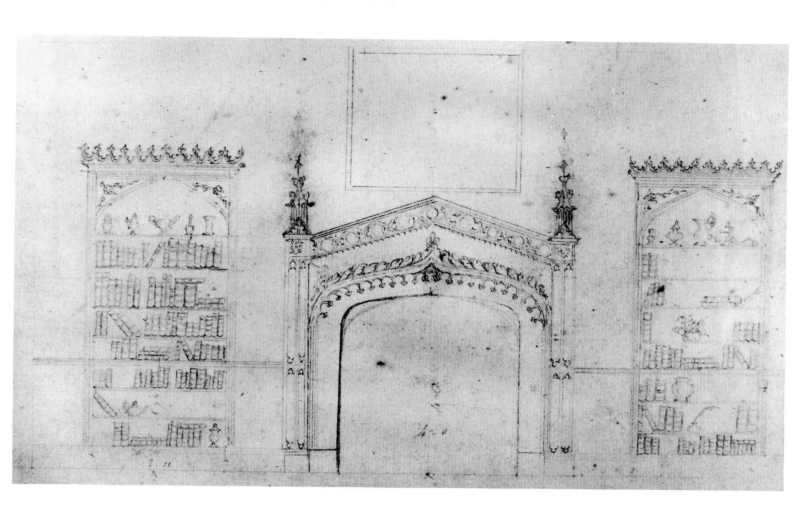

Door way to open at ye Dash lines

Chimney two

Chimney piece and Slabb with Inner Slips Measure about 20 ft Marble

173. Sir Roger Newdigate, *Design of a Chimney for Arbury Hall, Warwicks.*, ink and wash, 252 × 185 mm, 1766. Courtesy of The Victoria and Albert Museum, London.

pedestrian by comparison with the drawings of Newdigate and show no feeling for the third dimension. The comparison is bound to be unfair towards Miller because so few of his drawings have survived; but since these are the ones most firmly attributable to him, judgment of his place in the gothic revival must rest upon them and his surviving buildings and correspondence. This is not meant to slight his importance historically, since ironically the room depicted here had an admirer in Lord Dacre, who imitated it, as we have noted, in reconstructing Belhus. It should also be noted that when Lord Dacre refitted his dressing-room in 1763 he also fitted it with book-cases and referred to it as his study, so that too may be judged as a descendant of the Arbury dressing-room by Miller.[65]

132

174. Sir Roger Newdigate and Henry Keene, The Hall of University College, Oxford, 1766. Courtesy of Oxford City Libraries.

By that date the change in Sir Roger Newdigate's source of inspiration in architectural design became apparent in the chimney-piece of the parlour, delivered from its sculptor Richard Hayward on 4 November, 1763 (Plate 173).[66] This was modelled on the tomb of Aymer de Valence in Westminster Abbey, a source which was undoubtedly suggested by its use by Horace Walpole in the library at Strawberry Hill, though for some reason Walpole referred to quite different sources in his *Description of Strawberry Hill*, and later writers have accepted his account of its origin.[67] As he had simplified the Strawberry Hill model in designing the bays of the library, so Sir Roger simplified the upper structure of the chimney-piece, though not so radically as to disguise the source. The drawing for this work is among the Henry Keene drawings in the Victoria and Albert Museum, and I have previously attributed it to Keene because of its fine use of wash. But I remarked that the figure markings were in the hand of Sir Roger Newdigate and the drawings which have recently come to my notice include such superb examples of the deployment of wash in studies for doors and windows that there is no longer any reason to doubt his responsibility for this sheet.[68] A second version of this chimney-piece was carved by Hayward and erected for Sir Roger Newdigate by Henry Keene in the hall of University College, Oxford in 1766 (Plate 174).[69]

The bow window of the parlour was made to conform with that of the library across from it which was erected exactly ten years earlier in 1751 to Miller's designs.[70] Between these two windows lay the south front of the building, with the hall behind, and on 18 April 1761 Mr Keene came to Arbury for his first consultation and took the dimensions of this area. He came again for several days in June 1765 and after a further five years, on

133

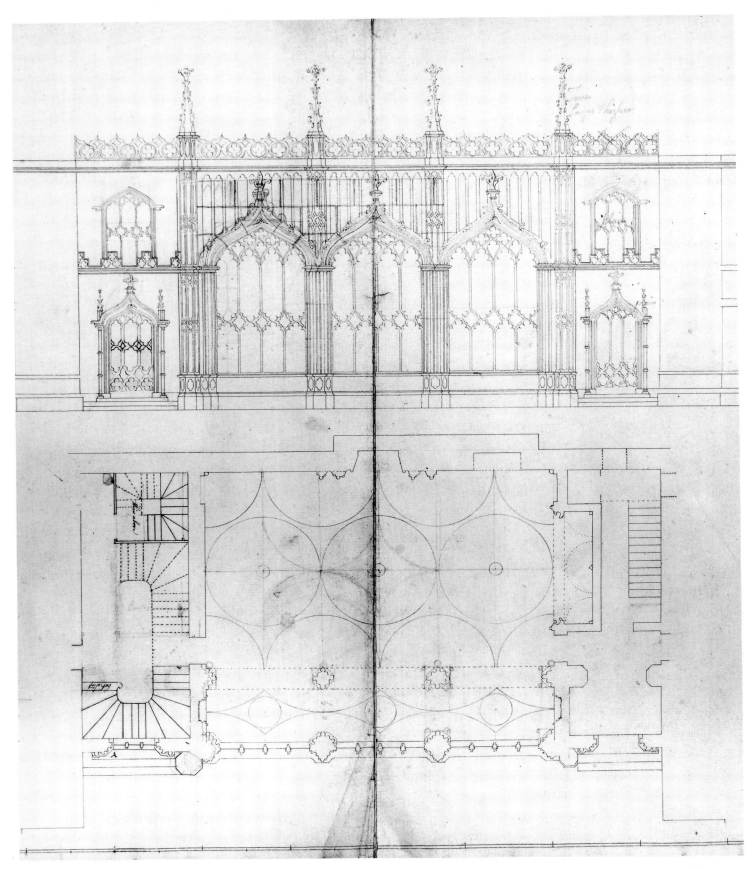

175. Sir Roger Newdigate, *Elevation and Plan for the South front of Arbury Hall, Warwicks.*, pencil and ink, 384 × 563 mm, 1765. Courtesy of Lord Daventry and the Warwick County Record Office.

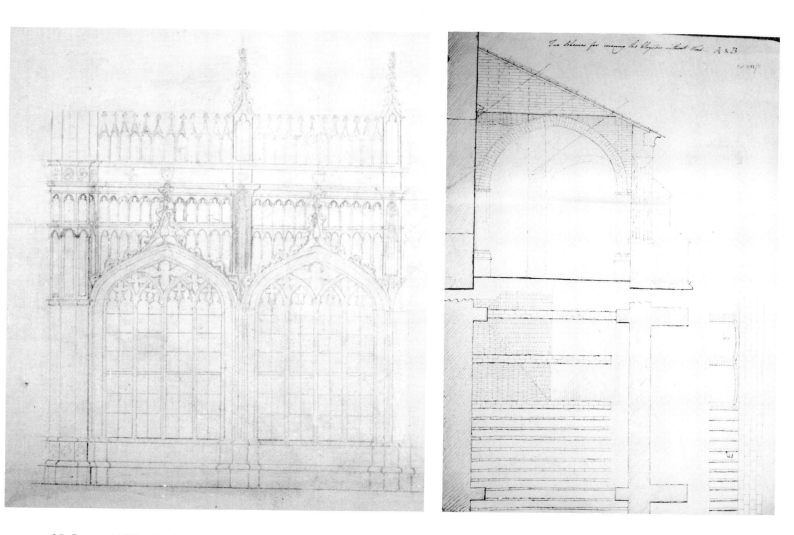

25 June, 1770, the keystone of the third arch of the new south front of Arbury was fixed.[71] The changes are recorded in a plan and elevation which demonstrate the precision and discipline of the draughtsmanship of Newdigate (Plates 175–6). The brattishing of the exterior and the towers at each end of the new bays were to be raised, an alteration noted in pencil to the right of the drawing, but otherwise the scheme is shown as it was effected (Plate X). The old front was demolished and the room brought forward by a three-bay loggia, and the internal decoration of columns, ceiling and chimney-piece conformed to the rich gothic decoration of the new exterior. It was not completed until 1788, though used for dining fifteen years earlier, in 1773, when Sir Roger had the satisfaction of noting that in the depths of December the family "breakfasted, dined and supped in the hall, the warmest room in the house".[72] The correspondence of Henry Keene with his patron demonstrates how closely the antique sources were followed. "I have therefore taken off casts in plaister at the Abbey," he wrote, "and shall have the leaves all carv'd from these exactly, only of different sizes ... I have taken the Joyner to the Abbey and taken off exact drawings from the best monuments which I shall closely follow—had this not been the case, I should have sent you copys of what I intended—but supposed as you were so well acquainted with these originals that would be needless."[73]

A covered walk existed in the courtyard of Arbury Hall, and this was converted into a cloister on the north and west sides from 1781 to 1784 (Plate 177). Henry Couchman was the consultant by that date, and with him Sir Roger "settled the north portico", on 16 August 1783. It took the form of a rather plain *porte-cochère* of three arches with battle-

176. Sir Roger Newdigate, *Alternative Elevation for the South front of Arbury Hall, Warwicks.*, pencil, 440 × 335 mm, 1765. Courtesy of Lord Daventry and the Warwick County Record Office.

177. Sir Roger Newdigate, *Design for the roofing of the Cloister of Arbury Hall, Warwicks.*, ink, 455 × 305 mm, 1781. Courtesy of Lord Daventry and the Warwick County Record Office.

178. Sir Roger Newdigate, *Elevation and Plan for the North front of Arbury Hall, Warwicks.*, ink, 334 × 456 mm, 1783. Courtesy of Lord Daventry and the Warwick County Record Office.

ments, but the preliminary elevation, plan and side-elevation shows more rich ornament and a more vertical emphasis given by rich finials to the buttresses (Plate 178). A very ornate doorway of flowing tracery was also proposed. Reconstruction of the north front of the house began ten years later, but was probably not completed until the early years of the new century when the east front was completed, since the towers shown in the drawing were built to conform to those of the east front (Plate 179). Ornament reached its height in the very rich bay window of the ground floor saloon on the east front, which was

179. Sir Roger Newdigate, *Elevation and part-Plan for the East front of Arbury Hall, Warwicks.*, ink, 325 × 465 mm, *c*.1795. Courtesy of Lord Daventry and the Warwick County Record Office.

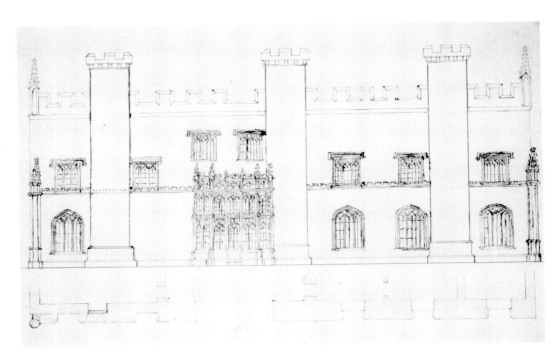

completed on 18 August, 1798, exactly fifty years after the rebuilding of Arbury had commenced.[74]

The best summary of Sir Roger Newdigate's work at Arbury is contained in the second notice of his death in *The Gentleman's Magazine*,[75] but the greatest tribute to it was paid by George Eliot when she cast Newdigate as Sir Christopher Cheverel and Arbury as Cheverel Manor in *Mr. Gilfil's Love Story*. Her description is so accurate and perceptive that quotation at length is justified.

The bow window was open, and Sir Christopher, stepping in, found the group he sought, examining the progress of the unfinished ceiling [Plate 181]. It was in the same style of florid pointed gothic as the dining-room, but more elaborate in its tracery, which was like petrified lace-work picked out in delicate and varied colouring. About a fourth of it still remained uncoloured, and under this part were scaffolding, ladders and tools; otherwise the spacious saloon was empty of furniture and seemed to be a grand Gothic canopy for the group of five human figures standing in the centre.[76]

Of the dining-room she wrote, "The room seemed less like a place to dine in than a piece of space enclosed simply for the sake of a beautiful outline." (Plate 180).[77]

For the convenience of her story, George Eliot gives Milan Cathedral as the source of inspiration for Arbury Hall, and she credits the sophistication of its detailing to Italian workmen rather than to the English craftsmen who were responsible.[78] But her general account is sufficiently accurate and full of insight.

For the next ten years, Sir Christopher was occupied with the architectural metamorphosis of his old family mansion; thus anticipating, through the prompting of his individual taste, that general reaction from the insipid imitation of the Palladian style, towards a restoration of the gothic, which marked the close of the eighteenth century. This was the object he had set his heart on, with a singleness of determination which was regarded with not a little contempt by his fox-hunting neighbours, who wondered greatly that a man with some of the best blood in England in his veins, should be mean enough to economise in his cellar, and reduce his stud to two old coach-horses and a hack, for the sake of riding a hobby, and playing the architect. Their wives did not see so much to blame in the matter of the cellar but they were eloquent in pity for poor Lady Cheverel, who had to live in no more than three rooms at once, and who must be distracted with noises, and have her constitution undermined by unhealthy smells. It was as bad as having a husband with an asthma. As for Sir Christopher, he was perfectly indifferent to criticism. "An obstinate, crotchety man", said his neighbours. But I, who have seen Cheverel Manor, as he bequeathed it to his heirs, rather attribute that unswerving architectural purpose of his, conceived and carried out through long years of systematic personal exertion, to something of the fervour of genius, as well as inflexibility of will . . . some of that sublime spirit which distinguishes art from luxury, and worships beauty apart from self-indulgence.[79]

18 ARLINGTON ST, LONDON

Sir Roger Newdigate communicated some of his "unswerving architectural purpose" to Henrietta Louisa, Countess of Pomfret, whose niece, Sophia Conyers, was his first wife.[80] Lady Louisa built the most outstanding, and perhaps the only, gothic revival house in London in the middle of the eighteenth century, 18 Arlington Street in St James's, which was promptly dubbed "Pomfret Castle".[81] She was noted as a lover of antiquity, and had a temperamental inclination to gothic architecture, remarking of Rochester Castle, "Surely to repair and make this place habitable wou'd be to erect a much Finer Family Seat than the very best of our Modern Buidings can pretend to", when she visited it in 1738.[82] In 1755 she asked Sir Roger Newdigate for gothic designs for a small farm in Bedfordshire and for a market house she proposed for Towcester in the same county.[83] Neither of these buildings seems to have been executed, but soon afterwards she began to build her own house in the gothic style, in the same street as Walpole's town house, indeed only two doors from it. The house seems to have been started without any involvement on the part of Sir Roger Newdigate, since she wrote to him in August 1756, after a visit to Arbury, "If I had the wings of an Eagle, I would perch on one of your bow windows, & take a lesson before my house gets above ground, to which it is pushing with all speed."[84]

There is considerable confusion about the identity of the architect of the street front of the house. Walpole attributed the building to Sanderson Miller, and yet Stiff Leadbetter, a Palladian architect as unimaginative as his Christian name suggests, received a payment of £200 in 1759, when the fabric was complete, and had been involved in the building plans since April 1756 at least.[85] Leadbetter need not have played any role more

181. Sir Roger Newdigate, Detail of Vaulting in the Saloon of Arbury Hall, Warwicks., 1798. Courtesy of *Country Life*.

182. Sanderson Miller (attributed), The Street front of No. 18 Arlington Street, London, 1756–9. Courtesy of *Country Life*.

decisive in the building than that played by his colleague, William Robinson in the Board of Works, during the building of Strawberry Hill in the same decade. Sanderson Miller could well have been Lady Pomfret's adviser at the start of the project, though it is curious that no reference to this has survived in his voluminous correspondence or that of Lady Pomfret. Certainly, Lady Pomfret had no high opinion of the architectural capacities of Stiff Leadbetter, to judge by her comments on Langley Hall, Buckinghamshire, built by him in these years.[86] It is very unlikely that she would have entrusted the planning of her London house to him.

The appearance of ''Pomfret Castle'' can be reconstructed from a drawing of 1760 in the Bodleian Library, Oxford, a watercolour by J. C. Buckler of 1831, and a series of photographs taken before its demolition in the 1930s (Plate 182).[87] Low octagonal towers framed a gateway from Arlington Street that gave on to a courtyard with screening walls painted to look like gothic arches. At the end of the courtyard lay the three-bay house of three storeys, framed by octagonal turrets, and with a *porte-cochère* before the entrance. The facade is a strange composition, topped as it is by a pediment sporting a quatrefoil opening and broad battlements. It is disappointing to see this classical feature in a work by Sanderson Miller of that date; and the round balls that surmount the *porte-cochère* are a throw-back to the work of William Kent at Rousham, with which Lady Pomfret was very familiar.[88] However, the turrets repeat those of Sanderson Miller at Lacock Abbey, recently completed, the fenestration is recognisably broad, and the low octagons of the gateway (heightened in later years), have the rather closed air that characterised his architecture. The facade is very close in feeling to an elevation by Sanderson Miller, based on *Ancient Architecture Restored and Improved*, for a house of three bays and two storeys, which may well be a preparatory drawing for ''Pomfret Castle'' (Plate 183).[89] Miller, as has

183. Sanderson Miller, *Elevation for a House, possibly No. 18 Arlington Street, London*, ink and wash, 277 × 222 mm, 1756. Courtesy of The British Architectural Library.

been pointed out, had recourse to the same volume for the windows of Lacock Abbey, despite the wishes of its owner, and the entrance arch at Lacock, built in 1755, had been very Kentian in its inspiration. The street elevation of Lady Pomfret's house therefore is thoroughly consistent in form with the *retardataire* nature of his domestic architecture at this period, and Walpole's attribution may be credited so far as the street front of the house is concerned. The park front, however, is very different. A watercolour of the nineteenth century shows two battlemented bow windows of three storeys, very open and light in character.[90] It was certainly designed by some architect other than the one who designed the street front, and in view of Lady Pomfret's letter of 1756, quoted above, the architect was probably Sir Roger Newdigate.

The probability of this attribution is strengthened to certainty by an examination of the photographs of the interior (Plates 184–6). Its principal feature was a top-lit stairwell, the walls of which were decorated with perpendicular gothic panelling in plaster, of the authenticity that had appeared elsewhere at this date only in the work of Henry Keene at Hartwell and Hartlebury, and was subsequently to appear at Arbury Hall. Newdigate is recorded as having visited the house to inspect the work in December 1760.[91] "Pomfret Castle" can therefore be seen as a trial run for the work of Keene with Newdigate at Arbury, which Keene first visited in April of 1761. The photographs show the woodwork of the panelling and the staircase carved with the same crisp fidelity to the originals that is apparent in the sophisticated plasterwork of the vaulted ceiling, and this is probably due to the practice Keene instituted, of working from casts rather than from drawings or prints.

Such fidelity to the antique was beyond the competence, and as far as we can tell, the inclination, of Sanderson Miller, so Walpole's attribution of the building to him cannot be taken at its face value. In his determination to exclude the work of Sir Roger Newdigate and Keene from his records of contemporary architecture, Walpole neglects the most important feature of the house in his attribution, and gives the architect of the facade, which is the less interesting feature, for the architect of the whole. So, in the case of Richard Bateman's house at Old Windsor, he associated the architecture with Richard Bentley, whose work was confined to the offices, rather than with Johann Heinrich Müntz, who had designed the more interesting cloister and octagonal room. This did not

185. Sir Roger Newdigate and Henry Keene, Interior of No. 18 Arlington Street, London, 1760. Courtesy of *Country Life*.

184. Sir Roger Newdigate and Henry Keene, Interior of No. 18 Arlington Street, London, 1760. Courtesy of *Country Life*.

prevent him from paying them the compliment of imitation in the design of his gallery at Strawberry Hill. The doors are taken from Müntz, and the ceiling is taken from Keene without acknowledgment.

LATER DEVELOPMENTS

Walpole need not have feared that the works of other amateurs and architects would overshadow his work at Strawberry Hill in importance or innovation. Sir Roger Newdigate showed no more appreciation of the importance of asymmetry in planning in gothic architecture than did Sanderson Miller. Under the impetus of the theory of the picturesque in architecture, exemplified by Richard Payne Knight at Downton Castle, Herefordshire, in 1771 and propagated in the villa architecture of John Nash, this was to be of first importance to the domestic architecture of the nineteenth century.[92] Sanderson Miller's domestic architecture was to have no relevance to subsequent practice, except in the coincidence of his collaboration with both Henry Keene and Sir Roger Newdigate at the beginning of their involvement in the gothic revival.[93] Newdigate took his major inspiration directly from Walpole's work in the library at Strawberry Hill, and recognised in Henry Keene the most accomplished practitioner of the reproduction of gothic ornament.[94] Despite their differences, personal and political, Walpole and Newdigate moved domestic architecture to the point where the demand for fidelity to antique sources led to a boom in the publishing of gothic architectural details during the first decades of the nineteenth century.[95] The greatest of these detailed works were A. C. Pugin's *Specimens of Gothic Architecture* (1821–3), L. N. Cottingham's *Working Drawings for Gothic Ornaments* (1823) and in the monograph category, J. C. Murphy's *Batalha* (1795).

These books were closely associated with the work of the gothic revivalists of the mid-eighteenth century. Cottingham's volume is a particularly eloquent testimony to the work of Walpole in that the frontispiece bears the elevation and details of the Chapel-in-the-Woods at Strawberry Hill, plate 30 is a detail of the cresting of that building (Plate 187), and plate 24 reproduces the chimney-piece of the great north bedchamber of Strawberry

Hill.[96] The rest of the plates are principally taken up with details of gothic architecture from Westminster Abbey, and can therefore be seen as a continuation of the work of Keene and Newdigate. The volume ends with Cottingham's ideal plan and elevation for a gothic mansion, which deploys the east end of King Henry the Seventh's Chapel as an entrance hall, and is ostentatiously unsymmetrical (Plate 188).[97] *The Specimen* books of the elder Pugin, which were continued by his more famous son, ranged more widely in their selection of examples but were similar in their character and intent. In the words of Kenneth Clark, they mark the stage at which ''Walpole's dream of correct Gothic was realisable.''[98] As we noted in the first chapter, there is a close connection between Murphy's *Batalha* and the work of Thomas Pitt, who had made designs for Strawberry Hill.[99] It is pleasant to note that both Horace Walpole and Sir Roger Newdigate subscribed to the publication of this superbly illustrated monograph which was to have considerable impact on the gothic revival in continental Europe in the nineteenth century.[100]

The influence of these volumes, and of the many similar studies published by John Britton and others, can be seen clearly in the buildings of the architects at the turn of the century, for example in the work of John Soane at Stowe, Buckinghamshire, (Plates 189–90) and of James Wyatt at Fonthill Abbey, Wiltshire.[101] It can also be seen in the works of amateur architects, for instance in the splended Toddington Manor, Gloucestershire, built by Charles Hanbury Tracy, Lord Sudeley.[102]

"My house", Walpole wrote to Thomas Barrett of Lee Priory, Kent, in 1788, "is but a sketch by beginners".[103] One wonders if even his foresight could have predicted what a vast and varied canvas would result from this brief sketch. He and Sir Roger Newdigate, and the other architects of the first phase of the gothic revival, suffered

188. Lewis Nockalls Cottingham, Plate 36 of *Working Drawings for Gothic Ornaments*, 1823. Courtesy of The British Library.

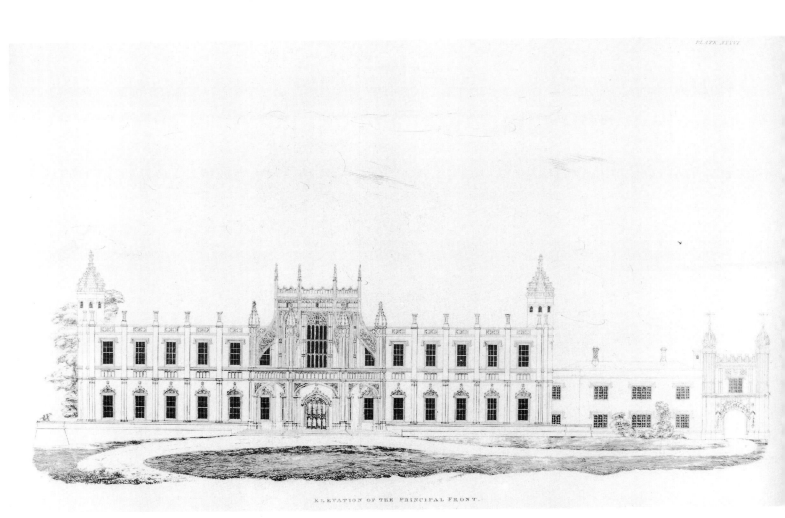

ELEVATION OF THE PRINCIPAL FRONT.

189. Sir John Soane, Interior of the Gothic Library, Stowe, Bucks., 1805–7. Courtesy of Stowe School.

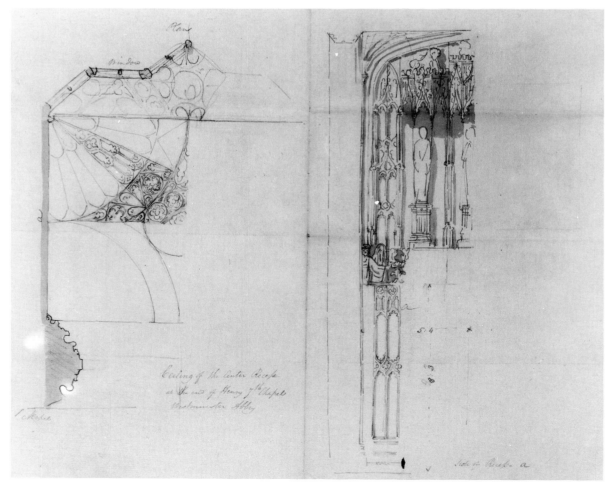

190. Henry Hake Seward for Sir John Soane, *Details from King Henry the Seventh's Chapel, Westminster Abbey*, ink and wash, 550 × 700 mm, 1805. Courtesy of The Sir John Soane Museum, London.

the incomprehension of their contemporaries because of their choice of style for domestic buildings, but the history of architecture has shown them to have been prophets rather than eccentrics, and there are many who, like George Eliot in 1857, "rather attribute that unswerving architectural purpose .. to something of the fervour of genius". Walpole continued his letter to Barrett, " If Mr. Matthew liked (Strawberry Hill), it was *en virtuose*, who loves the dawning of an art, or the glimmerings of its restoration."

VI. Ecclesiastical Architecture

WILLIAM KENT

When Horace Walpole visited Worcester in 1753, his fear of crowds prevented him from going to see the new chapel in Hartlebury Castle, the residence of the Bishop of Worcester. He did visit the cathedral however, braving election-day mobs to do so, and admired its "clusters of light pillars, of Derbyshire marble, lately cleaned". It was in this connection, rather than in the context of domestic architecture, that he made the famous comment, "Gothicism and the restoration of that architecture, and not of the bastard breed, spreads extremely in this part of the world."[1]

From Worcester he proceeded, via Malvern, to Gloucester, where he did visit the Bishop's residence, "restored to the Gothic by the last Bishop", of which unfortunately no visual evidence remains.[2] "The outside of the Cathedral is beautifully light," he remarked, "the pillars in the nave outrageously plump and heavy."[3] In this absence of appreciation for Norman architecture he is typical of his generation of gothic revivalists.[4] As we have seen, his search for "lightness" led to his rejection of Chute's first design for the long cloister at Strawberry Hill. However, he was enraptured by the beauty of the fan-vaulting of the Abbot's cloister, and we have noticed that it affected profoundly the course of his alterations to Strawberry Hill.[5] In the interior of the cathedral he found occasion to criticise the new screen designed by William Kent (Plate 191), which he would evidently have classed as an example of "the bastard breed" of gothic, that is to say, an unacceptable mixture of the classical and the gothic styles.

This is a fair description of Kent's screen, which was erected in 1741 and published by John Vardy, one of Kent's draughtsmen, in 1744.[6] The screen is an open arcade of three depressed ogee arches, with crocketed decoration, resting on sets of four octagonal colonettes spaced apart from each other in the form of a square. An emphatic course of dentils above the arches separates them from the attic, which repeats the regularity of the arcade in its spacing but reverses the incidence of the ogee arches which link fluted pilasters incongruously topped by crocketed finials. The screen looks very flimsy abstracted from its setting, but Vardy and Kent were careful to recall the setting to mind by a unique graphic device, hatching in at the bottom left and right corners of the print the relatively huge girth of the pillars abutting the new screen. Clearly the object of Kent and Bishop Benson, whose name is prominently inscribed in the central panel of the attic, was to induce an effect of the "lightness" Walpole had found praiseworthy in the west front of the cathedral. This is confirmed by a project which James Dallaway records: "It will scarcely be credited, in this age, that Kent recommended to the good bishop [Benson] to have the Norman pillars of the nave channelled or fluted; and that nothing but their being

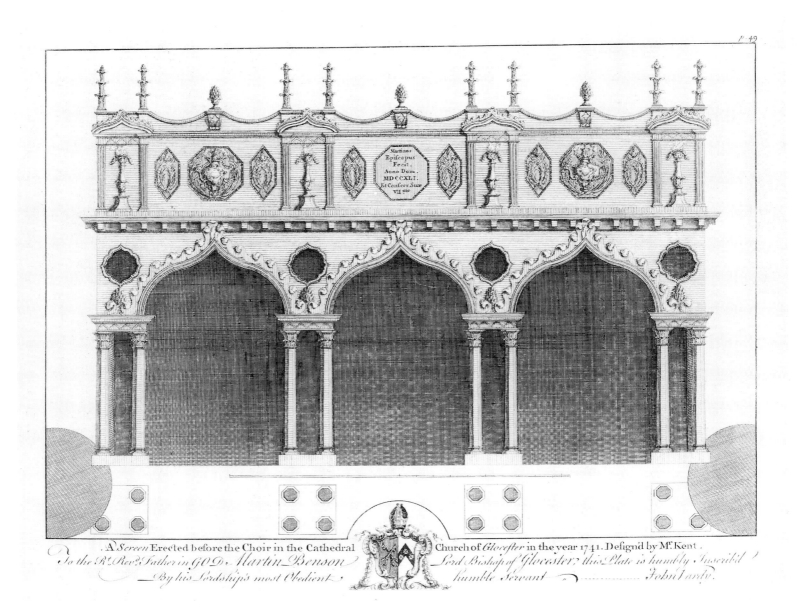

A *Screen* Erected before the Choir in the Cathedral Church of *Glocester* in the year 1741. Design'd by Mr Kent.

To the R.^t Revd Father in GOD. *Martin Benson* Lord Bishop of *Glocester*, this Plate is humbly Inscrib'd — By his Lordship's most Obedient humble Servant — *John Vardy*.

191. John Vardy after William Kent, *The Screen in Gloucester Cathedral*, 1744. Courtesy of the Lewis Walpole Library,. Farmington, Connecticut.

found to be unsolid, prevented this *bizarrerie* from taking place.''[7] One may remark that such a conversion of the Norman pillars to classical columns would have provided a kind of justification for the design of the screen; this is not to condone the notion, but to suggest the larger architectural intention of Kent, which was defeated by the force of circumstances.

In the same passage, Dallaway attributed this kind of alteration in ecclesiastical architecture of the eighteenth century to the influence of Batty Langley's *Ancient Architecture Restored and Improved*: ''This most absurd treatise is unfortunately much approved of by carpenters and stonemasons. Kent sanctioned such gross deviations from taste by his own practice.''[8] But, as in the case of garden buildings and domestic architecture, the book of Batty Langley follows the practice of William Kent and is better seen as an attempt to systematise the *ad hoc* solutions of Kent to specific architectural problems. The screen at Gloucester is a lighter, more open, version of the design for the alterations Kent had proposed for Westminster Hall in 1739, and that his solutions met with a considerable degree of acceptance in the 1740s is demonstrated by the publication of these designs in the form of prints.[9]

150

192. William Kent and Richard Bateman, St John the Evangelist, Shobdon, Herefs. – from the east. 1746–56. Courtesy of the Royal Commission on the Historic Monuments of England.

193. William Kent and Richard Bateman, St John the Evangelist, Shobdon, Herefs. – from the south. 1746–56. Courtesy of the Royal Commission on the Historic Monuments of England.

It is a pity that Walpole did not travel a little further west on this occasion, to visit the country house of his friend, Richard Bateman, at Shobdon in Herefordshire, because the finest and most complete example of Kent's gothic style applied to ecclesiastical architecture is to be found there at the Church of St John the Evangelist (Plates 192–3).[10] Its restoration did involve the shameful destruction of the beautifully sculpted Norman entrance of three arches, but the resulting interior is so delightful that Alec Clifton-Taylor has called it the gem among "the drawing-rooms of the Lord".[11] Contemporary opinion as to the success of this architectural programme was not unanimously favourable. Richard Pococke, Bishop of Ossorry, considered it "in very elegant taste".[12] But Charles Lyttelton referred to it slightingly in a letter to Sanderson Miller as a "pseudo-Gothic Church".[13] Edward Knight of Wolverley dispassionately noted in 1761 the "Gothic chapel lately erected by the direction of Mr. Rd. Bateman".[14] Recent commentary began with Marcus Whiffen, whose publications effectively brought the Church to the attention of art historians again, so that by 1963 Basil Clarke was able to refer to it as "this well-known Gothick church", and Sir John Summerson characterised it as "a pure example of the Gothic style of Kent".[15] The "pseudo-gothic" sneer of Charles Lyttelton, however, and the contemporary criticisms of the gothic style of Kent by Walpole, Gray and Dacre, previously noted, must make us wary of accepting it as a model of design in gothic ecclesiastical architecture of the period. The plans for the church were made first in 1746 and again in 1749 and the building was not completed until 1756.[16] By that date the gothic style of William Kent was looked upon with misgiving even by Richard Bateman, who was to call upon the considerably more sophisticated designs of Johann Heinrich Müntz when he altered his house at Old Windsor in 1760.[17]

The church at Shobdon has been traditionally associated with Richard Bentley because of the friendship between Horace Walpole and Richard Bateman, and the mistaken belief that Bateman had employed Richard Bentley to design the alterations to his house.[18] This attribution has been long discounted on stylistic grounds, but the architect of the church has remained a mystery.[19] The letters in the Herefordshire County Records Office which refer to the building mention "the architect" and "the surveyor" tantalisingly, without specifying his name,[20] but there is sufficient evidence in the papers and in the church to conclude that the building was executed by Henry Flitcroft to the designs of William Kent. Flitcroft is mentioned in the papers in connection with alterations to a passage at Shobdon Court in 1746, the year in which the first plans were drawn for the church,[21] so it is quite probable that he would on the same journey have

194. John Vardy after William Kent, *The Pulpit for York Minster*, 1744. Courtesy of the Lewis Walpole Library, Farmington, Connecticut.

overseen the execution of the designs of his colleague in the Office of Works, William Kent, who died two years later. Kent's authorship of the designs may be deduced from the evidence of the tester of the pulpit at Shobdon, which, though less ornate, is a clear transcription of the design for ''A Pulpit in the Cathedral of York'' by Kent (Plate 194), published by John Vardy in 1744.[22] Some credit, however, is due to Richard Bateman himself, who wrote to his steward, Mr Fallowes, in 1748:

> You promised me before I left Shobdon the plan of the Church with all its dimensions as it is now—Should be very glad to have this as soon as you conveniently could. That I might have my plans alter'd to begin upon the Church—for I am ready with the best ingredient for building and am therefore very impatient . . . be so kind to let me have the plan of the Church as soon as you can for mine will take up time to make compleat.[23]

The church is a Latin-cross in plan (Plates 195–6), the arms of the cross being wide and deep transepts and its head a chancel of the same dimensions as the transepts. Three

195. William Kent and Richard Bateman, Interior of St John the Evangelist, Shobdon, Herefs., 1746–56. Courtesy of the Royal Commission on the Historic Monuments of England.

196. William Kent and Richard Bateman, Interior of St John the Evangelist, Shobdon, Herefs., 1746–56. Courtesy of the Royal Commission on the Historic Monuments of England.

windows of two lights are in each wall of the nave, though those at the back are partly blocked by the gallery which is over the entrance. Windows of three lights are in the chancel and transepts, which are articulated internally by tripartite ogee hanging arches, the central arch wider than the sides and bearing a rich finial which breaks the line of the drip-course. That acts as a cornice around the church to separate the deep cove of the ceiling, which has a rectangular plaster frame but is otherwise unornamented. The wall areas are decorated with elegant gothic frames of plaster between the windows, except on the wall which holds a memorial tablet.

The chancel has a separate ceiling and its walls are very richly treated with six of the plaster panels and the window is of stained glass. It is furnished with gothic chairs and footstools which have all the weight and presence that one expects of furniture by Kent. The altar-rail runs into the substantial cluster of three-banded columns that separate the chancel and transepts from the body of the church, but since this area acts as the point of climax for the decoration of walls, windows and furniture throughout the church it effectively provides axial direction that is not weakened by the width of the opening of the transepts. The right-hand transept holds the Bateman family pew and is heated by a chimney-piece taken from Batty Langley's publication of 1742. Opposite is a private entrance, which is now blocked. The left-hand transept contains the baptistery area and is dominated by the richness of the pulpit with its tester above and a lectern and a desk for the clerk below. These are conceived and executed as one piece of furniture and are tied into the cluster of banded columns that turns the corner from the chancel into the transept. This richness of the composition is anticipated in the body of the church by the treatment of the ends of the pews for the congregation. Perhaps the most convincing argument for Kent's having designed the church is the extent to which furnishings conform with the architectural intention and confirm it. It is the unique and precious instance of ecclesiastical architecture of the gothic revival untouched by historicism.

HENRY KEENE

In the 1750s, archaeological accuracy became as much a requirement in ecclesiastical building of the gothic revival as in garden and domestic architecture. The chapel of Hartlebury Castle, redecorated for Bishop Maddox of Worcester by Henry Keene about 1750, is the earliest instance of this (Plates 197–8), and it is unfortunate that Walpole's agorophobia prevented him from visiting it and recording his impressions of it in 1753.[24] Hartlebury Chapel has been attributed to Sanderson Miller, but a letter among the Miller correspondence from Bishop Maddox seems to indicate that he was not responsible for the design. Its only date is 10 May: "The Chapel is finished, except the East Window, and [I] shall think myself happy if it does not displease a Gentleman of your just and elegant taste".[25]

However, as Colvin has pointed out, there was a lively co-operation between Keene and Miller at this time, and there is documentary evidence of their collaboration on designs for a house named Nelmes in Essex in 1749, and, on making furniture for the castle at Hagley and the supplying of a chimney-piece for Hagley Hall. There is every reason to suppose therefore that Miller's advice was sought by his friend and correspondent Bishop Maddox when he determined on alterations to the episcopal residence. But the decoration of the plaster ceiling of the chapel at Hartlebury is of archaeological derivation, modelled on the vault of King Henry the Seventh's Chapel in Westminster Abbey, and it should therefore be attributed to Henry Keene, who was to develop this motif. Keene was sufficiently well known in Worcester by this date for the cathedral

197. Henry Keene, Interior of the Chapel of Hartlebury Castle, Worcs., 1750. Courtesy of the Royal Commission on the Historic Monuments of England.

199. Henry Keene, St Mary's Church, Hartwell, Bucks., 1753–7. Courtesy of the Royal Commission on the Historic Monuments of England.

authorities to vote that he should be approached to design a new porch for the cathedral in 1750.[26]

There has never been any doubt as to Keene's authorship of the designs for St Mary's Church at Hartwell House in Buckinghamshire (Plate 199), built for Sir Thomas Lee from 1753 to 1757.[27] This was an octagonal building with a clerestorey of quatrefoil windows above a range of pointed windows, and a bell-tower above the entrance. It can be related to two drawings, an elevation and a section (Plates 200–1), though in execution solid buttresses replaced the slender colonnettes of the drawing, the honeycomb glazing of the lower windows was omitted and sturdy battlements crowned the composition in place of the lacy brattishing shown in the drawings.[28] This represents a process of simplification of ornament and strengthening of visual stability which may partly be accounted for by the difficulty of finding competent carvers and masons in the gothic style. A quotation from the correspondence of Henry Keene with Sir Roger Newdigate in connection with the redecoration of the Hall at University College, Oxford, provides an

198. (facing page) Henry Keene, Interior of the Chapel of Hartlebury Castle, Worcs., 1750. Courtesy of the Royal Commission on the Historic Monuments of England.

200. (*left*) Henry Keene, *Elevation and Plan for St Mary's Church, Hartwell, Bucks.*, pencil and wash, 475 × 275 mm, 1753. Courtesy of The Victoria and Albert Museum, London.

201. (*right*) Henry Keene, *Section and Ceiling for St Mary's Church, Hartwell, Bucks.*, pencil, ink and wash, 475 × 275 mm, 1753. Courtesy of The Victoria and Albert Museum, London.

insight into his commendable reaction to these difficulties. ''I have several hands at work in London on the Joyner's work: the carving I will venture to affirm will please you, for tho' we talked about turning in order to be cheaper, I find it will not please me . . . The expense is more than I calculated, but I shall be as much out of humour with it, as you would be, if it does not answer our wishes—and shall not therefore be penny wise and pound foolish.''[29]

In the light of the process of simplification noted above, two other drawings in the Victoria and Albert Museum collection may be associated with preliminary schemes for the Hartwell commission (Plates 202–4).[30] The first (Plate 202) is close to the building as executed, the principal difference being the battlemented sidewalls with niches, which buttress the main building effectively. The second (Plates 203–4) may well represent a refinement upon Keene's initial proposal. It shows the plan and elevation of a much smaller, jewel-like building, more richly decorated and insubstantial than that shown in the other drawings, but not fundamentally dissimilar. It seems to rest upon a square base, as though on a level hillock. It is more complex in plan, combining the Greek Cross form with that of the octagon. But it also displays the principal feature of the Hartwell Church, the elaborate fan-vaulting modelled in plaster on the ceiling of the Chapel of King Henry the Seventh in Westminster Abbey (Plate 204). This ceiling gave the church its aesthetic and antiquarian significance, and it was probably the factor that led to the long association of Henry Keene with Sir Roger Newdigate. Thanks to the fastidious care of Keene in directing the carvers in wood, the design of the gallery at Hartwell Church, as of the stalls in Hartlebury Castle Chapel, proved to be extremely effective, in a taut but graceful way.

The fan-vaulting of the ceiling reappears in contemporary ecclesiastical architecture in the chancel of the church at Wicken in Northamptonshire, rebuilt by John Sanderson for Thomas Prowse from 1754 (Plate 205).[31] Since Sanderson was Keene's collaborator in the building of the west front of Trinity College, Dublin, there is every reason to suppose that Keene would have supplied him with the drawings and casts, and perhaps also the artisans, for the execution of the work at Wicken.[32] Thomas Prowse is an *éminence grise* among the amateur architects of the middle of the eighteenth century; he was certainly a friend and correspondent of Sir Roger Newdigate in these years since he consulted Newdigate on the plans made by Sanderson Miller for the Shire Hall in Warwick in 1754.[33]

202. (*left*) Henry Keene, *Elevation and Plan for a Temple at Meswell, near Bridgewater, Somersetshire*, ink and wash, 485 × 285 mm, *c.*1753. Courtesy of The Victoria and Albert Museum, London.

203. (*right*) Henry Keene, *Elevation and Plan for a Gothic Church or Temple*, pencil and ink, 310 × 187 mm, *c.*1753. Courtesy of The Victoria and Albert Museum, London.

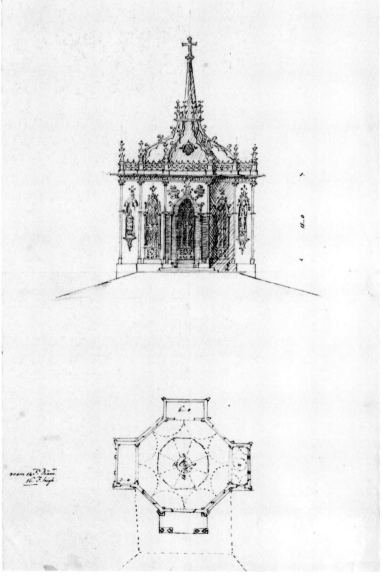

John Sanderson provides us with the date of completion of work on the ceiling of the chancel at Wicken in a letter to John Conyers of Copt Hall, Essex. dated 10 June, 1758, in which he speaks of his being about to go to Wicken ''to give directions for finishing the groyned ceiling of Esq. Prowse's Church there. The carcase of which has been built and used for service these 4 years past''.[34] However, there seems to have been a long lapse of time before all the work on the church was finished, for Elizabeth Prowse made the following note in her diary on 20 October, 1770: ''The Church at Wicken, the inside was finished by Mr. Sanderson and my mother P. paid for it, £240, and a drain round the Church was dug soon after.''[35] The alterations cannot have been begun before 1750, the year that Thomas Prowse had acquired the Wicken estate.[36]

The church has an uncomfortable spatial quality and there is a decided lack of relationship between the nave and the chancel, but there is no evidence to suppose that Thomas Prowse ever intended to extend the fan-vaulting from the chancel to the nave.[37]

The chancel again was the area of the church principally affected by the alterations made by Henry Keene to St Mary's Harefield, Middlesex, for Sir Roger Newdigate in 1768 (Plate 206).[38] The correspondence shows clearly that here the architect's function was to make the working drawings from designs supplied by the amateur architect, and

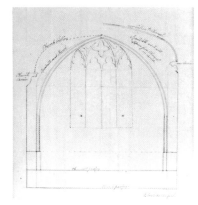

207. Henry Keene, *Design for the Chancel Arch in St Mary's Church, Harefield, M'sex*, ink, 460 × 364 mm, 1768. Courtesy of Lord Daventry and the Greater London Record Office.

206. St Mary's Church, Harefield, M'sex. Courtesy of the Royal Commission on the Historic Monuments of England.

one of these working drawings has survived.[39] The nature of the alterations is indicated in the "Estimate for Alterations, Repairs and Additions" which is in manuscript in the Warwick County Record Office.[40] The chancel was separated from the nave by a gothic arch (Plate 207), and its ceiling was decorated with plaster panels in the gothic style. It is not so elaborate as the other work of Keene and Newdigate but the same source supplied the formal models, as Keene makes clear in a letter accompanying the estimate, in which he states that he had completed the measuring of the stalls in Westminster Abbey and specifies those in the Chapel of King Henry the Seventh.[41] Newdigate had further alterations made to the south aisle of St Mary's Church, (called the Brackenbury Chapel), in 1802 and 1803, under the direction of one Thomas Martin, but these were not extensive, and Harefield Church remains today much as Henry Keene left it.[42] By and large, landowners interfered with their churches as little as possible in the eighteenth century, and attended to their structural care only when the erection of new family monuments, usually placed in the chancels, threatened the stability of the fabrics. This was the case at Harefield, where the monuments erected by Sir Roger Newdigate, and designed by him in a neo-classical manner, make a more rewarding study than the architectural alterations they occasioned.[43]

208. Church of All Saints, Wroxton, Oxon. Tower by Sanderson Miller, 1748. Courtesy of the Royal Commission on the Historic Monuments of England.

SANDERSON MILLER

Sanderson Miller's involvement in ecclesiastical architecture did not start auspiciously, since part of his first work, the rebuilding of the tower of All Saints' Church at Wroxton in Oxfordshire for Lord North (Plate 208), collapsed in 1748. This was a stone octagonal crown, which Miller's mason, William Hitchcox, had failed to cramp sufficiently strongly to the top of the tower, and though plans were made to re-erect it, the church remains without this feature to the present day. But the tower itself did not collapse, as is sometimes said. It still exists, and, together with the east window of the nearby Wroxton Abbey, inserted the same year, it shows a fragile and nervous handling of gothic elements by Miller, which is quite different from the heavy castellated style apparent in his garden buildings of the same period.[44] Perhaps this explains in part the fact that his ecclesiastical building has proved more perishable than his garden and domestic architecture; most of his work in churches has been destroyed or altered beyond recognition, and one can trace their history principally by means of documentary evidence only.

The alterations to the parish church at Hagley were decided upon in 1752, when Sir George Lyttelton asked Miller to prepare plans both for altering the window of the chancel, and for erecting a new gallery, on the occasion of the installation of a monument to the recently-deceased Sir Thomas Lyttelton.[45] A letter of 1 April, 1754, however, makes it clear that work had not been begun before that date.[46] By the following month, the scheme had been expanded to include the complete demolition of the existing chancel and the erection of a new one. Sir George wrote to Miller on 2 May, 1754:

Hollier sends me word that he thinks the pulling down and building up of the Chancel

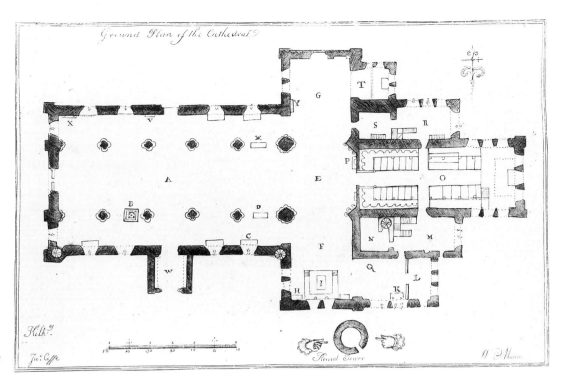

209. James Coffe, *Plan of St Canice's Cathedral, Kilkenny*, 1813.

will cost £200 or more. I hope he much over-reckons; otherwise I should not have undertaken the job. People will laugh at me for laying out so much money to so little purpose when I have so many necessary expenses to make. Hollier adds that he thinks they have taken down some (stone-work) which appear'd to be very firm and good, but I conclude they have acted according to your orders. Pray write to Hitchcox to do it as cheaply as he possibly can, and let me know exactly what it will cost. As my charge is so great, the Ceiling and Pavement must both be done by the Dean.[47]

It is evident from a manuscript account by the said Dean of Exeter, Sir George's brother, Charles, that he did not quite agree with this assessment of the share of financial responsibility for the work, which he describes succinctly.

The Church was rebuilt from the foundation A.D. 1754, with good freestone and the East Window decorated with rich painted glass, the floor also paved with fine white stone, the whole at the expense of the present Lord Lyttelton, as were the new windows throughout the body of the Church, together with the seats and gallerys. The ceiling and cornice of the chancel were ornamented at the same time, with shields of arms in their proper colours, at the expense of Dr Charles Lyttelton, Dean of Exeter.[48]

The rebuilding seems to have taken a year to effect, since William Shenstone wrote peevishly to Lady Luxborough in April 1755: "their new Chancel at Hagley is a mere Mausoleum and contains such a *display* of pedigree etc. as one would think must prove invidious to the last degree".[49] He also reported to his correspondent the fitting up of the new east window on 14 May of that year, but he did not elaborate.[50] Quite a different reaction came from Charles Lyttelton's successor as President of the Society of Antiquaries of London, Jeremiah Milles, who wrote to the Dean, by then Bishop of Carlisle, after visiting Hagley in 1768: "I admire the Church exceedingly, and am sensible that in so doing I pay my court to your Lordship".[51]

More immediately effective was the admiration Hagley Church evoked from Richard Pococke, Bishop of Ossory, who visited it in 1756.[52] Through his friend Charles Lyttelton, he immediately sent Sanderson Miller the plans of his cathedral, St Canice's at

Kilkenny, and asked him to prepare drawings for alterations in the Gothic style to the choir, the chapter house, and an area in the north transept known locally as "the Bishop's Court", which consisted principally of a seat on a podium (Plate 209).[53] The correspondence on the subject dates from 1756 and continues through the following year, and it shows that Miller had a model made of his proposals for the alterations and that he sent it to the Bishop in London. There the Bishop took the advice of his friends in the city, probably of the members of the Society of Antiquaries.[54]

The extent of Miller's responsibility for the alterations which were made to the lovely cathedral at Kilkenny was negligible in the long run, but the project is worth attention because of the light it throws on the policy and procedures of churchmen in the middle of the century. No alterations were made until 1762 and 1763, and the Bishop made it clear, in a letter to Sanderson Miller of 7 June, 1757, that the churchmen might be quite content to proceed with their own designing, aided by some pattern books: "I should also be obliged to you if you can inform me of any books for Gothic Architecture, besides *Canterbury* and *Westminster*, which may be a help to us in carrying on our work."[55] It seems clear from this, that the burden of the advice Bishop Pococke received from his friends in London had been that he should form his designs on models of attested historical accuracy rather than on the drawings of Sanderson Miller. However, Miller can be exempted from blame for the final designs of 1762, which were of stalls with Ionic columns, a barbarism which would have been decried by all gothic revivalists of the period.

The mixture was no more palatable to the critics of the following century, and even a staunch lover of St Canice's, J. G. A. Prim, wrote in 1844, "there is nothing remarkable in the choir, save the bad taste exhibited in its modern arrangements, which are all in the Grecian style".[56] It is indeed disappointing that Pococke, having taken so much trouble to acquire gothic designs, should have reverted to classical ornament in the woodwork of the choir, but it was probably as great a disappointment to Pococke. He had criticised the restorations made earlier to the cathedral in Waterford, precisely on this score: "The Quire has lately been much ornamented," he wrote, "if intermixture of Grecian and Gothick Architecture be called an ornament, by a Corinthian altar-piece."[57] Clearly the good Bishop meant well, but it is probable that the difficulty of finding workmen proficient in gothic design in Ireland made him decide to follow the example of the Bishop of Waterford, Thomas Milles, who was his uncle. A major concern of his letters to Sanderson Miller was the procuring of a wood-carver named Cobb, who would undertake to come to Ireland to oversee the local craftsmen.[58] Miller also promised to come in person to Kilkenny, but nothing seems to have come of the proposed visit of Miller or of Cobb. The Dean and Chapter at Kilkenny may have refused to approve the alterations so painstakingly formulated by the Bishop.

The difficulty of finding competent carvers in wood and stone for gothic detail was a major problem to the gothic revivalists, especially in places far from London. It must account in large part for the prevalence of the use of more malleable materials such as stucco, papier-maché and compositions of stone in the ornament of the period. In 1751, for instance, the Bishop of Durham, Richard Trevor, accepted a design for a gothic chimney-piece and accompanying wall-decoration from Sanderson Miller for a room in his residence, Durham Castle, but he too had to ask Miller to supply him with a carver, explaining, "I am afraid our People of Durham do not much understand this kind of Antique Work".[59] In the case of Kilkenny Cathedral, Bishop Pococke had proposed having a London carver provide models for the Irish craftsmen to follow: "I have thought of having one stall executed in London, by which we may judge of the expense & it will be a pattern for the Carver in Ireland who can afford to work cheaper: & one piece also of every kind of carv'd work."[60]

It is all the more surprising, therefore, to find above the Ionic choir stalls of the old St Canice's a splendid gothic revival organ-case with brittle and intricate carved ornament.[61] This must have been made in London when the organ itself was made, and I believe its design can be attributed to James Essex because it is so close to a design by him for a reredos signed and dated 1766, but used by Essex from 1757, as we shall see later. The preparatory drawing for the reredos is even closer to the Kilkenny organ in the stages of the slender shafts.[62] Pococke could well have commissioned the organ-case from James Essex through his good friend Charles Lyttelton, who was the moving spirit behind the alterations made by Essex at Ely Cathedral.

To return to Sanderson Miller, he supervised the rebuilding of the small Church of St Peter at Kineton, near Radway, in 1756 and 1757, but subsequent alterations have destroyed any trace of his work there.[63] The same is true of the Church of St Mary at Ross-on-Wye in Herefordshire, and indeed there is no documentary evidence that any alterations were made there in the middle of the eighteenth century. But it is a mark of Miller's widening popularity at the time that on 12 August, 1754, the incumbent, Reverend J. Egerton, asked him to prepare plans for alterations to the chancel of St Mary's, and by 24 September of the same year, had sent Miller the plans of the existing building.[64]

Miller's final church restoration was for James Leigh of Adlestrop, whose house he had altered. This involved the rebuilding of the Church of St Mary Magdalene to provide a family pew for the Leighs. An agreement of 17 March, 1758 between Edward Hitchcox and the wardens of the parish begins as follows: ''It is agreed that Edward Hitchcox shall execute the following Alterations and Repairs in the Church of Adlestrop and fulfill the whole in a workmanlike manner according to the Plan of Sanderson Miller, Esq. and to his satisfaction.''[65] Edward Hitchcox, the son of William who had been Miller's mason during the previous decade and died in 1757, signed his receipt of payment for the work on 29 September, 1759, so this can be taken as the date of completion. Further alterations to the nave of the church were made by Samuel Collett in 1765, and the agreement for this work specifically excludes interference with the chancel and the tower, so that Miller's earlier alterations were not affected by the later renovations.[66] But there is nothing to indicate that he was consulted or asked for designs in 1765, and it seems as though his effective career as an ecclesiastical architect ended with the sad nervous breakdown he suffered in 1759.

JAMES ESSEX

''His taste and his parsimony were nearly equally matched'', was the measured judgment of J. C. Buckler in his account of the cathedral restorations of James Essex, and it is seconded by Thomas Cocke in his recent essay on the subject.[67] James Essex, the architect responsible with his mentor, Sir James Burrough of Gonville and Caius College, for most of the architectural work done in Cambridge in the eighteenth century, found that this particular combination of qualities was much in demand by the bishops who sought alterations for their cathedrals or had alterations thrust upon them by the structural weaknesses of the buildings. They all pretended to taste and practised parsimony, and James Essex found himself called upon for designs for these alterations from the middle of the 1750s until his death in 1784.[68] As we have seen, his taste is in evidence even across the Irish Sea, in the organ-case for St Canice's Cathedral, Kilkenny.

The design for the organ-case will serve to demonstrate his parsimony and summarise his career in ecclesiastical architecture. Its central section is reproduced in the fullest

166

210. James Essex, *Design for a Reredos*, ink and wash, 280 × 445 mm, 1766. Courtesy of the British Library.

account of Essex, an essay by D. R. Stewart in the *Architectural Review*, and identified as a design for the altar and reredos of Ely Cathedral.[69] It is varied in a design for the screen at Ely (Plate 210), as the left-hand section of a drawing that proposed alternative schemes for panelling below the organ of the cathedral and it is shown again, this time as a proposal for an altar for Westminster Abbey. That proposal, datable to 1775, was not executed, nor was the design used at Ely, either for the screen or the altar.[70] However, it served as the drawing for the altar at Thaxted Church in Essex in about 1765, and for the screen in Lincoln Cathedral in about 1768, as well as for the organ in Kilkenny.[71] It appealed to Horace Walpole because it was based on a medieval tomb, that of Bishop Luda in Ely Cathedral. It is not surprising therefore to find it reappear in 1771, serving as the entrance gateway to Strawberry Hill.[72] It served James Essex very well indeed for almost twenty years!

It would evidently be a waste of time to look to Essex for prolific invention in gothic design; to quote Buckler again, he "never ran wild among the profuse gatherings of architectural splendour in any cathedral".[73] But in this respect, his practice is no different from that seen in the replication of the fan-vaulting of King Henry the Seventh's Chapel in Westminster Abbey by Keene and Newdigate. It is more "parsimonious" than their work because it remains a screen or panel and never reaches into the third dimension. What distinguishes him is that the work is executed in the genuine material, stone, or the look-alike composition of stone, so that among contemporaries he became valued for his engineering skills. "No man alive understands the technical part but himself", wrote his friend Michael Tyson, a fellow Cambridge antiquarian, to Richard Gough.[74] Thomas Cocke has remarked that the warning given by Thomas Gray to James Bentham on the subject of cathedral restorations went largely unheeded, and the impetus of the cathedral restoration movement can be dated from James Essex's alterations to Ely Cathedral and the publication of them by James Bentham in his monograph on the cathedral in 1771.[75] Gray had written, "This well-meant fury has been and will be little less fatal . . . than the reformation and the civil wars".[76] Nineteenth-century critics and historians found a scapegoat in James Wyatt for their denunciation of the restorations of the end of the eighteenth century, but with considerable injustice. By comparison with Wyatt, James Essex seemed to them innocuous in his restoration practices because the extent of his restorations was limited. But this is a relative judgment, and Gerald Cobb has rightly pointed out that Essex ran Wyatt a close second in the ruthlessness and insensitivity of the early recommendations he had made for Ely.[77] All commentators agree that the restorations of Essex are remarkable for their faithfulness to the spirit of the original.[78]

JOHN HOBCRAFT

The remarkable but not very satisfactory chapel at Audley End, Essex, built for Sir John Griffin in 1768, has been attributed to James Essex by his friend William Cole.[79] However, the documentary evidence indicates quite clearly that, though Essex may have advised at some stage, the making of the chapel was entirely the work of the London carpenter John Hobcraft (Plate XI).[80] A very fine set of drawings for the chapel has survived in an album at Audley End, and their authorship also presents problems (Plate 211). No comparable drawings from the hand of Hobcraft exist, and it is quite possible that since Robert Adam was engaged in work at the house in those years the drawings may be attributed to his office. In that case the design may also be attributed to him, but this speculation is not confirmed by any documentary evidence, nor do the drawings bear his signature, as one would expect had he been responsible for the design.

It is worth quoting Lord Braybrooke's description of the chapel dated 1836, as an instance of the taste of his generation as well as because it is the earliest description. He gives the dimensions as 51 ft in length by 26 ft 10 ins wide and 21 ft high, and continues:

> [it] originally occupied two stories; but the floor was raised about 1770 nearly to the level of the family seat, formerly a gallery, and the lower part converted into a housekeeper's room. The chapel, which has a nave and side aisles in miniature, was newly fitted up about the same period by Hobcraft, according to the fashion of the day, with pointed arches, clustered pilasters and a groined ceiling, in the style called after its patron, *Strawberry Hill Gothic*, a mode of decoration sufficiently objectionable under any circumstance, but perhaps never adopted with less judgment or a worse effect than in a building of the date and character of Audley End.[81]

In the circumstances, it is a minor miracle that the chapel has survived without alterations to the present day. It was fitted into an existing space and light comes from Jacobean windows which were fitted with stained glass. The congregation of retainers was ranged in benches facing each other in the miniature aisles and across from the window on the left was placed an elaborate gothic chair and lectern crafted in olive-wood and one of the most outstanding items of furniture of the period. The furniture is undistinguished otherwise, and decoration is confined to the pointed arches over the aisles and the thin ribs of the vaulting of the ceiling. The family must have been extremely low-church, since there is no effort to accent the area of the chancel; even the stained glass of the window is not effective as an axial agent, since its effect is negated by the stained glass of the north window and the richness of the design of the lectern opposite.

What is most confusing about the chapel is that the architectural decoration reaches its climax in the wrong place, namely in the family pew ranged along the back or entrance wall. This is heated by a modestly gothic chimney-piece, and is furnished by a set of richly decorated gothic chairs which contrast with the spartan seating of the body of the chapel. But the most astonishing element is the vaulting of the ceiling of the area, which is directly taken from the Chapel of King Henry the Seventh in Westminster Abbey and is rendered in plaster, painted pastel-pink, with a coloured heraldic shield in the centre. The patron, Sir John Griffin, must surely be responsible for this reversal of architectural and liturgical practice.

JAMES ESSEX AND JOHANN HEINRICH MÜNTZ

It is inevitable that one should compare the drawings of James Essex and those of Johann Heinrich Müntz in seeking to understand their contribution to the gothic revival, since

211. John Hobcraft, *Design for the Chapel at Audley End, Essex*, ink and wash, 590 × 780 mm, 1768. Courtesy of English Heritage.

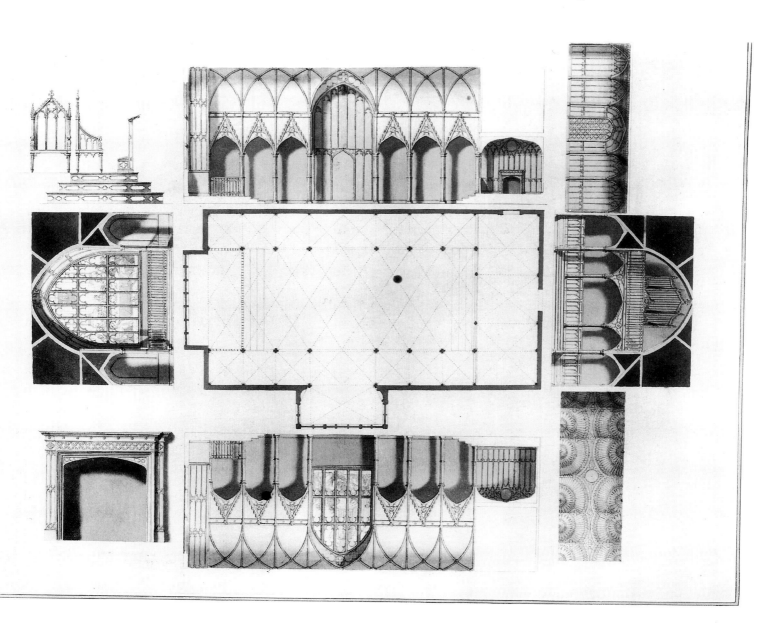

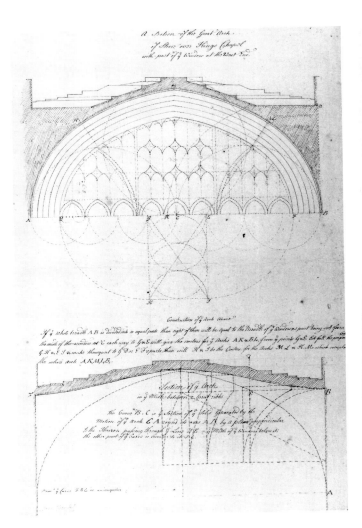

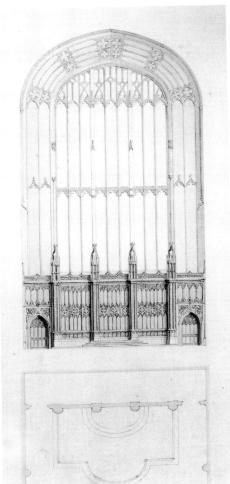

212. James Essex, *Section of the Roof of King's College Chapel, Cambridge*, ink, 491 × 300 mm, *c.* 1765. Courtesy of the British Library.

213. James Essex, *Design for the Reredos to King's College Chapel, Cambridge*, ink and wash, 385 × 200 mm, *c.* 1765. Courtesy of the British Library.

214. James Essex, *Design for a Gothic Window*, pencil and ink, 329 × 150 mm, *c.* 1765. Courtesy of the British Library

Essex was plainly aware of Müntz. The only copy of the *Proposals* for a treatise on gothic architecture printed by Müntz in 1760 is found among the notes James Essex had assembled for his own projected treatise on the subject.[82] Essex's drawings do not measure up to those of Müntz, for they are dryly descriptive even in their most finished state. Where hatching is used, as in the drawing of the vaults of King's College Chapel, Cambridge, it is gracelessly haphazard; and Essex's handling of wash can be described as bland at best and often watery (Plate 212). His best drawings are comparable to those of Müntz in their precision (Plate 213) and so too, incidentally, is his handwriting. He is similar to Müntz in his dependence on mathematical instruments for draughting, as is evident from the sketch for a two-light gothic window, built up on intersecting circles drawn by compass (Plate 214). But there is none of the intimacy and even mystery that make the drawings of Müntz so memorable, nor is there the feeling of ease with the style that Müntz shows in the ornamental invention and the fluidity of his tracery. Essex never moves far from the triangle, and one longs for an ogee, even a depressed one, after spending some time with his drawings. Because of Müntz's absence from England, Essex must be considered the more influential of the two. But in terms of immediate impact on the practice of the gothic revivalists, he takes second place to Henry Keene. The most attractive feature of the chapel at Audley End is the fan-vaulted ceiling, and that is a motif which Hobcraft, like Walpole at Strawberry Hill, had borrowed from Keene.

The projected treatise of James Essex has been described by Professor Pevsner and more recently by David Watkin, and no account of it will be given here because there is really no profit to be had from analysis in detail. The papers, deposited by Thomas

Kerrich in the British Library, are a rag-bag of odds and ends of architectural observation, architectural mythology and sheer irrelevancies that could never have been dragooned into presentable file.[83] Occasionally there are promising statements, such as, "The general practice of composing from fragments rather than from well established principles is one reason why so little progress has hitherto been made in that Stile", but the reader is cheated of any development of that statement.[84] As for "well established principles", this seems to boil down to the recognition of the importance of the pointed arch in gothic architecture. Essex claims to be original in this matter and he plays down the fact that Thomas Gray had seen the importance of this long before and had communicated it to James Bentham, who had duly published it in his monograph on Ely with suitable acknowledgment to the poet.[85] It was certainly a matter of common knowledge in the 1750s, since there are letters on the subject to Charles Lyttelton, from Charles Mason in 1753, and James Bentham in 1758.[86] In his printed *Proposals* of 1760 Johann Heinrich Müntz made the arch, systematised into eight different kinds, the principal subject-matter of his projected treatise, as Essex well knew.[87] His own claims, and those made for him, to originality of thought or insight on the principles of gothic architecture find no substantiation in the papers in the British Library, and there is little purpose in joining his friend, Michael Tyson, in lamentation over the failure of the publication of the treatise.[88] Walpole's scepticism as to the ability of Essex to handle the subject was well founded, and lamentations are better directed towards the lost treatise of Müntz, if only on visual grounds.[89]

JOHN CHUTE

Horace Walpole described the chapel at The Vyne to Horace Mann on 16 July, 1755, as "the most heavenly chapel in the world", and the hyperbole is pardonable (Plate 215).[90] Pevsner described it as "doubtless the best late medieval private chapel in England".[91] It was an irresistible temptation to any gothic revivalist, and Walpole could hardly wait to get his hands on it. He had already drawn up "An Inventionary of Alterations to be made at the Vine", the manuscript of which is dated 1 July, 1755.[92] The relevant parts concern the ante-chapel room, ("to be finished as the end is; the Windows to be painted by Price with the pedigree"), and the chapel itself, for which he prescribed pictures, an altar frontal, a reading-desk, and the "Walls above to be painted in a Gothic pattern; and a Closet with a Screen in the same pattern."[93] These suggestions were not made lightly. Walpole had concerned himself with alterations to the chapel at The Vyne as early as the previous 6 October, when he wrote to Mann: "Mr. Chute is much yours: I am going with him in a day or two to his Vine, where I shall try to draw him into amusing himself a little with building and planting".[94] By the following month he had determined on the necessity of painting the walls of the chapel, for he wrote to Richard Bentley on 3 November, 1754, in reference to Johann Heinrich Müntz, "I am sure you could make him paint delightful insides of the chapel at the Vine".[95] Walpole had not reckoned, however, on the independence of Chute and Müntz. The latter spent six months of the following year at The Vyne, but there is no indication that he set about schemes for painting the chapel, and none that John Chute wanted any at that time.

Most of Walpole's *Inventionary* was put into effect, but not as quickly as his temperament demanded, and his letters are full of grumbles about the slowness of Chute in executing alterations, and especially his failure to execute the designs made by Richard Bentley, who was then in Jersey and had never even seen The Vyne.[96] Given that circumstance, it is hardly surprising that his drawings for the ante-chapel were rejected by

215.(*facing page*) Interior of the Chapel at The Vyne, Hants. Courtesy of The Royal Commission on the Historic Monuments of England.

216. Richard Bentley, *Design for the Ante-Chapel of The Vyne, Hants.*, pencil and wash, 65 × 127 mm, 1754. Courtesy of the Lewis Walpole Library, Farmington, Connecticut.

John Chute. He reverted to the use of intersecting arches much like those he had proposed in the first scheme for the library of Strawberry Hill two years earlier, and their awkwardness is particularly apparent at the corners of the room, where the arches meet to dangle perilously in mid-air (Plates 216–17). The ante-chapel as executed has been described as ''a typical product of the Strawberry Committee's deliberations . . . panelled in thin strips of a flimsy fret-like pattern, of which the 'Gothickness' can deceive no one''.[97] Ironically, this is the most authentic part of the alterations. The pattern is not due to Walpole or Bentley or Chute, but was there already. Walpole had merely suggested that the room ''be finished as the end is'', and a break in the panelling indicates wood of different ages, so it would appear that Chute simply extended to the other walls the pattern of panelling already in place on the east or chapel end of the room (Plate 218). No designs for this have survived among his drawings and it is not in the least typical of his designing at any stage of his career.

Walpole's ideas for the chapel itself were honoured in the main, though he had to wait for seventeen years to see them realised by his less impetuous friend. Chute was also cautious in effecting the painting of the chapel ceiling, and did it in such a way that no structural changes were necessary and the new ceiling was easily removable. The painter Spiridione Roma succeeded Müntz as resident artist at The Vyne for two years from

217. Richard Bentley, *Design for the Ante-Chapel of The Vyne, Hants.*, pencil and wash, 140 × 260 mm, 1754. Courtesy of the Lewis Walpole Library, Farmington, Connecticut.

218. Interior of the Ante-Chapel of The Vyne Hants., *c. 1755*. Courtesy of the Royal Commission on the Historic Monuments of England.

1769, and he was responsible for executing the fan-vaulting painted in perspective on the ceiling.[98] The painting was done in distemper on canvas, which was then fixed to the upper walls and ceiling of the chapel, as appears in an old watercolour which may well be Roma's *modello* for the project, and which shows that it was a very skilful and attractive piece of illusionistic painting (Plate 219).[99] It is of interest that the model chosen breaks away from the Westminster Abbey precedent in favour of the fan-vaulting of the cloisters of Gloucester Cathedral, which Walpole had admired so much in 1753, and which had been so influential to the planning of the alterations to Strawberry Hill from 1758.[100] This instance of Chute's having recourse to archaeological precedent, therefore, may be ascribed in part to the influence of Walpole, like whom Chute owned copies of Dugdale's *St Paul's* and Dart's *Canterbury*.[101] However, the *Inventionary* had called only for "The walls above to be painted in a Gothic pattern", and no model had been specified.

One must conclude, therefore, that John Chute was himself convinced of the appropriateness of the use of archaeological models when designs for an ecclesiastical building were in question. An indication of this is that Thomas Gray, when visiting The Vyne, wrote to Walpole on 21 September, 1756, asking him to bring down a print of the interior of St George's Chapel, Windsor, on his next journey.[102] Certainly the designs Chute made about this time for the tomb-chamber of The Vyne have nothing in common with the quirky drawings for a columbarium, with urns and gesticulating saints, that Walpole

174

thought Richard Bentley had "drawn so divinely" (Plates 220–1).[103] Chute thought on a larger scale and designed a separate tomb-chamber to adjoin the existing chapel and serve as memorial to the founder of the family fame and fortune, his most illustrious ancestor, Challenor Chute, who had been Speaker of the Commons.[104] This twinning of chapel and tomb-chamber is a most extraordinary arrangement in plan, but the telling point is that it has a perfectly authentic source in historical precedent, which was to be seen quite close to The Vyne, in Basingstoke.

On reflection, it seems inevitable that Chute should have looked to the ruined medieval chapels of the Holy Ghost and the Holy Trinity in Basingstoke for inspiration in designing the alteration to the chapel of The Vyne. They were associated with the Sandys family who had preceded the Chutes in ownership of The Vyne. The ruins are in a more dilapidated condition today than they were in the eighteenth century, when the chancel of the earlier Holy Ghost Chapel was still partly standing, with the tomb-chamber of Lord Sandys, built against its south wall, and known as the Holy Trinity chapel. There is moreover, a direct connection between the splendid stained-glass windows of The Vyne and those formerly in the Basingstoke chapels, as H. G. Wayment has explained in the detailed study recently published in *Archaeologia*, to which I owe enlightenment as to John Chute's source for the tomb-chamber of The Vyne.[105]

219. Spiridione Roma (attributed), *Interior of the Chapel of The Vyne, Hants.*, watercolour, 457 × 545 mm, 1769. Courtesy of the National Trust and the Paul Mellon Centre, London.

220. Richard Bentley, *Design for a Columbarium for The Vyne, Hants.*, ink and wash, 178 × 154 mm, 1754. Courtesy of the Lewis Walpole Library, Farmington, Connecticut.

221. Richard Bentley, *Design for a Columbarium for The Vyne, Hants.*, ink and wash, 228 × 127 mm, 1754. Courtesy of the Lewis Walpole Library, Farmington, Connecticut.

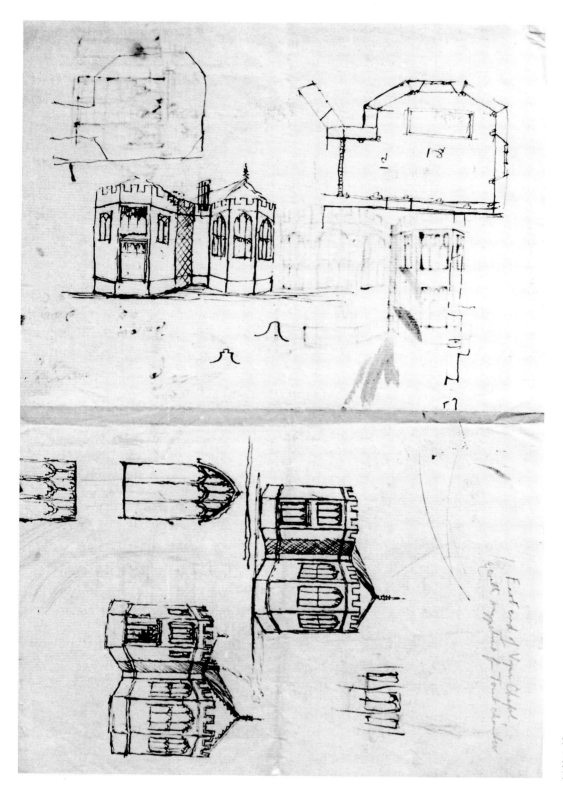

222. John Chute, *Sketches for the Tomb-Chamber of The Vyne, Hants.*, ink, 209 × 300 mm, *c.*1757. Courtesy of the Hampshire County Record Office.

Chute was especially careful to provide a fine stained-glass window for the new tomb-chamber, and he acquired it from the widow of John Rowell of Reading, after the artist's death in 1757.[106] Thus, this date may possibly be taken to be the date of two instructive drawings for the tomb-chamber which survive among his papers (Plates 222–3), since the subject of the window, *The Adoration of the Magi* after Van Dyck, is inscribed on the second drawing (Plate 223), shown *in situ* (though probably too faint to appear clearly in the

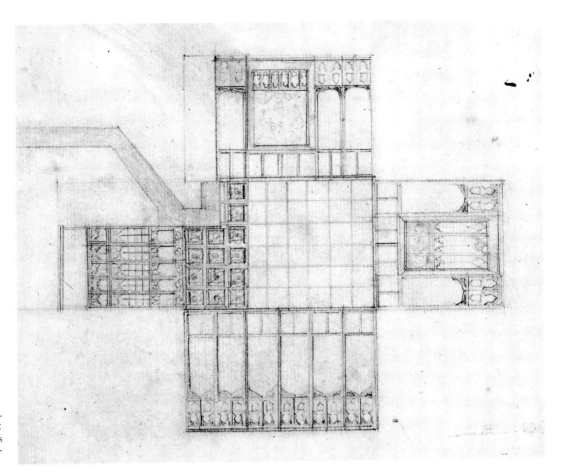

223. John Chute, *Design for the Tomb-Chamber of the Vyne, Hants.*, pencil, 228 × 191 mm, *c*.1757. Courtesy of the Lewis Walpole Library, Farmington, Connecticut.

photograph). The earlier sheet of drawings indicates that he had first determined on building a shallow rectangular addition and placing the tomb in the bay window to the south. But the final form is that of a rectangular room with the shallow bay window at the east end, adumbrated in the elevations of the earlier sheet which duplicate the east elevation of the Basingstoke chapels (Plate 224).[107]

The decoration of the room shown in the later drawing differs in detail from the tomb-chamber as erected, but it is not different in character. What is astonishing is that it is so very ecclesiastical and has absolutely nothing in common with the gothic decoration of Chute's domestic architecture at Strawberry Hill and Donnington Grove. The tomb itself is classical, with Ionic columns, and the mixture of the styles, though at first startling, is not disagreeable, perhaps because of the very high order of execution evident throughout. The success of the room can be measured by the fact that it has called forth no particular comment whatsoever from the chroniclers of the gothic revival. Like the tomb it houses, also designed by John Chute, it has the inevitability that is the mark of the unqualified masterpiece. With the assurance of its co-ordination of plan and elevation on historically determined precedents, it is the most neglected monument of the entire gothic revival and not simply of the beginning decades of the movement, which are the subject of this book.

This enigmatic man John Chute, emerges therefore as something in the nature of "the all-round man" of the gothic revival of the mid-eighteenth century. His drawings, from those based on the work of William Kent and the prints of Batty Langley for the first phase of the building of Strawberry Hill in 1753, to those made for the tomb-chamber of The Vyne, based on the ruins of the chapels of the Holy Trinity and the Holy Ghost in Basingstoke twenty years later, represent the course the revival was to run in the period. So much of the early work at Strawberry Hill depended on motifs drawn from tombs that

178

there is a poetic jusice in ending our account with a tomb-chamber holding an Ionic tomb. The sigificance of the change in attitude that this development involved was very early sensed and given expression by Chute's life-long friend Walpole in a letter to the third member of the Committee of Taste, Richard Bentley: "I own I grow to look on tombs as lasting mansions, instead of observing them for curious pieces of architecture."[108]

The work of the early gothic revivalists had been well done. They awakened the conscience of architects, craftsmen, antiquaries and landowners to the aesthetic and historical importance of the buildings in the gothic style. When the next generation gave practical expression to this newly-found sensibility in preserving and renovating the gothic cathedrals and churches of England, and of Europe, the principal criterion for success was to be fidelity to the intentions of the original architects of the buildings. There is reason enough to deplore the damage that was done in the cause of restoration, but that should not blind us to the fact that the early gothic revivalists had prepared a climate of opinion that would not tolerate destruction without question and that rejected utilitarian principles of restoration. The function of the gothic revival as guarantor of gothic survival is nowhere more evident than at The Vyne. Its triumph and essential rightness is manifest in the mastery shown by John Chute in the design of the tomb-chamber; it is equally manifest in the misgivings that prevented him from executing his many schemes for gothicising the house.

224. John Chute, *Elevation of the Chapel and Tomb-Chamber of The Vyne, Hants.*, pencil, 362 × 226 mm, *c*.1757. Courtesy of the Lewis Walpole Library, Farmington, Connecticut.

By permission of The British Library the document titled *Proposals for publishing by subscription a Course of Gothic Architecture*, signed and dated by Johann Heinrich Müntz, London 12 April, 1760, is here reproduced. It is a printed document, but is known in one version only, BL Add.MS. 6771, P.S.3/9168, found among the papers of James Essex which were deposited by Thomas Kerrich. Some of the illustrations for the proposed treatise have survived and are discussed in the first chapter above, and a comparison of the fragmentary evidence of this treatise with documents and drawings related to the proposal of James Essex to publish a comparable work will be found in the sixth chapter.

PROPOSALS FOR PUBLISHING BY SUBSCRIPTION A COURSE OF GOTHIC ARCHITECTURE

WHEREIN

The Fundamental Principles and Rules for the Disposition, Proportions, Use and Intentions of all the Parts and Members of that Stile of Building will be clearly stated and demonstrated.

Exemplified by Designs and Measures taken from the finest Fabrics and Monuments still existing in ENGLAND and abroad.

ALSO

Descriptions of the Instruments required for that Purpose, and the Machines our Forefathers used for the adorning their stupendous Fabrics, and particularly those by the Help of which they executed the curve Mouldings of their Arches and vaulted Roofs, &c. the Method of turning and working their slender round Pillars; a Scale to find the Centers of Force and Centers of Gravity of any of the Eight Arches, viz. Arches of 1,2,3,4,5,6,7,8, Centers or Segments of Circles as also the Consequence, Use, and Centers of Force of Exterior Pouterasses &c., &c.

by J. H. Müntz

This extensive Work will make one large Volume in Folio, printed upon the best Imperial Paper, and will consist of between Sixty and Seventy Copper Plates, divided in Four Parts, to be engraved by the best Hands in England, or, if a sufficient Number cannot be engaged to forward the Work, by some of the best Masters in Holland. Part the

First, which as it will be very intricate, and to have every Line true, the Author proposes to engrave himself. The Letter-Press cannot yet be ascertained, but as near as can be guessed will be about Sixty full Pages, including the Index Raisone of the technical Terms, which will be alphabetically digested, the Capital Letters whereof throughout the whole Alphabet will be Copper Plates, representing the Origin, Rise, Progress &c. of Architecture, all of which will be engraved by the Author.

Part the First will contain the whole Theory, or fundamental Principles and Rules, for the Disposition and Proportion of Piers and Pillars, for describing any of the Eight Arches, for finding and fixing the Center of Force and Center of Gravity of any of those Arches, with Tables of Calculation for what Superior Weight each Arch ought and can support, for the different Sections of the Rib-Stones and Key-Stones of those Arches, and how the Degrees of their Angles must be varied to give Solidity to each, &c. and what Ornaments are becoming to any curve Line to produce a good effect.

Part the Second will contain the foregoing Theory put into Practice; exemplified by different Gateways, Pillars, Doors, Windows, simple Arches and arched Roofs, Plans, Elevations, and Sections of whole Fabrics, plain and ornamented, useful and ornamental.

Part the Third will contain Designs of the finest Parts of ancient Buildings with Measures, Plans, and Sections, with occasional Remarks on their Merits, Meaning, and Proportions, and how to make Use of and introduce them in any Building.

This Part will also contain Designs of some remarkable fine and curious Remains of Moresque Fabrics, still existing in the Kingdoms of Murcia, Valentia, and the City of Saragossa in Spain, which the Author made there in 1743, with some historical Account of them, and their lofty Magnificence, and Remarks on some remarkable Particularities, &c. of which neither Drawing nor Print has ever been seen or done.

Part the Fourth will contain all the ornamental Parts and Members of the Three foregoing, detached and upon a larger Scale with their Sections; with Designs of Ceilings, Chimney-pieces, Windows, Alcoves, and other Furniture pieces, Chapels or Temples, Umbrellas, &c. for Gardens and Parks, Designs and Explanations of the Instruments and Machines for working ornamented Roofs and other curved Members, for turning the Pillars, &c.

CONDITIONS

The Price to Subscribers to be Three Guineas and a Half, Two Guineas to be paid at the Time of Subscribing, and a Guinea and a Half on the delivery of the Book, which will be in Fifteen Months after Three Hundred Subscriptions shall be received; Notice of which will be immediately given in all the Public Papers.

The Subscribers may be well assured that this Work will be carried on and executed in the most masterly manner in every respect; the most interesting Plates will be engraved under the Author's Inspection, and will certainly be published in the Time above mentioned.

There will be no more printed than what are subscribed for; and after the Subscription is closed, the Price will be advanced to Five Guineas.

The Names of the Subscribers will be prefixed.

SUBSCRIPTIONS are taken in by the Author, (at present) at his Lodgings at Mr. Helms, Little Castle Street, Oxford Market and by A. Webley, Bookseller, at the Bible and Crown in Holborn near Chancery Lane, and no where else, where some Drawings as Specimens and Proofs of all the Engravings may be inspected by the Subscriber during the whole Time until the Publication.

TO THE PUBLIC

As this Work is so extensive, and will be the Unique of this Kind, and will stand the Author in about Twelve Hundred Pounds at the lowest Computation, without reckoning the First Part which he intends to engrave himself, he should not go on with so heavy, laborious and expensive an Undertaking, if there are not Three Hundred Subscribers at the end of June, therefore hopes the above Clause will not be thought extraordinary. It would neither be prudent in him to expose the whole system before his being sure of the Means of putting it in execution; for, if he did expose the Principles and whole Theory, they being so simple, anybody of ordinary Talents might understand and master in an Hour what cost the Author several Years close Application, and either attribute to themselves the Invention, or take Advantage of the Author's Publication not taking place and publish what they might have seen and learned from the Author's Drawings; which if it would be very agreeable is left to the Generous to judge; the Author having undergone so many mortifying Experiences of this Kind cannot help being a little shy. But as soon as the Three Hundred Subscriptions shall be received, the whole will be laid open. All the Drawings, and Manuscripts for the Letter Press will be completely finished towards the end of July. At the time of publication of the Books, Three different Machines (of which the Drawings will be given in the Work) for working and moving heavy Masses, &c. will be produced, and everybody shall be at Liberty to move and work them. These Machines are entirely of the Author's own making for Wood, Iron and Steel Work, who spent Two Years in Contriving them. They are not only useful in Gothic Architecture, but will be of infinite Advantage in any other Branch of Building, &c.

By Permission, will also be given, the Plan, Elevation, Section and Perspective View, of a Temple for a Garden, in the Moresque Stile, of the Author's Composition, and which is going to be executed at a Nobleman's Country Seat.

The Author being conscious that what he shall advance will be strictly true, as Authorities will be cited for every thing, and as not one Book or Treatise on true Gothic Architecture has ever been written or existed as far as we know, therefore think it unnecessary to say any more. The Public will decide after Inspection.

N.B.

If any Nobleman, or Gentleman knows of any fine Remains, in any part of Great Britain, that might be worth taking Notice of, upon Information thereof the Author will transport himself upon the Spot to inspect and measure them, and if found interesting will be inserted.

If Three Hundred Subscriptions are not received at Midsummer the Work will not go on, and the Money will be returned.

Received the .... Day of .... 1760, of .... the Sum of Two Pounds and Two Shillings, being the first Subscription for A Course of Gothic Architecture, which (as soon as completed and finished) I promise to deliver upon the Payment of One Pound Eleven Shillings and Six Pence more.

Notes

CHAPTER I

1. Interest in the origins of romanticism has led to many exhaustive studies of the literary background of the gothic revival, and it will be sufficient to refer to A. Addison, *Romanticism and the Gothic Revival* (New York 1939); B. S. Allen, *Tides in English Taste* (New York reprint, 1969), Vol. I: Ch. 1–4; Vol. II: Ch. 14–15; P. Frankl, *The Gothic: Literary Sources and Interpretations* (Princeton 1960), 350–414; and M. Levy, *Le Roman "Gothique" Anglais* (Toulouse 1968), which is the most complete compilation of literary references. Important essays on topographical literature of relevance are H. M. Colvin, "Aubrey's Chronologia Architectonica"; J. Harris, "English Country House Guides, 1740–1840"; and J. M. Crook, "John Britton and the Genesis of the Gothic Revival"; all of these are published in *Concerning Architecture: Essays on Architectural Writers and Writing presented to Nikolaus Pevsner*, ed. J. Summerson (London 1968).

2. For the nineteenth century, see C. L. Eastlake, *A History of the Gothic Revival*, ed. J. M. Crook (Leicester 1970); K. Clark, *The Gothic Revival: An Essay in the History of Taste* (London 1928); P. Stanton *The Gothic Revival and American Church Architecture* (Baltimore 1968); G. Germann, *Gothic Revival in Europe and Britain: Sources, Influences and Ideas* (London 1972); T. Davis, *The Gothick Taste* (Newton Abbot 1974); J. Macaulay, *The Gothic Revival, 1745–1845* (Glasgow 1975).

3. A. Rowan, "Batty Langley's Gothic", *Studies in Memory of David Talbot Rice*, ed. G. Henderson (Edinburgh 1975), 197–215; E. 'Harris, "Batty Langley, Tutor of Free-Masons", *The Burlington Magazine*, CXIX, No. 890 (May 1977), 327–35.

4. Details of published works are from H. M. Colvin, *Biographical Dictionary of British Architects 1600–1840* (London 1978), which will hereafter be referred to as Colvin, *Biog. Dict.*

5. *The Early Eighteenth Century*, ed. P. Breman (London 1965), item 47.

6. "The Artist", *Man versus Society in Eighteenth-Century Britain*, ed. J. L. Clifford (London 1968), 70–84.

7. *Essay on Design* (London 1749), 70. For Gwynn see Colvin, *Biog. Dict.*, 372–4. His writings are discussed in M. S. Briggs, *The Architect in History* (London 1927), 304–17 and F. Jenkins, *Architect and Patron* (London 1961), Ch. 4–6.

8. E. Harris (1977), 329.

9. For further discussion see M. McCarthy, "The Education in Architecture of the Man of Taste", *Studies in Eighteenth-Century Culture*, Vol. V, ed. R. Rosbottom (Univ. of Wisconsin Press 1976), 337–53.

10. Sanderson Miller to Thomas Prowse, in L. Dickins and M. Stanton, *An Eighteenth-Century Correspondence* (London 1910), 315.

11. *Palladio and English Palladianism* (London 1974), 73–112. See also J. Archer, *The Literature of British Domestic Architecture, 1715–1842* (MIT Press, 1985).

12. Introduction to *The Art of Designing and Working the Ornamental Parts of Building* (London 1745), not listed by Colvin. The copy I have used is in the library of the Royal Ontario Museum, Toronto.

13. London, 1762, 60–1. It is worth pointing out that Allan Ramsay in the "Dialogue of Taste", Tract IV of *The Investigator* (London 1755), had defended gothic architecture vigorously and had posited that the classical style was an acquired taste rather than a norm with intrinsic validity.

14. Nikolaus Pevsner has remarked that the notes of James Essex, to be discussed later, also presuppose a classical basis for gothic architecture. See *Some Architectural Writers of the Nineteenth Century* (Oxford 1972), 3–4.

15. I am indebted to the late Professor H. W. Janson for this helpful reference. The first quotation is from Vol. I under item "Architecture" and the second is from Vol. II under item "Gothic". This edition is unpaginated.

16. Wittkower, 109–110.

17. Eastlake, 54.

18. A point made by R. B. Wragg, "John Carr: Gothic Revivalist", *Studies in Architectural History*, Vol. II, ed. W. A. Singleton (London 1966), 9–34.

19. Rowan (1975), 207. For a list of borrowings from the book see R. White, "The Influence of Batty Langley", in the unpaginated booklet of The Georgian Group, *A Gothick Symposium* (London 1984).

20. Rowan (1975), 208.

21. Rowan (1975), 202.

22. P. Breman (1965), item 46.

23. Wittkower, 73–92.

24. Morris at Clearwell Castle, Glos., for which see A. Rowan in *The Country Seat*, ed. H. M. Colvin and J. Harris (London 1970), 145–9; and Inverary, see L. Lindsay and M. Cosh, *Inverary and the Dukes of Argyll* (Edinburgh 1973). For Ware at Chicksands and Eythrope, see H. M. Colvin, "Eythrope House and its Destruction in 1810–11", *Records of Buckinghamshire*, Vol. XVII (1964), 219–27.

25. R. Morris, *Lectures on Architecture* (London 1734), third lecture, unpaginated.

26. The list could be extended indefinitely and would include the great neo-classicists, Sir William Chambers and Robert Adam, among the architects to the middle decades of the century.
27. Wragg, 13.
28. Discussion of these authors will be found below. In an unpublished manuscript in the Beinecke Library of Yale University (W. Salmon Jnr., *The Vitruvian Principles of Architecture Practically Demonstrated*, 1737), Batty Langley is accorded mention in the same sentence as Vitruvius, Palladio, Serlio, LeClerc, Inigo Jones and Gibbs! But most authors considered him beneath notice.
29. "He is an architect that has published a book of bad designs", Gray wrote to Walpole in explanation of his coining the expression "Battey-Langley-Manner" with reference to Kent's gothic alterations to Esher Place, Surrey, in 1733. This was written in 1754, and Walpole was certainly familiar with *Ancient Architecture Restored and Improved* long before then. But the following year we find the first derogatory comment by Walpole, in a letter to Bentley: "I want to write over the doors of most modern edifices *Repaired and Beautified: Langley and Hallet, Churchwardens!*" *Horace Walpole's Correspondence*, ed. W. S. Lewis, Vol. XXXV (New Haven 1973), 233 (hereafter referred to as *H.W.C.*). This was written in connection with Latimers in Buckinghamshire, which, since Walpole's last visit in 1750, had, as he phrased it, "undergone Batty Langley-discipline; half the ornaments are of his bastard Gothic, and half of Hallet's mongrel Chinese." Hallet was a fashionable cabinet-maker, for whose career see R. Edwards, *Dictionary of English Furniture*, Vol. II (London 1954), 252. The house was altered by Edward Blore from 1834 to 1838, as recorded in Colvin, *Biog. Dict.* 117. The decline of Langley's reputation in the nineteenth century is charted by Rowan (1975), 198–9. Beginning with Agnes Addison, 28–34, the modern commentators tend towards more favourable critical commentary, but the most balanced recent assessment of his career is the entry by John Harris in *Macmillan Encyclopedia of Architects*, ed. A. Placzek, Vol. II, (New York 1982), 607–8, which begins memorably "Batty Langley (1696–1751) deserves to be forgotten as an architect."
30. Chapter 3, below.
31. M. McCarthy, "John Chute's Drawings for The Vyne", *The National Trust Year-Book, 1975–76*, 70–80. Gate-piers erected at The Vyne were taken directly from Batty Langley, as noted by J. Lees-Milne in "John Chute and The Vyne", *The Connoisseur*, June 1960, 47.
32. *Letters of William Shenstone*, ed. M. Williams (London 1939), 204.
33. M. Williams, (ed.) (1939), 230.
34. Besides Williams, (1939), see T. Hull, *Select Letters* (London 1778); R. Graves, *Recollections of William Shenstone* (London 1788); and J. Hodgetts, *Letters of Lady Luxborough to William Shenstone* (London 1775). For Horace Walpole, *H.W.C.* is the most complete collection. For Sanderson Miller see L. Dickins and M. Stanton (1910).
35. T. Mowl, "The Case of the Enville Museum", *Journal of Garden History*, Vol. III, No. 2 (1983), 134–43. Alternative attributions are found in the paper by R. White cited in note 19 above and in W. Hawkes, "The Gothic Architectural Work of Sanderson Miller", also in *A Gothick Symposium* (London 1984), unpaginated.
36. Colvin, *Biog. Dict.*, 548–51.
37. *H.W.C.*, Vol. XXXV, 359.
38. As examples of his promotion of the talents of Richard

Bentley, for instance, see *H.W.C.*, Vol. IX (1941), 151, 216, 267, 284.
39. The works of Miller at Radway Grange and Walpole at Strawberry Hill will be considered below. For Shenstone's work at The Leasowes see J. Riely, "Shenstone's Walks: The Genesis of The Leasowes", *Apollo*, September 1979, 202–9.
40. Colvin, *Biog. Dict.*, 378–9.
41. W. Ison, *The Georgian Buildings of Bristol* (London 1952), 37–8.
42. *Macmillan Encyclopedia of Architects*, Vol. II, 297–8.
43. For attributions to Halfpenny see J. Lees-Milne, "Stout's Hill Uley and Hardwicke Court, Gloucestershire", *Country Life*, 5 July 1973, 16–20.
44. For Morris see Colvin, *Biog. Dict.*, 558–9. He collaborated with Halfpenny in the publication of *The Modern Builder's Assistant*, 1742 and 1757. For Swan see Colvin, *Biog. Dict.*, 799.
45. T. Wright, *Book of Arbours and Book of Grottoes*, ed. E. Harris (London 1979). Wright's designs are discussed below.
46. Colvin, *Biog. Dict.*, 934.
47. Colvin, *Biog. Dict.*, 603.
48. Colvin, *Biog. Dict.*, 603.
49. For his indebtedness to Batty Langley see Rowan (1975), 208, who notes a second edition in 1774. Colvin remarks that the book is sometimes titled *Original Designs for Temples*.
50. Plate 45 by Crunden and Plate 46 by Columbani. For these and other furniture designs in the gothic style, see P. Ward-Jackson, *English Furniture Designs of the Eighteenth Century* (London 1958), 14–21.
51. Plates 10 and 11, described as "gothic appliqué"!
52. Plates 3 and 5, described as "gothick antique"! The designs of Müntz are discussed below.
53. Crunden's two plates (three designs to each plate) are unnumbered at the end of the book.
54. Besides the plates bearing the names of Müntz and Crunden, there are eight designs bearing the names of Manwaring. But others are not attributed to any designer.
55. See D. Wiebenson, *Sources of Greek Revival Architecture* (London 1969), Ch. IV, and M. McCarthy, "Documents on the Greek Revival in Architecture", *The Burlington Magazine*, CXIV, No. 836 (November 1972), 760–9.
56. See J. M. Frew, "An Aspect of the Early Gothic Revival: The Transformation of Medievalist Research, 1770–1800", *Journal of the Warburg and Courtauld Institutes*, Vol. XLIII (1980), 174–85, and "Richard Gough James Wyatt and Late 18th Century Preservation", *Journal of the Society of Architectural Historians*, Vol. XXXVIII (December 1979), 366–74.
57. Colvin, *Biog. Dict.*, 863. The copy in the library of Dumbarton Oaks, Washington, is dated 1773 and claims to be "a new edition".
58. Colvin, *Biog. Dict.*, 822–3.
59. Colvin, *Biog. Dict.*, 687–8.
60. See J. Harris, *The Palladians* (London 1981).
61. See L. Lawrence, "Stuart and Revett: Their Literary and Architectural Careers", *Journal of the Warburg and Courtauld Institutes*, Vol. II (1938), 128–46.
62. See R. D. Middleton, "The Abbé de Coredemoi and the Graeco–Gothic Ideal: A Prelude to Romantic Classicism", *Journal of the Warburg and Courtauld Institutes*, Vol. XXV (1962), 278–320, and Vol. XXVI (1963), 90–123. See also W. Herrmann, *Laugier and 18th-Century French Theory* (London 1962), 71–83 and Appendix 8.
63. W. Herrmann, in the introduction to *M.-A. Laugier,*

An Essay on Architecture (Los Angeles 1977), notes translations into English of the *Essai* in 1755 and 1756. The works of Félibien des Avaux and of Louis Avril were also translated.

64. Above, p. 7.

65. R. Morris, (1734) Lecture four, unpaginated.

66. For Riou see Colvin, *Biog. Dict.*, 687–8.

67. *Short Principles for the Architecture of Stone Bridges* (London 1760), note to p. 13.

68. *Short Principles for the Architecture of Stone Bridges*, 17. Riou is here paraphrasing a passage from Sir Henry Wotton, *Elements of Architecture* (London 1624; reprint, Amsterdam, 1970), 51.

69. For Mylne see Colvin, *Biog. Dict.*, 570–7, and for Gwynn see note 7 above.

70. See Colvin, *Biog. Dict.*, 372. The writings of Gwynn and Robert Morris have been confused in the past, and the subject is clarified in Colvin, *Biog. Dict.*, 558.

71. J. Gwynn, *An Essay on Design* (London 1749), Preface, p. 5.

72. As will be seen below, Gwynn's strictures against this practice had no effect, even on the practitioners of the Gothic Revival.

73. J. Gwynn, *London and Westminster Improved* (London 1766), 46.

74. The copy I have used is in the Yale Center for British Art, New Haven, Conn., and I am grateful to Mr Paul Mellon for permission to use it before it entered the collection in Yale. It is catalogued under the name T. Osborne, who is known to have been a publisher, and who signed the Dedication which is to the King. The title page reads: "English Architecture: or, the Public Buildings of London and Westminster. With Plans of the Streets and Squares, represented in one hundred and twenty-three folio plates; with a succinct review of their history, and a candid examination of their perfections and defects. London, printed for T. Osborne in Gray's Inn". A preface of two pages precedes the text and plates. The plates are all by Samuel Wale, whose co-operation with John Gwynn is well documented; see E. Edwards, *Anecdotes of Painters* (London 1808), 116. Mr Ben Weinreb kindly looked over the volume with me some years ago and informed me that there is a second copy, whereabouts now unknown, listed in Weinreb Catalogue 3, ed. P. Breman (London 1964), item 57.

75. The entry in Weinreb Catalogue 3 reads as follows: "In 1756 Osborne had issued a new 2-volume edition of Maitland's *History and Survey*, with plates of individual buildings engraved by Benjamin Cole (who had previously done the plates to Oakley's *Magazine of Architecture* and to Hoppus's *Palladio*). These same plates were used for the present work, which contains an anonymous but extremely knowledgeable account of the building history and architectural curiosities of the public edifices illustrated. This text was re-issued only once (as an appendix to Osborne's 1760 Maitland), the present edition is its only separate issue. The author has remained undiscovered." The history of this book has been recorded, with a collation of the plates of the several editions, in Bernard Adams, *London Illustrated, 1604–1813: a Survey and Index of Topographical Books and their Plates*, London 1983, 96–104.

76. Gwynn (1758), 7.

77. See B. Little, *James Gibbs* (London 1955).

78. Gwynn (1758), 7.

79. Above, p. 11.

80. Gwynn (1758), 1–2.

81. See N. Pevsner, "Good King James's Gothic", *Studies in Art, Architecture and Design*, Vol. I (London 1968),

156–63.

82. J. Aheron, *A General Treatise on Architecture* (Dublin 1754), unpaginated, entries under "modern" and "gothic".

83. H. Walpole, *Anecdotes of Painting in England*, Vol. I (New York, reprint 1969), 121. First published in 1762.

84. James Dallaway noted in his edition of 1826: "The reason of the failure of these two most eminent architects was simply their *classically* confined views of architecture. They were unwilling to copy, and incompetent to invent designs, in any degree analogous to original examples of the different *Gothic* manners." *Anecdotes of the Arts in England* (London 1826), Vol. 1, 121, n. 2.

85. This uneasiness was widely expressed when it was proposed to build the new Hagley Hall in the gothic style in 1752. See M. McCarthy, "The Building of Hagley Hall, Worcestershire", *The Burlington Magazine*, Vol. CXVIII, No. 877 (April 1976), 214–25.

86. P. Toynbee and L. Whibley, *Correspondence of Thomas Gray*, Vol. I (Oxford 1955), 406.

87. K. Clark, 38.

88. K. Clark, 37.

89. *The Works of Thomas Gray*, ed. T. J. Mathias (London 1814), Vol. II, 98–103 and 600–3.

90. K. Clark, 32–46; P. Frankl, 411. See also N. Pevsner, *Some Architectural Writers* (1972), Ch. 1.

91. For Thomas Pitt see Colvin, *Biog. Dict.*, 639–40, and for his grand tour see M. McCarthy, "Art Education and the Grand Tour", *Art the Ape of Nature: Studies in Honor of H. W. Janson*, ed. M. Barasch and L. F. Sandler (New York 1981), 477–94.

92. Toynbee and Whibley, 659.

93. Pitt's thoughts on the origin of gothic are to be found in British Library Add. MS. 5845, ff. 142 verso and 143. He denies the Saracenic theory of Wren, a subject on which he had probably had previous discussions with his uncles Charles Lyttelton and George Lyttelton, the builder of Hagley Hall (n. 85 above). In *A Gentleman's Tour through Wales* (London 1781), 146–50, George Lyttelton discussed the origin of gothic and accepted a northern origin, citing Vasari in support of his conclusion. The tour was made in 1752, so the subject was clearly a lively topic in the family circle in that decade.

94. For the circulation of the manuscript see *Dictionary of National Biography*, Vol. XV (London 1921–2), 1236–8.

95. Toynbee and Whibley, 771.

96. Cole's transcript is British Library Add. MS. 5845, ff. 111–46.

97. Toynbee and Whibley, 659.

98. J. C. Murphy, *Plans, Elevations, Sections and Views of the Church of Batalha* (London 1795), for the importance of which see Frankl, 480; Germann, 32–3; and items 168–9 of Weinreb Catalogue 14, *The Gothic of Gothick*, ed. P. Breman (London 1966). Thomas Pitt, as Baron Camelford of Boconnoc, is listed as a subscriber to the book.

99. British Library Add. MS. 5845, f. 115.

100. Pitt's attribution is on f. 122. It is touching that Horace Walpole's final manuscript note should be one of gentle scepticism about this hopeful attribution. See *Horace Walpole's Miscellany 1786–1795*, ed. L. E. Troide (New Haven 1978), 155.

101. British Library, Add. MS. 5845, f. 142.

102. British Library, Add. MS. 5845, f. 117.

103. The following is a list of the drawings: f. 115 verso, Plan of the Old Cathedral, Lisbon: f. 116, Half-elevation of the west door of the Old Cathedral, Lisbon: f. 116 verso, Elevation of three bays of the Old

Cathedral, Lisbon: f. 120 Sketches of two Tombs in the South Transept of the Church at Alcobaça: f. 120 verso, Sketch of Pillars around the outside of the Choir of the Church of Alcobaça: f. 130, Plan of the Cathedral at Segovia: f. 131, Sketch of a Door and Windows in the East Front of the Cathedral at Cordova: f. 131 verso and f. 132, Plan of the Cathedral at Cordova, formerly a Mosque, built A.D. 789: f. 134, Section of the Arches in the Cathedral at Cordova: f. 135 verso, Sketches of Arches over the Ambulatory of the Cathedral at Toledo: f. 136, Plan of the Cathedral at Toledo: f. 137, Sketches of Moorish Arches in Toledo: f. 138 verso, Sketches of Moorish Arches in Carmona.

104. See M. McCarthy, "The Rebuilding of Stowe House, 1770–1777", *The Huntington Library Quarterly*, Vol. XXXVI, No. 3 (May 1973), 267–98, and M. McCarthy, "Soane's SAXON Room at Stowe", *Journal of the Society of Architectural Historians*, Vol. XLIV, No. 2 (May 1985), 129–46.

105. British Library Add. MS. 6771, P.S. 3/9168. This document, among the papers of James Essex, was kindly brought to my attention by John Harris. It is reprinted here by permission of the Trustees of the British Library, as *Appendix*.

106. For Müntz see Colvin, *Biog. Dict.*, 566–7, M. McCarthy, "Johann Heinrich Müntz: The Roman Drawings, 1749–1776", *The Burlington Magazine*, Vol. CXIX, No. 890 (May 1977), 335–40, and T. S. Badenoch, "Wilhelmshöhe: a unique record of a changing landscape by J. H. Müntz", *Journal of Garden History*, Vol. VI, No. 1 (Spring 1986), 50–61.

107. Above, p. 10.

108. These drawings are in the Lewis Walpole Library (Yale University), Farmington, Conn., and are reproduced by kind permission of the Trustees.

109. The first print, labelled "Fig. I" is 6 × 4 inches and the second, labelled "Fig. II" is 6¾ × 4½ inches. The drawing, labelled "Fig. 3", is in ink and wash, 3 × 7 inches.

110. For Müntz's quarrel with Walpole see *H. W. C.*, Vol. XVIII (1948), 34, E. Edwards, 15–16 and below 105–6.

111. See W. S. Lewis, "The Genesis of Strawberry Hill", *Metropolitan Museum Studies*, No. 5 (1934–6), 78 and fig. 23. The second drawing is recorded in J. Harris, *A Catalogue of British Drawings for Architecture, Decoration, Sculpture and Landscape Gardening, 1550–1900, in American Collections* (Upper Saddle River, N.J., 1971), 147, and is reproduced here, Plate V. This work will hereafter be cited as Harris, *A Catalogue*.

112. Musées Royaux de Peinture et de Sculpture, *Inventaire des dessins et aquarelles donnés à l'état belge par Madame la Doarrière de Grez* (Brussels 1913), no. 2671, mistakenly dated 1789. It is reproduced here, Pl. 16.

113. Harris, *A Catalogue*, 143 and Pl. 105. Reproduced here, Pl. 17, with the Plan, Pl. 148.

114. Hampshire CRO 31M57/639/157. The drawing is in ink and wash, 7 × 10 inches, and is reproduced here, Pl. 18.

115. Walpole records the printed proposal under the title *Principles of Gothic Architecture*, and states that Müntz went to Holland in 1763 (MS *Book of Materials*, Vol. 1, 7, in the Lewis Walpole Library). Müntz had been involved in the work of the Strawberry Hill Press since 1757, and Walpole had begun the printing of Müntz's book *Encaustic* (London 1760), so it is likely that the treatise on gothic architecture would have been printed at Strawberry Hill had they remained friends.

116. J. Frew (1980), stresses correctly the limitations of the research into the gothic style of antiquarians prior to 1770, and cogently relates these limitations to the sparsity of graphic studies of the gothic monuments. It may be conjectured that Müntz's graphic studies account for the wider range of style seen in his designs.

117. Two of Charles Lyttelton's manuscripts are preserved in the Library of the Society of Antiquaries of London: "The Genealogical and Historical Account of the Lytteltons of Frankley and Hagley" and "The Parochial Antiquities or Topographical Survey of Hagley". See T. H. Cocke, "The Rediscovery of the Romanesque", in the catalogue of the exhibition *English Romanesque Art* (Hayward Gallery, London, 1984), 360–6.

118. The letters are among the Miller Papers in the Warwick County Record Office, 125B/875–93. Only one of Miller's answers has been traced, and it is quoted below, p. 25. Thomas Lennard Barrett (later Lord Dacre) mentions Miller's having prepared plans for alterations to Charles Lyttelton's house in October 1747 (British Library, Stowe MS 753, f. 77), but their extent and style, and even the location of the house, are not detailed.

119. On 6 April, 1763, Walpole referred to him as "The Bishop of Carlisle, whom I have appointed Visitor of Strawberry", but political differences separated Walpole from all the Lytteltons (including their nephew Thomas Pitt) the following year, and in 1766 he referred to Charles Lyttelton as "Goody Carlisle". *H. W. C.*, Vol. X (1946), 57 and 202.

120. British Library, Stowe MS 753, f. 239.

121. British Library, Stowe MS 753, ff. 14–15, 20–1.

122. British Library, Stowe MS 753, f. 41. The alteration referred to, the moving of the choir from the crossing of the church to the east end, was not in fact effected until 1770–1. See T. Cocke, "The Architectural History of Ely Cathedral from 1540–1840", *Medieval Art and Architecture at Ely Cathedral* (British Archaeological Association, 1979), 71–7.

123. British Library, Add. MS 5834, f. 124.

124. *H. W. C.*, Vol. 1 (1937), 204.

125. *The History and Antiquities of the Conventual and Cathedral Church of Ely* (Cambridge, 1771), for the importance of which see Frankl, 411, and Weinreb Catalogue 31, *Church Architecture and Architects in Britain*, ed. H. Pagan, P. Wrightson and D. Chafee (London 1976), item 30.

126. *H. W. C.*, Vol. 1, 208.

127. N. Pevsner (1972), Ch. 1. A more recent summary is D. Watkin, *The Rise of Architectural History* (London 1980), 53–5.

128. *H. W. C.*, Vol. 1, 190.

129. Frankl, 491–539, demonstrates how slowly the membrological approach to analysis of gothic changed into the structural approach. J. Summerson, *Heavenly Mansions* (New York 1963), 12–14, argues the inadequacy of the structural interpretation.

130. For Miller see Colvin, *Biog. Dict.*, 548–51.

131. British Library, Stowe MS 752, f. 44.

132. British Library, Stowe MS 752, f. 167 verso.

133. British Library, Stowe MS 752, f. 172.

134. Warwick CRO 1382/1.

135. L. Dickins and M. Stanton, 30.

136. G. Lyttelton, 240. The tour was made in 1752.

137. British Library, Stowe MS 754, f. 225.

138. British Library, Stowe MS 754, f. 145.

139. "Journals of Visits to Country Seats", ed. P. Toynbee, *The Walpole Society*, Vol. XVI (1928), 36–7.

140. *Talboy's Collection of the Oxford English Prize Essays*, Vol. 1 (Oxford 1836), 35–38.

141. Department of Manuscripts, Henry E. Huntington Library, San Marino, California: Larpent Collection, LA 586 and LA 199; quoted by kind permission of the Trustees. It is printed as Appendix I of L. H. D.

Jestin, "Richard Bentley the Younger (1708–82): a Critical Biography", (Yale University Ph.D. thesis, 1985).

142. LA 199, f. 73. The references are to R. Wood, *The Ruins of Palmyra* (London 1753) and *The Ruins of Balbec* (London 1757), and to W. Chambers, *A Treatise of Civil Architecture* (London 1759).

CHAPTER II

1. M. Batey, "Shotover's Continuity with the Past", *Country Life* (29 December, 1977), 1978–9.
2. Colvin, *Biog. Dict.*, 833–5.
3. See H. M. Colvin, "Gothic Survival and Gothic Revival", *Architectural Review*, Vol. CIII (1948), 91–8; and, "The Origins of the Gothic Revival", *Accademia Dei Lincei, Problemi Attuali di Scienza e di Cultura*, Quaderno No. 241 (Rome 1978), 3–18.
4. Batey, 1978.
5. C. Hussey, *English Gardens and Landscapes* (London 1967), 78–83. Hussey emphasises the conservative or Tory character of the improvements effected by Lord Bathurst at Cirencester.
6. J. Lees-Milne, *Earls of Creation* (London 1962), 45.
7. J. Lees-Milne (1962), 54.
8. Hussey (1967), 89–113.
9. G. Clarke, "Grecian Taste and Gothic Virtue", *Apollo*, Vol. XCVII, No. 136 (June 1973), 566–71.
10. The most detailed treatment of the ideological implications of the gothic style in England is S. Kliger. *The Goths in England* (Harvard 1952).
11. G. Clarke (1973), 570–1.
12. K. Woodbridge, *Landscape and Antiquity* (Oxford 1970), 53–8.
13. Woodbridge (1970), 54.
14. Another set of buildings with historical associations constructed in these years was that at Kingsgate on the Isle of Thanet, designed for Lord Holland by John Gwynn, later Baron Newborough, who was not related to the architectural critic of the same name. For a description see T. Pennant, *London to the Isle of Wight* (London 1801), Vol. I, 109–10, and for their historical and ideological associations see Lord Ilchester, *Henry Fox, First Lord Holland* (London 1920), Vol. II, 280–2, and H. Honour, "An Epic of Ruin-Building", *Country Life*, 10 December, 1953, 1968–9.
15. Triangular towers remain a favourite form of building for commemorative purposes throughout the nineteenth century. Attention might be drawn here to Racton Tower at Stansted Park, Sussex, built for Lord Halifax to a design of Henry Keene in a rather retardataire style for its date. This was famous in its time for having cost, it was reported, ten thousand pounds. It is attributed to Theodosius Keene by Barbara Jones, (*Follies and Grottoes*, London 1953, 204) and more recently, by Clive Aslet (*Country Life*, 18 February, 1982, 411).
16. Batey, 1979.
17. K. Woodbridge, "William Kent's Gardening: The Rousham Letters", *Apollo*, Vol. C, No. 152 (October 1974), 282–91.
18. Hussey, (1967), 147–53.
19. "There is a beautiful cave called Fingal's", Walpole wrote to Cole, "which proves that Nature loves Gothic architecture". *H.W.C.* ed. W. S. Lewis, Vol. I, 329. For a less succinct account see Frankl, 417–88.
20. An engraving of the facade was published in *The British Inchanter and King Arthur, The British Worthy* (London 1735). The sectional elevation was published in J. Vardy, *Some Designs of Mr. Inigo Jones and Mr. William Kent* (London 1744).
21. J. Colton, "Merlin's Cave and Queen Caroline: Garden Art as Propaganda", *Eighteenth-Century Studies*, Vol. X, No. 1 (Fall 1976), 1–20.
22. J. Harris, "The Dundas Empire" *Apollo*, Vol. LXXXVI, No. 67 (September 1976), 234–9.
23. B. Jones, 366.
24. P. Leach, "In the Gothick Vein", *Country Life*, (26 September, 1974), 834–7.
25. Colvin, *Biog. Dict.*, 702–3 and M. McCarthy, "Sir Thomas Robinson: An Original English Palladian" *Architectura*, Bd. 10, No. 1, (1980), 39–57.
26. Colvin, *Biog. Dict.*, 332–4.
27. P. Leach, "In the Gothick Vein", *Country Life* (26 September, 1974), 834.
28. Leach (26 September, 1974), 835. For the Pugin phrase see Clark, 162–3.
29. Jones, 319.
30. Jones, 372–4.
31. P. Leach, "A Pioneer of Rococo Decoration", *Country Life* (19 September, 1974), 766–9.
32. See note 25 above.
33. J. Macaulay, 25–6 and 137–9.
34. Illustrated in T. Davis, 39.
35. Colvin, *Biog. Dict.*, 866–7.
36. The drawings are British Library, King's Maps, Vol. 30, 19u and 19w. See also H. M. Colvin (1964), 209–17.
37. Jones, 87–8.
38. Colvin, *Biog. Dict.*, 879. The attribution to Gibbs is by T. Friedman, "Romanticism and Neo-classicism for Parlington", *Leeds Art Calendar*, No. 66 (1970), 16–24.
39. The accounts are contained in the British Library, Strafford Papers, Add. MS. 22241. The builder of Stainborough Tower was Joseph Bower. He was paid £5. 3s. 1d. for work on the Lady Ann Tower on 14 September, 1727, and the following day undertook to build three towers, "which is Lady Luce Tower, and Lady Harriet Tower and Lord Wintworth Tower" for £4. 16s. 0d. each, which seems to indicate that these were at first only temporary structures. On 27 April, 1729 he undertook to build the walls between the towers at two shillings a rood. On 25 September, 1731, there is an entry, "Bower's Bill for the Castle", £57. 19s. 11d. A tower fell down in 1755, and John Platt of Rotherham submitted a sketch (f. 133) and estimate for the rebuilding amounting to ninety-eight pounds. He grudgingly accepted Lord Strafford's offer of eighty guineas however.
40. "Lord Strafford has erected the little Gothic building which I got Mr. Bentley to draw; I took the idea from Chichester Cross". *H.W.C.* Vol. IX, 295. The date 1756 is inscribed by Walpole on the drawing. The letter quoted is 1 September, 1760.
41. *H.W.C.*, Vol. XXV (1973), 102.
42. For Whately see M. Hadfield, R. Harling, L. Highton, *British Gardeners: A Biographical Dictionary* (London 1980), 302.
43. H. Walpole (1969), Vol. III, 89–90.
44. H. Walpole (1969), Vol. III, 81–2.
45. Quoted from Lewis, "Genesis", 65.
46. The inscription tells us that it was not built.
47. I. Taylor, "Bentley Bids the Pencil", P. Fritz and R. Morton, eds., *Women in the 18th Century and Other Essays* (Toronto 1976), 201–15. See also L. H. D. Jestin (1985).
48. For Wright's career see T. Wright (1979) and M. McCarthy, "Ireland Ancient and Modern: The Sketches in Architecture of Thomas Wright of Durham", *The Connoisseur*, Vol. 206. No. 828 (February 1981), 158–61; M. McCarthy, "Thomas Wright's

'Designs for Temples' and Related Drawings for Garden Structures'', *Journal of Garden History*, Vol. I, No. 1 (1981), 55–65; M. McCarthy, ''Thomas Wright's Designs for Gothic Garden Buildings'', *Journal of Garden History*, Vol. I, No. 3 (1981), 239–52. This section of the chapter is an amended version of the last article, and is dependent upon the drawings in the Wright Sketchbook in the Avery Architectural Library. Eileen Harris has recently identified another garden by Thomas Wright. See ''Villa for a Mortal Miss'', *Country Life*, 5 August, 1982, 392–4.

49. G. Mason, *Essay on Design in Gardening*, 2nd ed. (London 1795), 124–6, a reference for which I thank John Dixon Hunt.

50. E. Harris, ''Thomas Wright of Durham'' *Country Life* (26 August, 1971), 494.

51. S. Barton, *Monumental Follies* (Galashiels 1972), 74.

52. Barton, 138–9.

53. E. Harris (1971), 494: ''There was something flighty and eccentric in his notions, and a wildness of fancy followed even his ordinary projects''.

54. T. Wright (1979), cat. 14.

55. T. Wright (1979), 22.

56. Barton, 81.

57. T. Wright (1979), cat. 7.

58. T. Wright (1979), cat. 27.

59. A. Rowan (1972), fig. 12b.

60. E. Malins and The Knight of Glin, 118–22.

61. E. Malins and The Knight of Glin, 119, fig. 80.

62. Dickins and Stanton, 275.

63. Quoted from J. D. Hunt and P. Willis, 299–300.

64. Hunt and Willis, 323–4.

65. D. Stroud, *Capability Brown* (London 1975), 76.

66. Stroud, 77.

67. Stroud, figs 30b and 50b.

68. Stroud, figs 29b and 32a. The Bath House at Melton Constable, Norfolk, illustrated in Jones, 362, is very similar, and since Brown provided drawings for the garden buildings there in 1764 it should probably be added to the list of his works.

69. Stroud, 137 and fig. 30.

70. Stroud, fig. 16c. The pinnacles may have been added at a later date.

71. Stroud, 57–8. The accounts for the building of the Radway Tower were privately printed by Geoffrey Beard in 1951.

72. J. Hodgetts, (ed.), 227.

73. N. Pevsner and A. Wedgwood, *Warwickshire* (London 1966), 380.

74. Kidderminster Public Library Manuscripts, ref. 000287, quoted by kind permission of the Chief Librarian.

75. For the local history see G. Miller, *Rambles Round the Edge Hills* (Kineton 1967).

76. M. Williams, ed., *Letters of William Shenstone* (London 1939), 400.

77. *H.W.C.*, Vol. XXXV, 148–9.

78. Stroud, 140, perpetuates this misattribution and her lead has been followed in D. Watkin, *Athenian Stuart* (London 1982), 30. The letters are addressed to James Essex. British Library Add. MS 6771, f. 99 verso is from Wimpole, 6 April, 1768 and reads as follows: ''I was some time ago acquainted from my Lord that you had promised his Lordship that the Tower should be begun upon again the beginning of this month, and he now expects the workmen are about it, and is desirous to know what progress is made. Pay let no time be lost in carrying this business with all good speed, and the mean while pray favour me with a line by the bearer to let me know what answer I am to return to my Lord, and you will oblige, Sir, Your very humble Servant, Richd. Bartons.

''The carpenter tells me his work has been so far ready some time ago as to be of no hindrance to the masons going on.''

British Library Add. MS 6771 f. 178 verso is a note to Essex from Bartons at Wimpole dated Wed.Ap.22, informing him that Brown was expected the following day. No year is indicated, and there is no necessary connection, apart from the identity of the writer, between the two sheets. As for the attribution to Miller, the correspondence on this subject printed in Dickins and Stanton, 271–2, can be supplemented by one of the few extant letters of Sanderson Miller, hitherto unnoticed, British Library, Hardwicke Papers, Add. MS. 35679, f. 55. This is addressed from Radway to George Lyttelton on Feb.20, 1750. It confirms that Miller made plans for a castle for Wimpole, but it also confirms that Lord Hardwicke delayed about executing them. A print of the castle at Wimpole, which was hanging in Radway Grange, was sent to Sanderson Miller as a present as late as 1777, so this has no bearing on the issue. Warwick CR125B/72.

79. Warwick CR125B/150, dated December 13, 1750. Another instance of a stable-block dressed in style to harmonise with related buildings is that by Richard Bentley at Chalfont—dubbed Huohnynym Castle by Walpole—for the house John Chute designed in 1755. See G. C. Edmonds, *A History of Chalfont St Peter and Gerrard's Cross* (Gerrard's Cross 1968), 52. No drawings for this project are known.

80. J. Burnett-Brown, *Lacock Abbey, Wiltshire* (London 1969), 17.

81. T. Mowl, 134–43.

82. Colvin, *Biog. Dict.*, 481–4.

83. Warwick CR125B/61 and *H.W.C.*, Vol. XXV, 175–6.

84. M. McCarthy, ''The Building of Hagley Hall, Worcestershire''.

85. Williams, (ed.) (1939), 197. The seat, adorned with two pinnacles cost considerably more in execution and put Shenstone so out of humour with the ''cheap'' style that he exclaimed, ''The Devil take all Gothicism'' (240). For Shenstone's work at The Leasowes see J. Reily (1979), 202–9.

86. Hodgetts, (ed.), 174.

87. A list is given in A. C. Wood and W. Hawkes, ''Sanderson Miller of Radway and His work at Wroxton'', *Cake and Cockhorse* (Banbury Historical Society), Vol. IX, No. 6 (1969), 108–10, with indications as to the varying levels of probability of attribution.

88. For the vogue of the *fermes ornées* and the literary fame of Painshill and The Leasowes see Hunt and Willis, passim. See also N. and B. Kitz, *Pains Hill Park: Hamilton and his Picturesque Landscape*, London 1984.

89. Jones, 398–9.

90. Colvin, *Biog. Dict.*, 548–51.

91. *H.W.C.*, Vol. I, 178. A decline in the demand for gothic designs for furniture has also been noticed at this date. See A. Coleridge, *Chippendale Furniture* (New York 1968), 87–9.

92. M. McCarthy, ''Amateur Architects and their Gardens'', N. Pevsner, ed., *The Picturesque Garden* (Washington 1974), 31–55.

93. J. Harris, *Sir William Chambers* (London 1970), 38.

94. W. Chambers, *Plans, Elevations, Sections and Perspective Views of the Gardens and Buildings at Kew in Surrey* (London 1763).

95. F. Kielmansegge, *Diary of a Journey to England, 1761–1762* (London 1902), 77.

96. M. McCarthy, ''Documents on the Greek Revival in

Architecture'', *Burlington Magazine* (November 1972), 760–9.

97. Watkin, 27–8.

98. Hussey, (1967), 132–46.

99. Stroud, 139.

100. Williams (ed.), 280–4. Of similar instances one may cite Walpole's cousin General Conway, who built a bridge at Park Place out of the fabric of Reading Abbey with the assistance of Gainsborough's clerical brother, Humphrey, (P. Noble, *Park Place*, London 1905, 24–5), and in the west William Reeve despoiled St Werburgh's Abbey and other medieval buildings for his ''Black Castle'' in Bristol, (J. Latimer, *Annals of Bristol in the Eighteenth Century*, Bristol 1893, 285, 329, 377, 391). The most scandalous thoughtlessness was shown by Dicky Bateman, who had the Norman doorway of Old Shobdon Church erected in the park as an eyecatcher, with the inevitable result that its beautiful Romanesque carvings were destroyed by exposure and vandalism. Fortunately casts were made of these for the Exhibition of 1862, and are in the Victoria and Albert Museum.

101. N. Boulting, ''The Law's Delays: Conservationist Legislation in the British Isles'', J. Fawcett (ed.), *The Future of the Past* (London 1976), 14.

102. *H.W.C.*, Vol. XXXV, 520.

103. Harcourt procured this in 1786. Stroud, 191–2.

104. K. Woodbridge, *The Stourhead Landscape* (London 1982), 58–60.

105. *H.W.C.*, Vol. I, 225–35, 236, 244, 338. The drawing is reproduced in D. R. Stewart, ''James Essex'', *Architectural Review* (November 1950), 317–21, fig. 13.

106. P. Toynbee (ed.), *Strawberry Hill Accounts* (Oxford 1927), 153.

107. Toynbee (ed.), 14.

108. Toynbee (ed.), 15, 18.

109. Toynbee (ed.), 152.

110. This drawing was previously attributed to John Chute, (Lewis (1934–6), 82), but is attributed to Thomas Gayfere the Elder by Harris, (*Catalogue*, 105). Cottingham writes in his unpaginated *Preface*: ''The original of this beautiful composition forms the entrance to a chapel in Salisbury Cathedral, from which the working drawings, for the present erection, were made by the late Mr. Thomas Gayfere; for the use of which Mr. Cottingham is indebted to the liberality of his son Mr. Gayfere, the present Abbey mason''. The drawing in the Lewis Walpole Library, though a half-elevation, resembles so closely the frontispiece in markings and style that its authorship cannot be doubted. In the same volume Cottingham printed details of the ornament and cornice of the Chapel-in-the-Woods, but the drawings for these are attributable to Cottingham himself. Walpole would have been pleased that the Gayfered and Cottinghams were valued by their contemporaries particularly for their care in the restoration of church architecture. see *The Gentleman's Magazine* (March 1828), 275–6, and J. S. Hawkins, *History of the Origin and Establishment of Gothic Architecture* (London 1813), 225–6.

111. Hants CRO 31 M57/639, 113–17 and 119. Other drawings for the building are in the Lewis Walpole Library, Farmington, Connecticut.

112. Harris, *Catalogue*, 69. This drawing is inscribed by Walpole ''Gate for the Flower Garden/designed by Mr. Chute'', but the only gate erected in these years was that designed by Essex, which is quite different in scale as well as in style. Perhaps there was a lapse of memory on the part of Walpole, since the drawing is not in the *Chute Album*, but is pasted into Walpole's grangerised copy of the edition of *Description of*

Strawberry Hill of 1784. The inscription may therefore date from the time of the insertion of the drawing into the book, that is to say, after 1784.

113. *H.W.C.*, Vol. XXXV, 406–7.

114. *H.W.C.*, Vol. XXXV, 407.

115. On p. 141. Toynbee (ed.) (1928), 146.

116. *H.W.C.*, Vol. XXXV, 487.

117. Eastlake, 49.

CHAPTER III

1. *H.W.C.*, Vol. XX (1960), 111.

2. *H.W.C.*, Vol. XX, 119.

3. *H.W.C.*, Vol. XX, 127. Sir John Summerson has emphasised the importance of this early committment to asymmetry on Walpole's part (*Architecture in Britain, 1530–1830*, Harmondsworth, 5th ed., 1969, 241), but it has been questioned for no good reason by James Macaulay, (58–9) and more recently Alistair Rowan has neglected its importance to boost that of Richard Payne Knight at Downton in ''Lo Stile Castello'', *Accademia Dei Lincei, Problemi Attuali di Scienza et di Cultura*, Quaderno, no. 241 (Rome, 1978), 29.

4. *H.W.C.*, Vol. XXXVII (1974), 270.

5. H. Walpole (1969), 83–4.

6. *H.W.C.*, Vol. XX, 361.

7. *H.W.C.*, Vol. XV, 361. When Walpole leased Strawberry Hill in May 1747, it was a small three-bay house standing in five acres beside the Thames. When he bought it the following year, he added a small wing of two storeys which, like the original house, has been concealed by his later additions. William Robinson, an official of the government Board of Works, was the architect of this early addition, which was not gothic in style.

8. *H.W.C.*, Vol. XXXV, 184.

9. *H.W.C.*, Vol. XXIV (1967), 207. The papers of John Chute are in the Hampshire County Record Office.

10. For comparable designs in Batty Langley, see Plates XVII and LXI. It is probable also that Walpole and Chute, through information from their executive architect William Robinson, an officer of the Board of Works, were familiar with these features from the recent designs made for Sir William Stanhope's Eythrope House, discussed in the previous chapter.

11. I am grateful to the late Mrs Ruth Day of Farmington for having brought this volume to my attention, and for many other kindnesses.

12. J. W. Lindus Forge, ''Kentissime'', *Architectural Review*, Vol. CVI (1949), 187–8 and J. Harris, ''William Kent's Gothick'', *A Gothick Symposium*, London 1984, unpaginated.

13. *H.W.C.*, Vol. 9, 71.

14. Toynbee and Whibley, 404.

15. C. F. Bell, ''Thomas Gray and the Fine Arts'', *Essays and Studies by Members of the English Association*, Vol. XXX (Oxford 1945), 70–7, is a curiously unsympathetic assessment.

16. *H.W.C.*, Vol. XIII–XIV (1948), 24.

17. I. Tayler, ''Bentley Bids the Pencil'', *Woman in the 18th Century and Other Essays*, ed. R. Fritz and P. Morton (Toronto 1976), 201–15. See note 47 to Chapter 2 above.

18. There is a note by Walpole on Bentley's drawing for the tribune, ''First idea for the Chapel Tribune at Strawberry Hill, but rejected tho' beautiful, because it must have been too large or too small''. The drawing is reproduced in Lewis (1934–6), fig. 24.

19. W. S. Lewis, *A Guide to the Life of Horace Walpole* (New Haven 1973), item 52, provides a reproduction of this

drawing and mistakenly credits Richard Bentley with the design of the east front.

20. These drawings are in the Lewis Walpole Library, Farmington, Connecticut.

21. It is shown as an entrance in the plate reproduced opposite page 64 of Toynbee, *Accounts*, and this was first used as the title-page of *The Life of Edward Lord Herbert of Cherbury*, printed at Strawberry Hill in 1764.

22. Toynbee (1927), 8.

23. Toynbee (1927), 83. The lantern is now in the Lewis Walpole Library.

24. T. S. Perkins, *The Churches of Rouen* (London 1900), illustration p. 44.

25. Lewis (1973), item 53.

26. *H.W.C.*, Vol. XXXV, 150–1.

27. *H.W.C.*, Vol. XXXV, 150–1.

28. *H.W.C.*, Vol. XXXV, 140.

29. *H.W.C.*, Vol. XXXV, 154.

30. *H.W.C.*, Vol. XXXV, 154.

31. This was first brought to my notice by Michael Snodin, and his acute observation has since been confirmed by an examination of the fabric in 1983 which revealed two cantilever beams in the floor of the Holbein Chamber. These formerly supported the bay window. I am grateful to Mrs Catherine Jestin of Farmington for informing me of the progress of the examination, and for much help with my researches in connection with Horace Walpole.

32. S. Calloway, "Horace Walpole and Strawberry Hill", *The Victoria and Albert Album*, No. 1 (1983), 151–2. The date 1762 is confirmed in Toynbee (1927), 9.

33. The inscriptions on the drawing are by Walpole. They read, "Entrance from the road at Strawberry Hill. N.B. there is a rose Window added under the battlements". "The Breadth of the window with ye frames 5: foot". "The shields must project in a ridge down the middle".

34. *H.W.C.*, Vol. XXI (1960), 238.

35. It was designed by James Essex and finished in September 1776. Toynbee (1927), 166.

36. *H.W.C.*, Vol. XXXV, 110–11.

37. Toynbee (1927), 146.

38. Toynbee (1927), 107.

39. For changes made to Strawberry Hill during the nineteenth century see J. M. Crook, "Strawberry Hill Revisited—III", *Country Life*, 21 June, 1973, 1794–7.

40. M. I. Wilson, *The English Country House and its Furnishings* (London 1979), 73, suggests an aesthetic basis for this arrangement.

41. C. Wainwright, "Horace Walpole and his Collection", *Horace Walpole and Strawberry Hill* (Richmond upon Thames, 1980), 14–17.

42. Toynbee (1972), 110–11.

43. M. Snodin, "Horace Walpole, Builder and Designer", *Horace Walpole and Strawberry Hill* (Richmond upon Thames 1980), 9–13. Walpole wrote to Lord Harcourt on 1 July, 1782: "I have little time left to enjoy anything, and who knows what will become of Strawberry, and how soon it may be put up to auction? I am infinitely sensible of all your goodness to me, and much prouder of it than of a collection, were it the Tribune of Florence". *H.W.C.*, Vol. XXXV, 516. The association of collection and tribune was evidently almost automatic for him.

44. Bentley designed the chimney-pieces in the Yellow Bedchamber—called The Beauty Room after copies of the Lely portraits were hung there—the Blue Bedchamber, the refectory or dining-room, and the little parlour.

45. Toynbee (1927), 102–3.

46. It is an elaboration of the unit of design used by Bentley for the "soffito" of the Galfridus Mann monument erected in 1757 and very highly praised by Walpole and Chute. *H.W.C*, Vol. XXI, 250.

47. Toynbee (1927), 76–8. Walpole's sketch for the ceiling is in the Lewis Walpole Library.

48. "For the library, it cannot have the Strawberry imprimatur: the double arches and double pinnacles are most ungraceful; and the doors below the bookcases in Mr. Chute's design had a conventual look, which yours totally wants. For this time we shall put your genius in commission, and, like some other regents, execute our own plan without minding our sovereign". *H.W.C.*, Vol. XXXV, 157–8.

49. "We have determined upon the plan for the library, which we find will fall in exactly with the proportions of the room, with no variations from the little doorcase at St. Paul's, but widening the larger arches". *H.W.C.*, Vol. XXXV, 164.

50. *H.W.C.*, Vol. XXXV, 184.

51. Toynbee (1927), 129–30.

52. After Müntz had left Strawberry Hill, Walpole acquired in 1762 the more detailed of the two drawings of this door, which is Plate V.

53. A second drawing, probably for the chimney-piece of the gallery, is reproduced in *H.W.C.* Vol. XXII, (1960), 338.

54. Toynbee (1927), 118. Further discussion of the ceiling of the gallery will be found below.

55. Toynbee (1927), 108.

56. Toynbee (1927), 115.

57. *H.W.C.*, Vol. IX, 384.

58. Toynbee (1927), 114.

59. Toynbee (1927), 122.

60. W. Hefford, "Thomas Moore of Moorefields", *Burlington Magazine*, Vol. CXIX (December 1977), 840–8.

61. Toynbee (1927), 110.

62. See p. 69 above, Pl. 92.

63. McCarthy, "The Building of Hagley Hall, Worcestershire".

64. N. Pevsner, "Rococo Gothic: Walpole, Bentley and Strawberry Hill", *Architectural Review*, Vol. XCVIII (December 1945), 151–3. The term seems to have originated in the title of the third chapter of Clark, "Ruins and Rococo: Strawberry Hill". J. Isaacs, "The Gothic Taste", *Journal of the Royal Institute of British Architects*, Vol. LIX (1952) proposed the refinement of "Baroque Gothic" to be used of Kent and Miller and "Rococo Gothic" to be used of Walpole. That distinction was not adopted however, and "Rococo Gothic" alone reappeared in J. M. Crook's introductory essay to the edition of Eastlake published in Leicester in 1970. Terence Davis titled his second chapter, perhaps wittily, "Rococo at Random".

65. Bentley himself seems to be responsible for having started this error. Sir Egerton Brydges, *Restituta*, Vol. IV (London 1816), 384–6, quotes Bentley as having claimed in conversation on 22 December, 1772 that "He designed the Gothic architecture in his [Walpole's] house, both inside and outside, and the paintings of the ceilings".

66. M. Girouard, "English Art and the Rococo", *Country Life* (13 and 27 January, 3 February, 1966), 59–61, 188–90, 224–7.

67. Hants CR0 31M57 639–131.

68. *H.W.C.*, Vol. XXXV, 37.

69. Colvin, *Biog. Dict.*, 496.

70. The inventory, Hants CR0 31M57/649, is dated 1842. An inventory of books dated 1682, (Hants CR0 31M57/642), allows us to distinguish the architectural

books owned by John Chute from those that had been in The Vyne earlier, and there can be little doubt that he was responsible for the acquisition of architectural books dated from 1754, the year he succeeded to The Vyne.

71. Girouard (1966), 190.
72. H. Walpole (1969), 254–7.
73. Note 3 above.
74. *H.W.C.*, Vol. II (1937), 24.

CHAPTER IV

1. *H.W.C.*, Vol. XXXV, 233.
2. Walpole, in his "Account of Richard Bentley", relates: "He gave Mr. Churchill several designs for his house at Chalfont, but they have not been followed exactly". *H.W.C.*, Vol. XXXV, 644. See G. C. Edmonds, 51–2.
3. *H.W.C.*, Vol. IX, 284. "The house and grounds are still in the same condition; in short, they finish nothing but children; even Mr. Bentley's gothic stable (which I call Huohnynm-Castle) is not rough-cast yet".
4. M. Fraser, *Gerrards Cross and the Chalfonts* (London 1967). For Salvin's work see N. Pevsner, *Buckinghamshire* (London 1960), 83.
5. Pevsner, *Berkshire* (London 1966), 128–9.
6. C. Hussey, "Donnington Grove, Berkshire", *Country Life* (28, 25 September; 2 October, 1958), 588–91, 654–7, 714–17. There is also a gothic fishing-house, attributed to John Chute, at Donnington. M. Drury, "The Architecture of Fishing", *Country Life* (27 July, 1972), 202–5.
7. An inscription on one of the sketches in the Chute Album provides the date 1763. The elevations by John Hobcraft are framed and exhibited in the Ante-Room at The Vyne, and are wrongly ascribed to John Chute in the National Trust Guidebook, *The Vyne, Hampshire* (London 1978), 17.
8. Colvin, *Biog. Dict.*, 422–3.
9. Hussey (1958), 655.
10. Hussey (1958), 591.
11. *H.W.C.*, Vol. XXXV, 642.
12. The following section is based in part on M. McCarthy, "John Chute's Drawings for The Vyne", *National Trust Year-Book 1976–7*, 70–80. See also C. W. Chute, *A History of The Vyne* (Winchester 1888). The drawings of John Chute in the Hampshire County Record Office have been catalogued by the author, and numbers given here refer to that catalogue. Those for gothicising the south front are principally Hants CR0 31M57/639, 19–39. Other drawings in the Chute Album in the Lewis Walpole Library are listed in Harris, *Catalogue*, 71–2. Others are still at The Vyne, either framed for display or in the books in which they were inscribed by John Chute. I am grateful to the staff of the Hampshire County Record Office and the custodians of The Vyne for their help with the cataloguing, and I am also deeply indebted to Dr Walter Leedy, who took time from his own work to photograph the drawings.
13. *H.W.C.*, Vol. XXXV, 58.
14. Anthony Chute's work at The Vyne is not recorded in detail, but he certainly effected renovations to the ground-floor gallery in 1753 (Hants CR0 31M57/632).
15. *H.W.C.*, Vol. XXXV, 84, n. 6; 232, and 639–40.
16. *H.W.C.*, Vol. XXXV, 185.
17. This was a copy of *The Last Supper* by Santi di Tito, procured through Horace Mann. *H.W.C.*, Vol. XX, 485.
18. *H.W.C.*, Vol. IX, 216.
19. Hants CR0 31M57/639, 44–6, 50, 56–99, 144. Several pages of the sketchbook which is Hants CR0 31M57/652 are also devoted to the staircase, and there are some drawings related to it in the Chute Album in the Lewis Walpole Library.
20. Hants CR0 31M57/639, 49–50.
21. Hants CR0 31M57/639, 44, 61, 68, 71–5, 144.
22. Edward Marshall's accounts for the building of the portico and for work in the chapel of The Vyne are Hants CR0 31M57/627–9.
23. An account of his management of The Vyne was written W. L. W. Chute in August, 1872, and is now Hants CR0 31M57/1097. "On the north front little change has been made. The centre has been battlemented to correspond to the battlements over the Chapel, and I have put in two blind stone windows to relieve the plainness of the previously dead wall of the Chapel, and added the buttress which forms the flue of the stove in the Chapel Hall".
24. Hants CR0 31M57/1097: "On the west side of the Gallery I brought forward the stone work of the entrance door and thus made a porch to relieve the plainness of the front" . . . "In later years I determined to throw out the present (south) porch".
25. *The Vyne, Hampshire* (London 1978), 20.
26. Hants CR0 31M57/639, 154–6. There is also a drawing for a rococo girandole, Hants CR0 31M57/639, 152.
27. Harris, *Catalogue*, plate 15.
28. Lewis (1934–6), fig. 18.
29. Harris, *Catalogue*, 29.
30. *H.W.C.*, Vol. IX, 120 (Ragley); 138 and 146 (Roel); 151 and 216 (Greatworth); 267 (Hinchinbrooke); 284 (Aston). For Cassiobury, *H.W.C.*, Vol. XXXV, 177. Walpole frequently sought to use his influence and that of his friends to secure official posts for Bentley. See *H.W.C.*, Vol IX, 146, 262, 272, and *H.W.C.*, Vol. XXX, 154.
31. In 1760 Müntz published in London, *Encaustic: or Count Caylus's Method of Painting in the Manner of the Ancients*. His description of his experiments (124–33) provides an interesting insight into life at Strawberry Hill during the preceding years. The book was started on the Strawberry Hill Press, but printing was not continued after he and Walpole had quarrelled. Müntz was praised as "a late very ingenious author" on page 16 of Robert Manwaring, *The Cabinet and Chair Maker's Real Friend and Companion* (London 1765). But apart from this notice, his book on encaustic painting seems to have been forgotten even before Edward Edwards consigned it to oblivion in his *Anecdotes of Painters* (London 1808), 15–16. For Müntz's involvement with the Strawberry Hill Press see *Journal of the Printing Office at Strawberry Hill*, ed. P. Toynbee (London 1923), 3–9. George Montagu acquired two of Müntz's landscapes and wrote to Walpole of Müntz, "I fancy Scot has debauched him to set up landscape painter". Samuel Scott was a Twickenham neighbour, *H.W.C.*, Vol. IX, 261.
32. Walpole was deeply hurt by this quarrel, as appears from his account of it to George Montagu, where the pain of the old quarrel with Thomas Gray recurs: "— a cause much more familiar to me has separated us — nothing but a tolerable quantity of ingratitude on his side, both to me and Mr. Bentley. The story is rather too long for a letter; the substance was, most extreme impertinence to me, concluded by an abusive letter against Mr. Bentley, who sent him from starving on seven pictures for a guinea, to £100 a year, my house, table and utmost countenance. In short, I turned his

head and was forced to turn him out of doors. You shall see the *documents*, as it is the fashion to call proof-papers. (Gray) I suppose will naturally think me to blame. Poets and painters imagine *they* confer the honour when they are protected—and they set down impertinence to the article of their own virtue, when you dare to begin to think that an ode or a picture is not a patent for all manner of insolence''. *H.W.C*, Vol. IX, 259. This passage is preceded by a reference to his action being comparable to that of driving Hannah and Ishmael into the wilderness, which has given rise to the supposition that Müntz's love affair with one of Walpole's servants caused the quarrel. Edward Edwards, (15–16), even stated that Müntz had married this servant before leaving Strawberry Hill. I have found no documentary evidence to support this reading, and Müntz's extensive travels in later years make it unlikely that he was married. Even if he did, it is not likely that Walpole, who was so tolerant of the marital complications of Richard Bentley, would have reacted so strongly to his marriage. In the absence of the documents or proof-papers referred to by Walpole, it is not probable that the true story will be known, and my suggestion that the Bateman commission was at the root of the quarrel seems more to the point. Müntz wrote a very dignified letter to Walpole on 2 November, 1759, but it does not clarify the cause of their disagreement. It is printed in *H.W.C.*, Vol. XL, 169–70.

33. *H.W.C.*, Vol. X, 43.

34. *H.W.C.*, Vol. XXXV, 644. Prior to these alterations the house of Richard Bateman at Old Windsor, known then as The Grove and subsequently as The Priory, was dismissed by George Lyttelton as ''half-gothic, half-attick, half-Chinese and completely fribble''. E. J. Climenson, *Elizabeth Montagu, 1720–61*, (London 1906), 192. By kind permission of the Trustees of the Lewis Walpole Library, I quote in part a letter to Mr Lewis from a woman who lived in the house from 1922 to 1934: ''The eighteenth-century Gothic flavour of the house, during our time there was most marked; it had a brittle, elegant monasticism, rather toylike, grafted on a substantial brick and stone structure, said to have been originally an Elizabethan inn. None of the Chinese features for which it was first noted remained . . . The ''monkish apartments'' which would have given Mrs Delany ''the vapours to inhabit'' were still there in our time, and still cell-like and gloomy, the upper part of the pointed arches of their windows filled with the ''pretty painted glass'' she admired, and there was more of this Flemish glass, blue and yellow, in passage-windows downstairs . . . The octagon-room which was his (Richard Bateman's) refectory was our drawing-room, and I enclose two photographs of it. It is as he created it, except for the blocking of two doors which led into the garden. We uncovered from countless layers of paint and varnish the fine Gothic moulding of the stone mantelpiece, over which hung in Bateman's time Alan Ramsay's portrait of Mary, Lady Hervey, in its Grinling Gibbons frame . . . Having known and loved Horace Walpole for very many years in his Letters it was a special joy to live for some time in a house with which he had been most closely associated . . . I regret that the very characteristic and perfectly preserved ceiling is not shown in these photographs.'' Pevsner records that the date 1762 was found inscribed in the octagon room. N. Pevsner, *Berkshire*, 190.

35. *H.W.C.*, Vol. XXXV, 103: ''I saw my Lord Lyttelton and Miller at Ragley; the latter put me out of all patience. As he has heard me talked of lately, he thought it not below him to consult me on ornaments for my Lord's house—I who know nothing but what I have purloined from Mr. Bentley and you (Chute), and who have not forgot how little they tasted your real taste and charming plan, was rather tart''.

36. Now in the collection of the Musées Royaux de Peinture et de Sculpture in the Musée des Beaux-Arts in Brussels. *Inventaire des dessins et aquarelles donnés à l'état belge par Madame la Doarrière de Grez* (Brussels 1913), no. 2674. The drawing is there misdated 1789, in spite of two signatures and dates that read clearly 1759. On the verso is the following inscription in the hand of Müntz: ''Funeral Monument of Caducanus once Bishop of Hereford. J. H. Müntz Hereford 1759. The same erected at Old Windsor for the Honble. R.:Bateman''.

37. J. Harris, ''Father of the Gardenesque'', *Country Life* (7 June, 1979), 1838–40.

38. For Lord Charlemont's garden see C. O'Connor, ''Gardening at Marino'', *Morrea: Journal of the Irish Garden Plant Society*, Vol. II (Spring 1983), 29–38. I am grateful to Mrs O'Connor for her help and company in field-work at Marino. The foundations of a gothic brick building were uncovered by us, but there is not sufficient of it to judge how closely it corresponds to the drawings by Müntz. However, a Greek relief sculpture was rediscovered as a result, and is recorded in C. O'Connor and B. Cook, ''A Greek Stele in Dublin'', *The Antiquaries Journal*, Vol. LXI, part 1 (1981) 29–34.

39. M. McCarthy, ''Johann Heinrich Müntz: the Roman Drawings''. Further sets of these vase drawings have since come to light. The best biography of Müntz is by Elizabeth Budzinska, *Polski Slownik Biograficzny*, Tome XXII/2 (Warsaw 1977), 324–5. See now also T. S. Badenoch-Watts, ''The Life and Work of Johann Heinrich Müntz'', Ph.D. thesis, University of Toronto, 1986.

40. For Hogarth on the oval and the egg see *The Analysis of Beauty* (London 1753), 23. Müntz's aesthetic position in relation to the writings of his contemporaries and predecessors is currently under investigation by Teresa Badenoch-Watts at the University of Toronto, and I have learned much in discussion with her on the subject. The term *architecture parlante* does not seem to have been invented until the mid-eighteenth century, but Emil Kaufmann has detected its intent in the writings of Germain Boffrand. See *Architecture in the Age of Reason* (New York edition 1968), 130.

41. M. Craig, *The Volunteer Earl* (London 1958), 123–4, and *Historic Manuscripts Commission, 12th report, Appendix Part X*, Vol. I (London 1896), 286. A drawing by T. S. Roberts, reproduced in E. Malins and The Knight of Glin, 139, shows a striking gothic building at the head of the lake at Marino. Its date is uncertain however, and it is too indistinct to allow for visual comparison with the known works of Müntz.

42. H. Walpole (1969), 104 n. 7.

43. Müntz's promise, in the printed *Proposals* of 1760, (Appendix I below), to have his plates printed in Holland if that were necessary, suggests that he was well acquainted with Dutch artists before this date, though there is no evidence of his having been there before he left England in 1763. Dr Terry Friedman has drawn to my attention a splendid elevation and plan for a pavilion with colonnades and a clocktower, by Müntz, with inscriptions in Dutch. Two of Mr Lewis's drawings also have Dutch inscriptions, but no evidence of buildings erected by Müntz after leaving England has come to light, except the villa at Korsun, for which see A. Busiri-Vici, *I Pontatowski e Roma* (Florence 1971), 100.

44. I am grateful to Jacob Simon, formerly Assistant Curator at Kenwood, for having clarified the nature of this building for me and showing me the watercolour by Barrow, which was once titled *Strawberry Hill*. The house is illustrated in E. Miles, *Thomas Hudson 1701–79* (London 1979), item 78. I have never been able to see the drawing, so I give only a tentative opinion as to its authorship.

45. Walpole later made enquiries about Müntz in Madrid, as J. Nichols records in *Literary Illustrations of the Eighteenth Century*, Vol. VII (London 1858), 536. Müntz was not known there however. He returned to England for a brief visit in 1788, for which see *H.W.C.*, Vol. XII, 263. At this date, and until his death in 1798, he was living in Kassel, Germany, and important new information on his activities there is contained in T. S. Badenoch (1986), 50–61.

CHAPTER V

1. M. Williams (ed.), (1939), 322.
2. Smart Lethulieur to Charles Lyttelton, 23 October, 1752: "Mr. Pitt and I had half an hour's chat this evening about Hagley. He sincerely concurs with me in rejoycing that the scheme for a Gothick House is laid aside, it being I find as unintelligible to him as to me, unless executed at a vast useless expense". (British Library, Stowe MSS 752, f. 74 verso). Lord North to Sanderson Miller, "If an Italian House is built at Hagley it is by my Lady". (Warwick CR0 125B/956).
3. McCarthy, "The Building of Hagley Hall, Worcestershire".
4. *H.W.C.*, Vol. XX, 127.
5. For the landscape garden see above, and J. Sambrook, "Parnell's Garden Tours: Hagley and the Leasowes", R. P. Maccubin and P. Martin (eds.) *British and American Gardens in the Eighteenth Century*, Williamsburg 1984, 51–64.
6. M. McCarthy, "The Building of Hagley Hall, Worcestershire", 224. George Lyttelton wrote to Miller encouraging him to visit Holkham Hall: "The only Danger is that it should putt you out of conceit with your Gothick Architecture; but you are a man of too large Ideas to be confined to one Taste". (Warwick CR0 125B/645).
7. This has been quoted above on p. 5. Dickins and Stanton, 315.
8. N. Pevsner and A. Wedgwood (1966), 457.
9. Colvin, *Biog. Dict.*, 419–20.
10. Miller died in 1780 and Arbury was not completed until 1798. See M. McCarthy, "Sir Roger Newdigate; Drawings for Copt Hall, Essex, and Arbury Hall, Warwickshire", *Architectural History*, Vol. XVI (1973), 26–36.
11. Wood and Hawkes, 94, note 34.
12. Dickins and Stanton, 268, "It is hard to forgive the ridiculous little turrets that disfigure the angles of the walls, and the south-eastern front . . . is frankly hideous".
13. C. Hussey, *English Country Houses: Mid-Georgian* (London 1963), 43.
14. Dates are taken from Appendix I of A. C. Wood, "The Diaries of Sir Roger Newdigate 1751–1806" *Transactions of the Birmingham Archaeological Society*, Vol. LXXVIII (1962), 40–53. The agreement for the second bow window "in the same form & with all the carvings and ornaments as that now erected at the end of the library" is dated 8 June, 1760, and specifies that the window was to be erected twelve months later. Sir Roger was to pay £40 and supply materials. It is signed by A. Harris, T. Cheshire and T. Morris. (Warwick CR0 136B/2419).
15. *H.W.C.*, Vol. XLII (1980), 220.
16. Warwick CR0 125B/452.
17. Warwick CR0 1382/1, p. 21.
18. Dickins and Stanton, 543.
19. Hussey (1956). Hiorne and Hitchcox had worked together for Miller at Radway Grange. (Wood and Hawkes, 94, note 34.) The Newdigate accounts in the archives of Glyn Mills & Co., (among the ledgers of Child & Co., 1749–55), record a payment by Sir Roger Newdigate to David Hiorne of £22.19s on 25 September, 1750. Hussey noted the dependence of the library bays upon Strawberry Hill, but was wrong about the painting of the ceiling, for which see A. C. Wood (1962), 53.
20. E. G. D'Oench, *The Conversation Piece: Arthur Devis and his Contemporaries* (New Haven 1980), "Chronology", X–XI, 23 and fig. 16. See also R. C. Lines, "Arbury 'Gothick' and the Newdigates", *The Connoisseur Year Book 1960*, 11–17, and A. C. Wood (1962), Appendix 2.
21. Hussey (1956), suggests that Newdigate's panelling above the arches of the bays, which is a development of the Strawberry Hill model, "sensitively imitates the Late Perpendicular that is so much in evidence at Oxford". For Newdigate's long political association with the university, see L. Namier, 59–77.
22. Walpole wrote to Mann on 14 November, 1775: "So the Pretender is in a dying way: and wants an heir—it is not a race of Phoenixes. Sir Roger Newdigate is at Rome, and formerly would have been proud to be chief mourner at the funeral". *H.W.C.*, Vol. XXIV, 144.
23. A more recent account of the house is G. Nares.
24. In his *Observations on English Architecture*, Dallaway mentions Newdigate's gift of the candelabra by Piranesi to Oxford (p. 154), and he praises the work of Henry Keene for the university (p. 159). But he does not mention the more outstanding gothic revival work of either Newdigate or Keene. For the candelabra see M. McCarthy, "Sir Roger Newdigate and Piranesi".
25. See below, chapter 6.
26. D. Verey, *Gloucestershire: The Cotswolds*, 80.
27. Shakespeare's Birthplace Trust, Stratford-on-Avon, Leigh MSS, Series B, Gloucs. Papers, Box 7, Bundle 4. The work was finished by 7 January, 1754, when Sanderson Miller witnessed the payment of £300 to William Hitchcox by James Leigh.
28. The detailed "Articles of Agreement" are in the Warwick County Record Office, as is Collett's receipt of payment of £947.10s. for this stage of the building.
29. Warwick CR0 125B/963: "Admiral Smith has bought Cordel House and Estate, and as he proposes to lay out three or four hundred pounds upon the buildings, and that as soon as possible, Sir Thomas (Lyttelton) is extreamly desirous that he should have your advice before he sets about it". This is from Molly West to Sanderson Miller, simply dated 8 June, with no indication of the year. Wood and Hawkes give 1750.
30. Mr Hawkes kindly showed me the photographs taken before its demolition. Dickins and Stanton, 275, note 2 remark that the house was subsequently altered and enlarged.
31. Colvin, *Biog. Dict.*, 551, also attributes to Miller tentatively the octagonal lodges to Siston Court, though D. Verey, *Gloucestershire: The Vale and the Forest of Dean* (London 1970), 338, says that they are of the nineteenth century. Sanderson Miller's involvement with building at Siston is evidenced by a plan and elevation of "a poorhouse" for Siston, inscribed on the

verso of Warwick CR0 125B/678, which is dated 1759. It does not seem to have been executed.

32. Ambrose Isted of Ecton Hall, Northamptonshire, is not known to have been a correspondent of Sanderson Miller, but they were contemporaries at Oxford from 1735, and Miller made designs for several of the close friends of Isted. For Ambrose Isted see R. Cumberland, *Memoirs* (London 1806), 121–3 and *Verney Letters of the Eighteenth Century*, ed. Lady Verney, Vol. II (London 1930), 113, 123 and 178. The house is dated 1756. See N. Pevsner, *Northamptonshire* (London 1961), 198–9.

33. N. Pevsner, *Wiltshire* (London 1963), 258; Dickins and Stanton, 298–310; H. A. Tipping, "Lacock Abbey, Wiltshire", *Country Life*, (17 March, 1923), 357–9; see also J. Burnett-Brown.

34. Dickins and Stanton, 301.

35. Dickins and Stanton, 304.

36. Dickins and Stanton, 303.

37. Dickins and Stanton, 317–19.

38. Dickins and Stanton, 310–12.

39. "Journals of Visits to Country Seats", ed. P. Toynbee, *The Walpole Society*, Vol. XVI, 34. The visit of 1754 is recorded in a letter to Richard Bentley, "What he (Dacre) has done is in Gothic, and very true, though not up to the perfection of the committee". (*H.W.C.*, Vol. XXXV, 183–4).

40. *H.W.C.*, Vol. XLI, 360.

41. An account of Belhus shortly before demolition is N. Pevsner, *Essex* (London 1954), 71–2, which describes the gothic decoration as "rather thin". I am grateful to Mrs Nancy Edwards at the Essex County Record Office for constant helpfulness in my researches.

42. Essex CR0 D/DL 428.

43. Warwick CR0 125B/414 and 418.

44. Warwick CR0 125B/422.

45. A letter from Lord Dacre to Sanderson Miller, dated 28 October, 1747, is British Library, Stowe MS 754, ff. 77 and 78. It makes no reference to building work at Belhus that year, though he writes, "I am not a little pleased to find myself back at my old habitation, and to revisit my Gothic rooms and my young plantations."

46. Warwick CR0 125B/431.

47. Warwick CR0 125B/433.

48. Warwick CR0 125B/434, 440 and 441.

49. Warwick CR0 125B/448. For Lovell's work and that of Sanderson Miller at Wroxton Abbey, Oxfordshire, see Wood and Hawkes, 99–106. Lovell's career is clarified in M. McCarthy, "James Lovell and his Sculptures at Stowe".

50. Warwick CR0 125B/452.

51. Warwick CR0 125B/455: "I wish you cou'd put me in a way to get a reasonable stucco man to do the ceiling of Lady Dacre's dressing-room: which is to have the same cornish which Sir. R: Newdigate has in his study or rather I believe in Lady Newdigate's dressing-room".

52. Warwick CR0 125B/456 and 457.

53. Warwick CR0 125B/458 and 461.

54. For Moore see G. Beard, 168, and J. Lane.

55. Warwick CR0 125B/467.

56. *ALS*, Lyttelton MSS, Hagley Hall, quoted by kind permission of Lord Cobham.

57. Essex CR0 D/DL/E 13.

58. Lord Dacre left a manuscript account of the stained glass. See F. S. Eden.

59. Walpole's letter, cited in note 40 above, continues interestingly: "You know I love the spirit of *ancienne noblesse*; and since Cheesemongers can be peers, I would have the mansions of old barons powdered with quarterings, for distinction; and since Mr. Adam

builds for so many of them, I wish he would deviate from his style of filigraine, and load them with the Tuscan Order, which admits very speaking columns".

60. Warwick CR0 764/216.

61. For Keene see Colvin, *Biog. Dic.*, 481–4. There is an autobiography by Couchman available in photostat, (Warwick CR0 Z14/1–7L), but it unfortunately stops at 1766, the year he came to work in Warwickshire.

62. In the Warwickshire County Record Office. Warwick CR0 764/214, 216, 217. For the earlier publication, McCarthy, "Sir Roger Newdigate: Drawings".

63. A drawing from Dart's *Westminster* (Warwick CR0 764/216) demonstrates that Newdigate used printed sources of the Abbey as well as his sketches.

64. Warwick CR0 764/214. There is a third drawing by Miller for this room, in the same folio.

65. Note 56 above.

66. A. C. Wood (1962), 53.

67. The most detailed account of the library at Strawberry Hill is W. S. Lewis, *Horace Walpole's Library*, (Cambridge 1958), which repeats, p. 40, the sources given in Walpole's *Description of Strawberry Hill*, (London 1784), namely p. 107 of Dart's *Westminster* and p. 67 of Dart's *Canterbury*. These are present in ornament for the chimney-piece, but do not account for its principal features, the pointed arch, triangular top and rich pinnacling, which are taken from the tomb of Aymer de Valence and comparable tombs.

68. McCarthy, "Sir Roger Newdigate: Drawings", 30.

69. Correspondence relating to Newdigate and Keene's work at University College, executed between 1766 and 1768, is Warwick CR0 136B/1860, 2322, 2324, 2323, 2325, 1785, 2326, 1730, 1731, 1732, 1733, 2327, 2328 in the chronological order. There is a further letter on the subject from Henry Keene in the Greater London Council Record Office, Acc. 1085, CR 136, Mx. Pec. 7.

70. See note 14 above.

71. A. C. Wood (1962), 52.

72. A. C. Wood (1962), 52.

73. Warwick CR0 136B/1785. The passage refers to the alterations at University College, but may fairly be taken as representative of the working methods of Keene and Newdigate.

74. A. C. Wood (1962), 54.

75. "He new-cast and rebuilt the whole house, on the site of an ancient priory, in the gothic style, in which he professed himself merely an humble imitator". The account was written by R. Churton, whose letter to Francis Newdigate on the subject (Warwick CR0 136B/3548) asks: "Any dates of newbuilding the house? as when he set about it, and do that 'very impudent thing' as he used to call it, of cutting through the solid wall of the front & making those beautiful Gothic arches & Gothic windows?"

76. G. Eliot, *Scenes of Clerical Life*, ed. D. Lodge (London 1980), 141.

77. G. Eliot, 134.

78. G. Beard, 166, states that the saloon was plastered by W. Hanwell with the assistance of G. Higham and R. Hodgson in 1786, but this conflicts with the dates of construction and painting given in A. C. Wood (1962). George Higham was certainly paid £58-1-2½ for plasterer's work done in 1784 and 1785, but not for work in the saloon. The bill is Warwick CR0 136B/2421A. The Arbury accounts merit further study.

79. G. Eliot, 158–9. Judging by the internal evidence, *Mr. Gilfil's Love Story* is set in the early 1770s, which means that George Eliot brings forward the building of the saloon by twenty-five years. It is worth remarking that she was not misled into giving so early a date for

the ceiling of the library as has been common: "The oriel window was overshadowed by the great beech, and this, with the flat heavily-carved ceiling and the dark hue of the old books that lined the walls, made the room look sombre, especially on entering it from the living-room, with its aerial curves and cream-coloured fretwork touched with gold." (p. 137).

80. For Lady Pomfret's antiquarian pursuits see S. Houfe, "Diaries of The Countess of Pomfret", *Country Life* (24 and 31 March, 1977), 728–30 and 800–2.

81. J. Cornforth, "A Countess's London Castle", *Country Life Annual* (1970), 138–9.

82. Houfe, 730.

83. Warwick CRO 136B/2220 and 2980.

84. Warwick CRO 136B/2224.

85. Houfe, 729–30. The attribution to Sanderson Miller occurs on p. 145 of Walpole's "Book of Materials, 1757–", in manuscript in the Lewis Walpole Library. It was published in *Anecdotes of Painting in England*, Vol. IV (New York reprint 1969), 161.

86. Houfe, 229–30: "It is a large plain-stone Building, with three pairs of stairs & many rooms, but nothing like an Apartment, & only two Rooms to lodge Company—there is another building joyn'd by a cover'd passage, in which is a kitchen, capacious enough to dress a Coronation Dinner, & with all conveniences imaginable for the *Cookes*, as also for all the *Servants*."

87. For illustrations of the drawing in the Bodleian Library, and the Buckler drawing, see H. Phillips, *Mid-Georgian London* (London 1964), 70, fig. 79 and 269, fig. 358. The photographs are published in Cornforth.

88. Houfe, 729–30, comments on the friendship of Lady Pomfret with William Kent and the Dormer brothers of Rousham, Oxfordshire.

89. This elevation is now in the collection of the Royal Institute of British Architects. See J. Lever, *Catalogue of Drawings in the Collection of the Royal Institute of British Architects*, Vol. L–N (London 173) 71, fig. 45. The drawing is there associated with a barn for Ambrosden, Oxon., which is not probable. Some sketches quite similar in character and form are to be found on the verso of Warwick CRO 136B/2227, a letter of Lady Pomfret to Sir Roger Newdigate, 23 December, 1757, in which she refers to "my house . . . so far advanced and so near perfection".

90. Illustrated in Houfe, fig. 3.

91. Houfe, 801.

92. J. Summerson, *The Life and Work of John Nash, Architect* (London 1980), 23–4 and Ch. 4.

93. Colvin, *Biog. Dict.*, 482, discusses the early associations of Miller and Keene.

94. G. Nares, 20, has given currency to the idea that the relationship between Sir Roger Newdigate and Henry Keene did not end happily, but this mistake arises from a mis-dating of bills for work executed at Sir Roger's town house in Spring Gardens. The item brought into evidence on this subject is an entry in Sir Roger's account-book for 1779, which reads, "Enlarging the rooms under the direction of H. Keene, Builder, who after receiving £500 to pay workmen paid £180 and became insolvent" (A. C. Wood, 1962, 49). The *H. Keene* is evidently an error, for Henry Keene had died in 1776 and the event was reported to Newdigate by Joseph Eyre. "Your acquaintance Mr. Keene had been dead more than two months, and that his son, a young man of 22 years of age had got into all his business". (Warwick CRO 136B/1667) The letter is not dated precisely, and Eyre is

reporting at second hand.) Accounts for the work in Spring Gardens clarify the matter. There are two receipts of £500, the first dated 17 August, 1772, and the second dated 3 July, 1778, the latter evidently the one referred to in the account book of the following year. Both receipts are signed by Theodosius Keene, son of Henry; they are now to be found inserted inside the cover of Sir Roger's diary for 1785, (not 1786 as A. C. Wood, 1962, 48, reports), but there is no mistaking the dates inscribed on the receipts. The unfortunate bankruptcy of Theodosius Keene, therefore, has no relevance to the relationship of Sir Roger Newdigate with his father, and letters of Theodosius Keene on the grand tour show that Sir Roger extended his friendship to the son, as well as his patronage. See M. McCarthy, "Art Education and The Grand Tour".

95. For the illustrated architectural literature of the early nineteenth century see J. M. Crook, "John Britton and the Genesis of the Gothic Revival", *Concerning Architecture*, ed. J. Summerson (London 1968), 98–119. New material on the subject is available in the Phil.M. thesis of M. Aldrich, "Thomas Rickman and Architectural Illustration of the Gothic Revival", (University of Toronto 1983). For Cottingham and Pugin the Elder see Colvin, *Biog. Dict.*, 234–5 and 677–8.

96. This chimney-piece was designed by Walpole himself from the prints of the tomb of Bishop Dudley, in Dart's *Westminster*. It was built by Thomas Gayfere, who built the Chapel-in-the-Woods at Strawberry Hill, and is accounted for with the payment for that building.

97. The architects of the Gothic Revival do not seem to have been concerned that there was a decided disparity of style in the middle ages between domestic and ecclesiastical architecture, though E. Aitkins, *Designs for Villas* (London 1808), 709 is an exception to this generalisation. Perhaps people were so used to the application, by Palladian and other neo-classical architects, of elements of temple architecture to domestic purposes, that they assumed Gothic Revival architects would follow the same practice in the alternative style. For the connections and continuities that may be discerned between classical architecture and that of the Gothic Revival see the remarks of Beresford Pite following S. H. Goodhart-Rendel, "English Gothic Architecture of the Nineteenth Century", *Journal of the Royal Institute of British Architects*, 3rd series, Vol. XXVI (1924), 340, and S. Lang, "Principles of the Gothic Revival in England", *Journal of the Society of Architectural Historians*, Vol. XXV, No. 4 (December 1966), 240–67.

98. Clark, 95.

99. See above, p. 17.

100. P. Breman (ed.), (1966), item 169. The statement of G. Germann, 33, that Murphy was "a practising architect" seems to have no basis in documentation.

101. Michael McCarthy, "Soane's SAXON Room at Stowe". For Wyatt's work at Fonthill see J. Wilton-Ely, "The Genesis and Evolution of Fonthill Abbey", *Architectural History*, Vol. 23, (1980), 40–9.

102. For the work of this outstanding amateur architect see M. McCarthy, "Tracy of Toddington Manor", *Transactions of the Bristol and Gloucestershire Archaeological Society*, Vol. LXXXIV (1965), 161–74 and also "The Work of Hanbury Tracy, Lord Sudeley, At Hampton Court", *Woolhope Transactions*, Vol. XXXVIII, Part I (1964), 71–5.

103. *H.W.C.*, Vol. XXXXII, 220.

CHAPTER VI

1. *H.W.C.*, Vol. XXXV, 150.
2. "This was the old abbot's lodging, much altered and rebuilt by various bishops; it was replaced by a modern house in 1857–72". *H.W.C.*, Vol. XXXV, 153, n. 59.
3. *H.W.C.*, Vol. XXXV, 153.
4. On the growth of appreciation of Norman architecture, see J. M. Frew (1980), and C. H. Krinsky, "Romanesque Architecture and Some Eighteenth-Century Critics", *Gesta*, Vol. II (1964), 20–1, and T. H. Cocke, "The Rediscovery of the Romanesque".
5. See above, 69–73.
6. J. Vardy, *Some designs of Mr Inigo Jones and Mr William Kent* (London 1744), pl. 49.
7. J. Dallaway, *Observations on English Architecture* (London 1806), 78, no. U.
8. Dallaway (1806), 78, no. S.
9. Vardy, pl. 48.
10. N. Pevsner, *Herefordshire* (London 1963), 287–8.
11. A. Clifton-Taylor, *English Parish Churches as Works of Art* (London 1974), 131.
12. M. Wight, *The Churches of Shobdon and their Builders* (Hereford 1961), 8.
13. Warwick CR0 125B/882.
14. Kidderminster Public Library, ref. no. 000294.
15. B. F.Clarke, *The Building of the Eighteenth-Century Church* (London 1963), 63, and J. Summerson, 239. M. Whiffen, "Shobdon Church, Herefordshire, an Unnoticed Example of Rococo Gothic", *Country Life* (12 February, 1943), 315–16. G. Grigson, "Who Wins at Shobdon?", *Country Life* (17 December, 1953), 2034–5.
16. The dates have been established from the correspondence of Richard Bateman with his steward at Shobdon, Mr Fallowes, now in the Herefordshire County Record Office, unlisted at time of writing. This is summarised in Wight.
17. See above, 105–11.
18. Whiffen (1943).
19. Summerson (ed.) (1968), 356, n. 3 to Ch. 24. As in the case of the problem of the architect of Strawberry Hill, Summerson opts for William Robinson, but more tentatively.
20. Letters dated 18 January, 1749, and 24 March, 1749, Richard Bateman to Mr Fallowes, Herefordshire CR0, Hanbury Collection.
21. For Flitcroft's work at Shobdon Court see the letter dated 3 April 1746, and for the first planning of the church, letters dated 16 April and 8 May, 1746, Richard Bateman to Mr Fallowes, Herefordshire CR0, Hanbury Collection.
22. Vardy, pl. 51, which is not found in some copies of the first edition.
23. This letter is dated simply "Thursday the 16th", and a later hand has added "1748" (perhaps mistakenly for 1746), Richard Bateman to Mr Fallowes, Herefordshire CR0, Hanbury Collection.
24. E. H. Pearce, and J. Lees-Milne, 23 September (1971), 740–3.
25. Warwick CR0 125B/809.
26. Colvin, *Biog. Dict.*, 482 for Nelmes and Hagley, and 483 for Worcester Cathedral.
27. H. C. Smith, "Henry Keene, A Georgian Architect", *Country Life* (30 March, 1945), 556–7, and W. H. Smyth, *Addenda to the Aedes Hartwellianae* (London 1864), 20–1, where the name is mistakenly given as B. Keene.
28. Victoria and Albert Museum, A 189. 1921. Colvin,

Biog. Dict., 483, notes designs in the Bodleian Library, Ms. Top. Gen. b. 55, ff. 29–34, which seem to be later in date, drawings after the building rather than for it.
29. Warwick CR0 136B/1785.
30. Victoria and Albert Museum, A 189. 1921.
31. N. Pevsner, *Northamptonshire* (London 1961), 460–1 and M. Whiffen (1943), 70–1.
32. For the collaboration of Keene and Sanderson on the execution of Theodore Jacobson's design for the west front of Trinity College, see E. McParland, "Trinity College, Dublin—II", *Country Life* (13 May, 1976), 1242–5.
33. Warwick CR0 125/36. For Prowse see Colvin, *Biog. Dict.*, 666–7.
34. Essex CR0 D/DW E.36. 7. There is an inscription at the Church which gives the year 1758 also. See Clarke, 71. The work on the chancel was undoubtedly occasioned by the erection of the two fine monuments, to Charles Hosier and to his daughter, Anna Maria Sharp. Mrs Prowse had inherited the Wicken estate from Hosier on his death in 1750. The monuments were installed in 1758.
35. I am grateful to Colonel Lloyd-Baker for permission to study a typescript of the diary of Elizabeth Prowse, made available to me through the kindness of the staff at the Gloucestershire County Record Office.
36. Biographical notes on Thomas Prowse are available in E. F. Wade, "Notes on the Family of Prowse of Compton Bishop, Co. Somerset", *Miscellanea Genealogica et Heraldica*, N.S. Vol. III, 162 and 165.
37. The correspondence between the ceiling of the chancel at Wicken Church and that of St Mary's Hartwell, was noted in Whiffen, 71. E. F. Instone, in a letter to *Country Life* (24 December, 1953), 2116, pointed to the similarity of the ceiling design and the ceilings at Arbury.
38. N. Pevsner, *Middlesex* (London 1951), 88–92, notes "The chancel especially is as cram-full of curious objects as the rooms of the Soane Museum".
39. Middlesex CR0 135/Mx. Pec. 2.
40. Warwick CR0 136B/251 2B, "A General Abstract of the Workmen's Bill at Harefield Church—Anno 1768 & 9", in Henry Keene's hand, reads as follows:

			£.	s.	d.
Carpenter	Thomas Bush	1st Account	71	1	0
		2nd Ditto	8	8	3
Mason	Thomas Gayfere	Pd. 23rd	53	4	2
Plasterer	Dormer Heafford	Pd. 25th	51	9	4
Painter	(illegible)		2	0	8
Glazier	Joseph Summers		12	8	5
Carvers	Messrs. Hayter & Bond		6	5	4
Smith	John Elwell		8	16	6
Ditto	Eleanor Randall		2	12	10
			250	10	0
Cr by Cash. recd. for some old materials			7	8	6
			243	1	6
				H. Keene	

N.B.

The estimate was £201 4s. 6d; Altarpieces & Cold. Glass £31-1-0. Additions afterwards, as repairs to old pews and desks, gratis, + air-holes—but nich additional; in old arch—alteration of Stalls & new hand-rail instead of old one—setting monument in Brackenbury Chapel, and some other little matters.

This account establishes the date of installation of the monument to Diana Ball, a classical urn in a gothic niche and Keene's responsibility for the niche. The urn itself would have been designed by Sir Roger Newdigate, who designed the monuments to his mother and his first and second wives, which were sculpted by Richard Hayward and John Bacon Jnr. Pevsner thought it ''pretty, if somewhat sentimental''. A detailed account of the carpenter's work at Harefield of the same date is Warwick CR0 136B/2512A.

41. Middlesex CR0 136/Mx. Pec. 4, dated 29 March, 1768.

42. The bills for this work, totalling £177. 8s. 7½d. are Middlesex CR0 136/Mx. EF. 22 and 24.

43. A. Esdaile, ''Harefield Church and its Monuments'', *The Architect*, Vol. CXIV (27 November and 4 December, 1925), 386–8 and 568–9.

44. Wood and Hawkes.

45. Warwick CR0 125B/671.

46. Warwick CR0 125B/661.

47. Warwick CR0 125B/660.

48. ''The Parochial Antiquities of Topographical Survey of Hagley'', in manuscript in the Library of the Society of Antiquaries of London. I am indebted to the librarian, Mr Hopkins, and the Secretary, Mr Thompson, for many kindnesses in the course of my work.

49. M. Williams (ed.), (1939), 446.

50. Williams (ed.), (1939), 449.

51. British Library, Stowe MS. 754, f. 235, dated from York, 6 June, 1768.

52. Dr Pococke's account is given in Whiffen, 68.

53. The alterations proposed for St Canice's Cathedral, and the correspondence of Bishop Pococke with Sanderson Miller on the subject is detailed in M. McCarthy, ''Eighteenth-Century Cathedral Restoration: Correspondence Relating to St Canice's Cathedral, Kilkenny'', *Studies* (Winter 1976), 330–43 and (Spring 1977), 60–76.

54. The correspondence is printed in full in the Appendix to McCarthy, ''Eighteenth-Century Cathedral Restoration'', 63–75.

55. McCarthy, ''Eighteenth-Century Cathedral Restoration'', 74–5.

56. J. G. A. Prim, ''A Sketch of the History, Architecture and Antiquities of the Cathedral Church of St Canice, Kilkenny'', *The Church of England Magazine*, No. 465 (25 May, 1844), 337–9. Prim was to be co-author with J. Graves of *The History of the Cathedral Church of St Canice, Kilkenny* (Dublin 1857). Bishop Pococke is less severely condemned there, and ''the bad taste of the age'', is blamed for the Ionic decoration of the choir stalls. When St Canice's was restored to its present state by Sir Thomas Deane from 1866, Graves obtained the Ionic stalls and altered them to form the gallery of the lovely little church at Inisnag, about eight miles from Kilkenny on the Waterford road. They are still there and look very nice.

57. G. T. Stokes (ed.), *Pococke's Tour in Ireland in 1752* (Dublin 1891), 128.

58. McCarthy, ''Eighteenth-Century Cathedral Restoration'', 75. The Bishop had stipulated that the carver, ''must be a sober man, live in my house, and not be above eating at the servant's table, & must keep out of other company otherwise he will be undone'' (p. 70).

59. Warwick CR0 125B/795.

60. McCarthy, ''Eighteenth-Century Cathedral Restoration'', 64–5.

61. McCarthy, ''Eighteenth-Century Cathedral Restoration'', figure 3. I am indebted to Mr Wilde, the verger of St Canice's, for finding me the fine old photographs, and to Dr McAdoo, since translated to the Archdiocese of Dublin, for permission to publish it.

62. The drawings are Britist Library, Add. MS. 6776, f. 60, which is the finished drawing with signature and date, and f. 61 which is the preparatory drawing.

63. Whiffen, 68. Colvin, *Biog. Dict.*, 550 records references to this work in Miller's diary. See also P. Titchmarsh, *The Parish Church of St Peter, Kineton, Warwickshire* (Kineton 1983), 11–13.

64. Warwick CR0 125B/786–7. No work is recorded in Whiffen or Clarke.

65. Shakespeare's Birthplace Trust, Stratford-on-Avon, Leigh MSS., Series B, Gloucestershire Papers, Box 2, Bundle 6. The text continues:

> To take down the south wall and rebuild the same of the same height with the north wall and make a recess of ten feet square with a pew for Mr. Jas Leigh at the east end of the said south wall with a Burying Vault underneath of the same dimensions, with steps, doors, seats, windows and other necessaries as shall be judged proper by the said Mr. Miller. And also to take off the roof of the said Church of Adlestrop to new frame it and find such slabs and timber which shall be found proper and necessary to put the same in good condition and to new ceil the roof and plaister the sides of the said Church and also to make 2 doors into the Church thro' the Bellfry and to put a new floor for the ringers and raise the old floor to a height proper for the bell ropes. And also to build a Gallery at the West End of the said Church of four rows of Benches the breadth of the Church, with stairs up to the Gallery etc.

James Leigh was to pay Hitchcox £52, and the Churchwardens were to pay him a further £63 for this contract, subject to the approval of Sanderson Miller. It was signed by Leigh and Hitchcox and by Joseph Hanks and John Simonds for the Churchwardens. The witness was Edward Turner of Ambrosden House, Oxfordshire, who had also previously employed Sanderson Miller and William Hitchcox. He was brother-in-law to James Leigh and contributed five pounds to the alterations to the Church at Adlestrop, as appears by his account book, which is also deposited in the Shakespeare's Birthplace Trust in Stratford-upon-Avon.

66. This work is recorded in Clarke, 60.

67. T. H. Cocke, ''James Essex, Cathedral Restorer'', *Architectural History*, Vol. XVIII, (1975), 12–22.

68. Colvin, *Biog. Dict.*, 297–300 for James Essex, and 168–70 for Sir James Burrough.

69. Figure 8 of D. R. Stewart, 317–21.

70. See figures 5 and 7 of Stewart. For an account of this scheme see G. Cobb, *English Cathedrals: The Forgotten Centuries* (London 1980), 11. Horace Walpole was also consulted about the alterations to the altar of Westminster Abbey, and proposed that a design based on the market cross of Chichester (used twenty years earlier for the building in the Menagerie at Wentworth Castle, as we have seen), be the model, ''elevated on a flight of steps with the altar in the middle, and semicircular arcades to join the stalls, so that the Confessor's chapel and tombs may be seen through in perspective.'' (Walpole to Mason, 10 July, 1775, quoted from W. S. Lewis, *Horace Walpole* (New York 1961), 113). For James Essex's proposals for alterations to Ely Cathedral, see R. R. Rowe and G. Scott, ''The Octagon and Lantern of Ely Cathedral'', *Proceedings for the Royal Institute of British Architects*, Vol. XXVI (1876), 69–85, and T. H. Cocke (1979), 71–77.

71. Fot Thaxted Church see Colvin, *Biog. Dict.*, 299, and for the Lincoln Screen see Cocke (1980), fig. 12b.

72. P. Toynbee (ed.) (1927), 132–3. Walpole seems to have developed some qualms of conscience, for he

wrote to Cole when sending the design in 1769, "Bishop Luda must not be offended at my converting his tomb into a gateway".

73. Cocke (1979), 21.
74. Stewart, 320.
75. J. Bentham.
76. Cocke (1975), 21, n. 3.
77. Cobb, 76–7. Since they are not discussed by Cobb, a note may be added here on the alterations to the cathedrals of Carlisle and Norwich which involved Thomas Pitt and his uncle Charles Lyttelton. As we have noted, Pitt became a neighbour of Walpole and designed features of the Gallery and Tribune of Strawberry Hill, and his uncle, President of the Society of Antiquaries was appointed "Visitor of Strawberry" in 1763. In that year Charles Lyttelton was elevated from the Deanship of Exeter to the Bishopric of Carlisle, and Walpole wrote, urging him to "change it for Hartlebury or Farnham Castles—to these Pitt and I can come with our Gothic trowels." (*H.W.C.*, Vol. XL, 288.) In the following year Bishop Lyttelton asked Sanderson Miller to provide him with a design for a screen for Carlisle Cathedral, but nothing seems to have come of this initiative, and in 1765 he turned to his gifted nephew, as appears by the following letter recorded by John Nichols in his *Literary Illustrations of the 18th Century*, Vol. III, 310: "My nephew, the young Mr. Pitt, has promised me a design for a new altar-screen at Carlisle Cathedral, in case I can send him a proper person to *draw* it. If you could recommend such a one who will do it well under Mr. Pitt's eye, and reasonable, I should be greatly obliged if you would immediately send him to Mr. Pitt's". The fullest account of the alterations is that in R. W. Billings, *Carlisle Cathedral* (London 1840), 6–9. A manuscript of John Chambers in the Library of the Royal Institute of British Architects, "Biographies of English Architects", under the entry *Carlysle, Thomas*, provides us with the information that this gentleman was the carpenter employed for the extensive woodwork in the choir, the ceiling of which was stuccoed to resemble fan-vaulting at the same time. The woodwork is very fine. Alterations cost £1,300, of which the Bishop contributed £100 personally.

Pitt was next involved in alterations to Norwich Cathedral, but in what capacity or how extensively does not appear clearly. Jeremiah Milles wrote in commendation of these alterations to Bishop Lyttelton in 1768: "Your nephew Pitt I find is entitled to some merit on that account as is also the Dean's Lady". (British Library, Stowe MS 754, f. 235.)

78. N. Pevsner (1972), 2.
79. British Library, Cole MS, 5834, f. 110.
80. J. D. Williams, *Audley End: The Restoration of 1762–1797* (Chelmsford 1966), 31, pl. VIII.
81. Lord Braybrooke, *The History of Audley End* (London 1836), 127. See also P. Drury, "No other place . . .", Architectural History, Vol. XXIII, (1980), 1–39. I am most grateful to Paul Drury for his advice on matters relating to the work at Audley End.
82. The *Proposals* is printed as the Appendix.
83. The manuscripts are British Library Add. MS 6760–6773 and 6776, though manuscripts not in the hand of Essex are to be found in these papers also.
84. Quoted from Stewart.
85. Pevsner (1972), 5 states that Bentham did not make reference to Gray in expounding the importance of the arch, but Bentham is generous in acknowledgment of his debt to Gray in the Preface to the Cambridge edition of 1771. Perhaps Professor Pevsner was using the London printing of the essay, published by John

Taylor along with essays by Grose, Warton, and Milner in 1800 as *Essays on Gothic Architecture*, which omitted the Preface.
86. Bentham's letters to Lyttelton are in the British Library, Stowe MS 754, ff. 14–15, and 20–1. They were published in the second edition of the *History and Antiquities . . . of Ely* (Norwich 1812), 7–11. The letter of Charles Mason is British Library, Stowe MS 753, f. 239. Bentham's letters were also published in *The Gentleman's Magazine*, 17 April, 1784.
87. See Appendix.
88. It may be argued that Essex lifted the discussion of the arch from the window to the vault, or to use Frankl's unsatisfactory shorthand, from the membrological to the scientific stage of discussion, and that his originality is to be found therein. But I have not found that discussion of the arch in the eighteenth century is centered on the window; it is always associated with the support system in the first place, and I may quote from the first of Bentham's letters to Lyttelton, dated 17 April, 1758, as an example: "The Characteristics of this stile of Building; its pointed Arches, & slender & delicate Pillars, its richness & sometimes profuseness in the ornamental parts;—& the vast variety of tracery that is found both in the Roofs & Windows of this mode of Building". Essex stressed the technical role of arches and the interaction of buttress and pinnacle, but his scattered remarks in their unpublished state can hardly be credited with having influenced technical discussion to any extent greater than the notes of Thomas Gray. Unlike Gray, the structural consideration of Gothic architecture made Essex rather blind to the decorative possibilities of the arch, and he censures the Gothic architects very firmly: "When they began using the intersecting Arches, they became absurd and ridiculous". Clearly Richard Bentley was lucky he had left Cambridge before Essex started practice!
89. See above, Ch.1.
90. *H.W.C.*, Vol. XX, 465.
91. N. Pevsner and D. Lloyd, *Hampshire and the Isle of Wight* (London 1967), 637–8.
92. Hants. CR0 31M57/633, which is printed as Appendix I to *H.W.C.*, Vol. XXXV, 639–40.
93. The screen was built and placed in front of the gallery at the back of the chapel, as seen in plate 215.
94. *H.W.C.*, Vol. XX, 449.
95. *H.W.C.*, Vol. XXXV, 186.
96. *H.W.C.*, Vol. IX, 216: "I don't know what sight I have to come in Hampshire, unless it is Abbotstone, I am pretty sure I have none to come at The Vine, where I have done advising, as I see Mr. Chute will never do anything. The very altarpiece that I sent for to Italy is not placed yet. But when he could refrain from making the little Gothic columbarium for his family which I proposed and Mr. Bentley had drawn so divinely, it is not probable he should do anything else".
97. The National Trust, *The Vyne* (London 1969), 19.
98. Roma signed for receipt of payment for this on 5 October, 1771. For Roma see H. Walpole, Vol. IV (1969), 72–8, and E. Croft-Murray, *Decorative Painting in England*, Vol. II (London 1970), 270–1. Some of his work, not in the best state of repair, can still be seen in the gallery of the chapel of The Vyne. See also item 29 and plate 45 of the catalogue of the Royal Academy exhibition, *English Taste in the Eighteenth Century* (London 1955–6). The bill for his work at The Vyne amounts to £363. 13s. 0d. It is on the verso of a drawing by Chute, Hants CR0 31M57/639, 27.
99. The painting is at The Vyne and was published in McCarthy, "John Chute's Drawings", fig. 27.

100. See above, chapter 3.
101. They are listed in the inventory referred to above, p. 88.
102. Toynbee and Whibley, Vol. II, 481.
103. Above, n. 98.
104. C. W. Chute, Ch. 4. For the documents relating to the tomb see C. L. Chute, ''A Monument by Thomas Carter'', *Country Life* (27 May, 1954), 1733–4.
105. H. G. Wayment, ''The Stained Glass of the Chapel of The Vyne and the Chapel of the Holy Ghost, Basingstoke'', *Archaeologia*, Vol. CVII (1982), 141–52.
106. S. M. Gold, *John Rowell* (The Ranelagh Press 1965), 35–6, pls. 5 and 6.
107. Hants CR0 31M57/639, 39 for the sheet of sketches, and Lewis Walpole Library Collection for the second drawing. The building accounts do not seem to have survived, so dating must rest on probabilities. The tomb was begun in 1775 and was not finished for several years, and the ceiling of the chapel was done in 1771, as we have seen. Although Chute bought the window in 1757, therefore, the more probable date for the drawing is in the early 1770s. John Chute died in 1776.
108. *H.W.C.*, Vol. XXXV, 250. Walpole and Chute undoubtedly had serious discussions about tombs in the early 1770s, since Chute, as we have seen, made designs for the Chapel-in-the-Woods at Strawberry Hill, built to house the tomb of Capoccio. Walpole had first written of this tomb, ''these materials will make me a beautiful chimney-piece'', (407). As we have seen, he also half-apologised to Bishop Luda for using his tomb as a design for the entrance gateway to Strawberry Hill. Perhaps the Chapel-in-the-Woods should be read as his act of atonement for any disrespect shown in his earlier pillaging of tombs for architectural motifs!

Manuscripts and drawings

Arbury Hall, Warwickshire—drawings of Sir Roger Newdigate.

Avery Architectural and Fine Arts Library, Columbia University, New York—drawings of Thomas Wright of Durham.

Beinecke Library, Yale University, New Haven— The Book of Architecture of John Shrimpton.

Bodleian Library, Oxford University—Gough Maps, Ms. Top. Oxon., North Papers.

British Library, London—King's Maps, Stowe MS 752–4, Cole MS. 5834–6, Add MS. 5845, 14260, 22241, 22257–61, 33099, 35679, 41133–5.

Essex CRO—Dacre Papers, Copt Hall Papers.

Hagley Hall, Worcs.—Lyttelton Manuscripts.

Hampshire CRO—drawings and papers of John Chute.

Henry E. Huntington Library, San Marino, California—Stowe Papers, plays of Richard Bentley, letters of William Kent and Thomas Pitt.

Hereford CRO—Hanbury Papers.

Kidderminster Public Library—notebooks of Edward Knight of Wolverley.

Lewis Walpole Library, Farmington, Connecticut— drawings of Richard Bentley, John Chute, Horace Walpole, J. H. Müntz and others.

Middlesex CRO—Newdegate Papers.

Musée Royale des Beaux Arts, Brussels—drawings of J. H. Müntz.

National Trust, The Vyne, Hampshire—drawings of John Chute, John Hobcraft and J. H. Müntz.

Royal Institute of British Architects, London— drawings of Sanderson Miller, Sir Roger Newdigate and Thomas Wright of Durham, John Chambers MS "Biographies of English Architects".

Shakespeare's Birthplace Trust, Stratford-on-Avon—Leigh Papers.

Sir John Soane's Museum, London—drawings and letters of Thomas Pitt.

Society of Antiquaries of London—manuscripts of Charles Lyttelton.

Victoria and Albert Museum, London—drawings of Henry and Theodosius Keene and manuscript and drawings of J. H. Müntz.

Warwickshire CRO—drawings and papers of Sanderson Miller and Sir Roger Newdigate.

Windsor Castle, Royal Library—drawings of Thomas Wright of Durham.

Yale Center for British Art—drawings and manuscript of Stephen Riou.

Unpublished works in typescript

Aldrich, M., *Thomas Rickman and Architectural Illustration of the Gothic Revival*, thesis (1983), University of Toronto.

Aunt Prowse's Diary, Hardwicke Court, Glos.

Badenoch, T., *Dessins de Müntz de Wilhelmshoehe*, thesis (1983), University of Toronto.

Badenoch-Watts, T., *The Life and Work of Johann-Heinrich Müntz*, thesis (1986), University of Toronto.

Briggs, N., *Thomas Lord Dacre and His Circle* (1960).

Hawkes, W., *Sanderson Miller of Radway*, thesis (1964), Department of Architecture, Cambridge University.

Jestin, L. H. D., *Richard Bentley the Younger (1708–1782); A Critical Biography*, thesis (1985), Yale University.

McCarthy, M., *Amateur Architects in England*, thesis (1972), Courtauld Institute of Art, University of London.

Rowan, A. J., *The Castle Style in English Domestic Architecture*, thesis (1965), University of Cambridge.

Sparkes, J. G., *Belhus* (1964), Essex CRO.

Stroud, D., *Index to the Architectural Society Publications Dictionary*, Library of the Royal Institute of British Architects, London.

Published works

Adams, C. K., and Lewis, W. S., "The Portraits of Horace Walpole", *The Walpole Society*, Vol. XLII (1968–70), 1–34.

Addison, A., *Romanticism and the Gothic Revival* (New York 1939).

Addison, W., *Audley End* (London 1953).

Aheron, J., *A General Treatise on Architecture* (Dublin 1754).

Aikins, E., *Designs for Villas* (London 1808).

Aldrich, M., "Gothic Architecture Illustrated: The Drawings of Thomas Rickman in New York", *The Antiquaries Journal*, LXV, Part II (1985), 427–33.

Allan, Juliet, "New Light on William Kent at Hampton Court Palace", *Architectural History*, Vol. XXVII (1984), 50–8.

Allen, B. S., *Tides in English Taste 1619–1800* (New York reprint 1969).

Ames, D. S., "Strawberry Hill": Architecture of the "as if", *Studies in Eighteenth Century Culture*, Vol. VIII (Wisconsin 1979), 351–63.

Anon., *A Gleam of Gothic* (Bath, Holbourne of Menstrie Museum, 1972).

Archer, John, *The Literature of British Domestic Architecture, 1715–1842* (M.I.T. Press 1985).

Aubin, R. A., "Grottoes, Geology and the Gothic Revival", *Studies in Philology*, Vol. XXXI (1934), 408–16.; "Some Augustan Gothicists", *Harvard Studies and Notes in Philology and Literature*, Vol. XVII (1935), 15–25.

Badenoch, T. S., "Wilhelmshoehe; a unique record of a changing landscape by J. H. Müntz", *Journal of Garden History*, Vol. 6, No. 1 (Spring 1986), 50–61.

Barton,S., *Monumental Follies* (Worthing 1972).

Bate, W. J., *From Classic to Romantic; Premises of Taste in Eighteenth-Century England* (New York 1961).

Batey, M., "Shotover's Continuity with the Past", *Country Life* (29 December, 1977), 1978–9.

Beard, G. W., *Georgian Craftsmen and Their Work* (London 1966).

Beard, G. W., and Folkes, J. H., "John Chute and Hagley Hall", *Architectural Review* (March 1952), 199–200.

Beer, E. S. de, "Gothic—Origin and Diffusion of the Term", *Journal of the Warburg and Courtauld Institutes*, Vol. II (1948), 143–62.

Bell, C. F., "Thomas Gray and the Fine Arts", *Essays and Studies by Members of the English Association*, Vol. 30 (1945), 50–81.

Bentham, J., *History and Antiquities of the Conventual and Cathedral Church of Ely* (Cambridge 1771).

Bentham, J., and Willis, B., *The History of Gothic and Saxon Architecture in England* (London 1798).

Billings, R. W., *Architectural Illustrations, History and Description of Carlisle Cathedral* (London 1840).

Blunt, R. (ed.), *Diaries and Letters of Mrs. Montagu* (London 1923).

Boe, A., *From Gothic Revival to Functional Form* (Oxford 1947).

Boulting, N., "The Law's Delays. Conservationist Legislation in the British Isles", J. Fawcett (ed.), *The Future of the Past* (London 1976).

Braybrooke, Lord, *The History of Audley End* (London 1836).

Breman, P., (ed.), *The Gothic of Gothick (Weinreb Cat. 14)*

(London 1966); (ed.) *The Early Eighteenth Century* (London 1965).

Briggs, M. S., *The Architect in History* (London 1927); *Men of Taste* (London 1947); *Goths and Vandals* (London 1952).

Briggs, N., "Lord Dacre and Morant's History of Essex", *Essex Journal*, Vol. 2, No. 1, 6–11.

Brown, R. (ed.), *The Architectural Outsiders* (London 1985).

Brydges, E., *Restituta* (London 1816).

Budzinska, E., *Jana Henryka Muntza podroze malownicze po Polsce i Ukrainie* (Warsaw 1982).

Burke, E., *A Philosophical Enquiry into the Origin of our Ideas on the Sublime and the Beautiful* (London 1756).

Burnett-Brown, J., *Lacock Abbey, Wiltshire* (London 1969).

Bury, A., "Paintings and Prints of Twickenham and Richmond in the Collection of the Hon. Mrs. Ionides", *The Connoisseur* (April 1956), 93–100.

Busiri-Vici, A., *I Poniatowski e Roma* (Florence 1971).

Caisse nationale des monuments historiques et des sites, *"Le Gothique" retrouve* (Paris 1979).

Calloway, S., Snodin, M., and Wainwright, C., *Horace Walpole and Strawberry Hill* (Richmond 1980).

Chambers, W., *A Treatise of Civil Architecture* (London 1759); *Plans, Elevations, Sections and Perspective Views of the Gardens and Buildings at Kew in Surrey* (London 1763).

Chancellor, E. B., *Lives of the British Architects* (London 1907).

Cherry, B. and Pevsner, N. B. L., *London 2: South* (Harmondsworth 1983).

Chute, C. L., "A Monument by Thomas Carter", *Country Life* (27 May 1954), 1733–4.

Chute, C. W., *A History of The Vyne* (Winchester 1888).

Clarke, K., *The Gothic Revival* (London 1928).

Clarke, B. F. L., *The Building of the Eighteenth Century Church* (London 1963).

Clarke, G., "Grecian Taste and Gothic Virtue", *Apollo* (June 1973), 566–71; "William Kent: Heresy in Stowe's Elysium", *Furor Hortensis*, P. Willis, (ed.), (Edinburgh 1974), 48–56.

Clarke, M. and Penny, N., *The Arrogant Connoisseur: Richard Payne-Knight 1751–1824* (Manchester 1982).

Clifford, J. L. (ed.), *Man Versus Society in Eighteenth-Century Britain* (London 1968).

Clifton-Taylor, A., *English Parish Churches as Works of Art* (London 1974).

Climenson, E. J. (ed.), *Diaries of Mrs. Phyllis L. Powys* (London 1899); *Letters of Elizabeth Montagu* (London 1906).

Cobb, G., *English Cathedrals: The Forgotten Centuries* (London 1980).

Cobbett, R. S., *Memorials of Twickenham* (London 1872).

Cochran, H. S., *St. Mary's Harefield* (London 1926); *More about Harefield Church and Parish* (London 1927).

Cocke, T. H., *The Ingenious Mr. Essex, Architect* (Fitzwilliam Museum, Cambridge 1984); "James

Essex, Cathedral Restorer'', *Architectural History*, Vol. XVIII (1975), 12–22; ''The Rediscovery of the Romanesque'', *English Romanesque Art* (Hayward Gallery, London 1984), 360–6; ''The Architectural History of Ely Cathedral'', *Medieval Art and Architecture at Ely Cathedral* (BAA Transactions, London 1979), 71–7.

Coke, Lady M., *Letters and Journals* (London 1889–96).

Coleridge, A., *Chippendale Furniture* (New York 1968).

Colton, J., ''Merlin's Cave and Queen Caroline: Garden Art as Propaganda'', *Eighteenth-Century Studies*, Vol. X, No. 1, 1–20.

Colvin, H. M., ''Gothic Survival and Gothic Revival'', *Architectural Review*, Vol. 103 (1948), 91–8; ''Eythrope House and its Destruction in 1810–11'', *Records of Buckinghamshire*, Vol. 17 (1964), 219–27; ''Aubrey's Chronologia Architectonica'', *Concerning Architecture*, ed. J. Summerson (London 1968), 1–12; *A Biographical Dictionary of British Architects 1600–1840* (London 1978); ''The Origins of the Gothic Revival'' *Accademia Dei Lincei, Problemi Attuali di Scienza e di Cultura*, Quaderno no. 241 (Rome 1978), 3–18.

Colvin, H. M. and Harris, J. (eds.), *The Country Seat* (London 1970).

Cornforth, J., ''A Countess's London Castle'', *Country Life Annual 1970*, 138–9.

Cottingham, L. N., *Working Drawings for Gothic Ornaments* (London 1823); *Smith and Founder's Dictionary* (London 1824).

Craig, M., *The Volunteer Earl* (London 1958).

Croft-Murray, E., *Decorative Painting in England 1537–1837* (London 1970).

Crook, J. M., ''John Britton and the Genesis of the Gothic Revival'', *Concerning Architecture*, ed. J. Summerson (London 1968), 98–119; ''Northumbrian Gothick'', *Journal of the Royal Society of Arts* (April 1973), 271–83; ''Strawberry Hill Revisited'', *Country Life* (7, 14 and 21 June 1973), 1598–602, 1726–30, 1794–7; ''Walpole's Concept of Gothic'', *Country Life* (28 June, 1973), 1886.

Crunden, J., *Convenient and Ornamental Architecture* (London 1770); *The Joyner and Cabinet-Maker's Darling or Pocket Director* (London 1770).

Crunden, J., Milton, T. and Columbani, P., *The Chimney-Piece Maker's Daily Assistant* (London 1766).

Cumberland, R., *Memoirs* (London 1806).

Dallaway, J., *Anecdotes of the Arts in England* (London 1800); *Observations on English Architecture* (London 1806).

Darly, M., *The Ornamental Architect* (London 1770).

Davis, R. M., *The Good Lord Lyttelton* (London 1939).

Davis, T., *The Gothick Taste* (Newton Abbot 1974).

Decker, B., *Gothic Architecture Decorated* (London 1759); *Chinese Architecture Civil and Ornamental* (London 1759).

Dickins, L., *History of Radway* (London 1937).

Dickins, L. and Stanton, M., *An Eighteenth Century Correspondence* (London 1910).

Dimier, L., ''Le Paysagiste Müntz'', *Bulletin de la Société de l'histoire de l'art francais* (1923), 108–10.

D'Oench, E. G., *The Conversation Piece: Arthur Devis and his Contemporaries* (New Haven 1980).

Doig, A., ''James Adam, James Essex and the Altarpiece for King's College Chapel, Cambridge'', *Architectural History*, Vol. XXI (1978), 79–82.

Drury, M., ''The Architecture of Fishing'', *Country Life* (27 July, 1972), 202–5.

Drury, P., ''No other place'', *Architectural History*, Vol. XXIII (1980), 1–39.

Ducarel, A. C., *Anglo–Norman Antiquities Considered in a Tour through Part of Normandy* (London 1767).

Eastlake, C. L., *History of the Gothic Revival*, ed. J. M. Crook (Leicester 1970).

Eden, F. S., ''The Belhus Heraldic Glass'', *Country Life* (5 May, 1923), 600–3.

Edmonds, G. C., *History of Chalfont St Peter's and Gerrards Cross* (London 1968).

Edwards, E., *Anecdotes of Painting* (London 1808).

Edwards, R., *Dictionary of English Furniture* (London 1954).

Eliot, G., *Scenes of Clerical Life*, ed. D. Lodge (London 1980).

Esdaile, A., ''Harefield Church and its Monuments'', *The Architect*, Vol. CXIV, (27 November and 4 December, 1925), 386–8, 403–4.

Esdaile, K. A., ''Some 18th Century Works on Architecture'', *Architect and Building News*, Vol. CXVI (1 October and 12 November, 1926) 384–5, 568–9.

Evans, J., *History of the Society of Antiquaries of London* (London 1956).

Fawcett, W. M., (ed.), *James Essex: Journal of a Tour through Flanders and France in 1773* (Cambridge 1888).

Fleming, J., ''Adam Gothic'', *The Connoisseur* (October 1958), 75–9; ''An Adam Miscellany'', *Architectural Review*, Vol. CXIII (1958), 103–7; ''Robert Adam's Castle Style'', *Country Life* (23 and 30 May, 1968), 1356–59, 1443–7; ''A Retrospective View'' by John Clerk of Eldin, with some Comments on Adam's Castle Style'', *Concerning Architecture*, ed. J. Summerson (London 1968), 75–9.

Fothergill, Brian, *The Strawberry Hill Set; Horace Walpole and his Circle* (London 1983).

Frankl, P., *The Gothic: Literary Sources and Interpretations through Eight Centuries* (Princeton 1960).

Franklyn, J., ''The Incomparable Baronet of Arbury'', *Coats of Arms*, Vol. IV (1955–8), 274.

Fraser, M., *Gerrards Cross and the Chalfonts* (London 1967).

Frew, J. M., ''Richard Gough, James Wyatt and Late 18th Century Preservation'', *Journal of the Society of Architectural Historians*, Vol. XXXVIII, No. 4 (December 1979), 366–74; ''An Aspect of the Early Gothic Revival: The Transformation of Medievalist Research 1770–1800'', *Journal of the Warburg and Courtauld Institutes*, Vol. XLIII (1980), 174–85; ''Gothic is English: John Carter and the Revival of the

Gothic as England's National Style'', *Art Bulletin*, Vol. LXIV, No. 2, 315–9; ''Salisbury Cathedral Choir-Screen reconsidered'', *Architectural History*, Vol. XXVII (1984), 481–5; ''The Destroyer Vindicated? James Wyatt and the Restoration of Henry VII's Chapel, Westminster Abbey'', *Journal of the British Archaeological Association*, Vol. LXXIV (1981), 100–7; ''Some Observations on James Wyatt's Gothic Style, 1790–1797'', *Journal of Society of Architectural Historians*, Vol. XLI (1982), 142–50; ''Gothic in Transition: Wyatt and Bernasconi at New College, Oxford. (1788–1794)'', *Burlington Magazine*, Vol. CXXVI (1984), 683–8.

Friedman, T., ''Romanticism and Neo-Classicism for Parlington'', *Leeds Art Calendar*, No. 66 (1970), 16–24; *James Gibbs* (London 1984).

Gerard, A., *An Essay on Taste* (London 1759).

Germann, G., *Gothic Revival in Europe and Britain: Sources, Influences and Ideas* (London 1972).

Gibbon, M., ''A Manifesto in Ironstone'', *Country Life* (1 June, 1972), 1416–17.

Girouard, M., ''The Castle Revival in English Architecture, 1610–1870'', *Historismus und Schlossbau*, ed. Wagner-Renate and Krause (Munich 1975), 83–6; ''English Art and the Rococo'', *Country Life* (13, 27 January and 3 February, 1966), 59–61, 188–90, 224–7.

Gloag, J., *Georgian Grace* (London 1956).

Goatman, W., *Harefield and Her Church* (London 1947).

Gold, S. M., *Life of John Rowell* (Ranelagh Press 1965).

Graves, J. and Prim, J. G., *History of the Cathedral Church of St. Canice, Kilkenny* (Dublin 1857).

Graves, R., *Recollections of William Shenstone* (London 1788).

Greening-Lambourn, E. A., ''The Shields in Ratley Roundhouse'', *Notes and Queries*, Vol. CLXXXIII (1943), 157, 233.

Grigson, G., ''The Origin of Grottoes'', *Country Life* (1 September, 1950), 688–93; ''Who Wins at Shobdon?'', *Country Life*, (17 December, 1953), 2034–5.

Gunn, W., *Inquiry into the Origins and Influences of Gothic Architecture* (London 1819).

Gunnis, R., *Dictionary of British Sculptors 1660–1851* (London 1964).

Gwynn, J., *An Essay on Design* (London 1749); *London and Westminster Improved* (London 1766).

Gwynn, J. (attr.), *English Architecture, or the Publick Buildings of London and Westminster* (London 1758).

Hadfield, M., Harling, R., Highton, L., *British Gardeners: A Biographical Dictionary* (London 1980).

Hakewill, J., *History of Windsor and its Neighbourhood* (London 1813).

Halfpenny, W., et al., *The Modern Builder's Assistant* (London 1742).

Halfpenny, W. and J., *Chinese and Gothic Architecture Properly Ornamented* (London 1752); *Rural Architecture in the Gothic Taste* (London 1752).

Hall, I., ''Architecture and Ancestry'', *Country Life* (6 May 1982), 1278–81; ''Antiquity and Fashion'', *Country Life* (13 May, 1982), 1358–61.

Halsband, R., ''The Rococo in England: Book Illustrators, mainly Gravelot and Bentley'', *Burlington Magazine*, (December 1985), 870–80.

Harbron, D., ''The Modern Proteus'', *Architectural Review*, Vol. LXXX (1936), 167–70.

Harcourt, L., *Mr. Methuen's House* (Slough 1981).

Harris, E., ''Thomas Wright of Durham'', *Country Life* (26 August, 2 and 9 September, 1971), 492–5, 546–50, 612–15; ''Batty Langley: Tutor to Freemasons'', *The Burlington Magazine* (May 1977), 327–35; ''Villa for a Mortal Miss'', *Country Life* (5 August 1982), 392–4.

Harris, J., ''Exoticism at Kew'', *Apollo*, Vol. LXXVII (August 1953), 103–8; ''Sir William Chambers, Friend of Charlemont'', *Irish Georgian Society Bulletin*, Vol. VIII (1965), 67–100; ''Pritchard Redivivus'', *Architectural History*, Vol. II (1968), 17–24; ''Father of the Gardenesque'', *Country Life* (7 June 1979), 1838–40; ''The Dundas Empire'', *Apollo*, Vol. LXXXVI (September 1976), 234–9; *The Palladians* (London 1981); ''William Kent's Gothick'', *A Gothick Symposium* (Georgian Society, London 1983) unpaginated; *A Catalogue of British Drawings for Architecture, Decoration, Sculpture and Landscape Gardening, 1550–1900, in American Collections* (Upper Saddle River, N.J. 1971); *Sir William Chambers* (London 1970).

Harwood, T. E., *Windsor Old and New* (London 1929).

Hawkes, W., ''The Gothic Architectural Work of Sanderson Miller'', *A Gothic Symposium* (Georgian Society, London, 1983), unpaginated.

Hawkins, J. S., *History of the Origin and Establishment of Gothic Architecture* (London 1813).

Heely, J., *Letters on Hagley, Envil and the Leasowes* (London 1777).

Hefford, W., ''Thomas Moore of Moorefields'', *The Burlington Magazine* (December 1977), 840–8

Heilman, R. B., ''Fielding and the First Gothic Revival'', *Modern Language Notes*, Vol. LVII (1942), 671–3.

Herrmann, W., *Laugier and 18th Century French Theory* (London 1962).

Herrmann, W. (ed.), *Langier: An Essay on Architecture* (Los Angeles 1977).

Hersey, G. L., ''Associationism and Sensibility in Eighteenth-Century Architecture'', *Eighteenth-Century Studies*, Vol. IV, No. 1 (1970), 71–89.

Hipple, W. J., *The Beautiful, the Sublime and the Picturesque* (Carbondale 1957).

Historic Manuscripts Commission, Twelfth Report, Appendix Part X, Vol. 1 (London 1896).

Hobhouse, H., *Lost London* (London 1971).

Hodgetts, J., (ed.), *Letters of Lady Luxborough to William Shenstone* (London 1775).

Hogarth, W., *The Analysis of Beauty* (London 1753).

Honour, H., *Horace Walpole* (London 1957); ''An Epic of Ruin-Building'', *Country Life* (10 December, 1953), 1968–9.

Hooker, E. N., "The Discussion of Taste from 1750 to 1770, and the New Trends in Literary Criticism", *Modern Language Association of America*, Vol. LIXXX (1934), 577–92.

Houfe, S., "The Diaries of the Countess of Pomfret", *Country Life* (24 and 31 March 1977), 728–30, 800–2.

Hull, T., (ed.), *Selected Letters* (London 1778).

Hunt, J. D., "Emblem and Expressionism in the 18th Century Landscape Garden", *Eighteenth Century Studies*, Vol. IV, No. 3 (1971), 294–317.

Hunt, J. D. and Willis, P., *The Genius of the Place* (New York 1975).

Hunt, J. F., et al., *History of Radway* (London 1937).

Hurd, R., *Letters on Chivalry and Romance* (London 1762).

Hussey, C., *The Picturesque* (London 1927); *English Country Houses: Early Georgian* (London 1955); *English Country Houses: Mid-Georgian* (London 1956); *English Gardens and Landscapes 1700–1750* (London 1967); "Donnington Grove, Berkshire", *Country Life* (18 and 25 September and 2 October, 1958), 588–91, 654–7, 714–17.

Hyams, E., *Capability Brown and Humphry Repton* (London 1971).

Ilchester, Earl of, *Henry Fox, First Lord Holland* (London 1920).

Inventaire des dessins et aquarelles donnés a l'état belge par Madame la Doarrière de Grez (Brussels 1913).

Ironside, E., *History and Antiquities of Twickenham* (London 1797).

Isaacs, J., "The Gothick Taste", *Journal of the Royal Institute of British Architects*, Vol. LIX, No. 9 (July 1952), 337.

Ison, W., *The Georgian Buildings of Bristol* (London 1952).

Jackson, T. G., *Modern Gothic Architecture* (London 1873).

Jenkins, F., *Architect and Patron* (Oxford 1961).

Jenkins, J. G., *The Dragon of Whaddon* (London 1953).

Jones, B., *Follies and Grottoes* (London 1953).

Jourdain, M., *The Work of Wiliam Kent* (London 1948).

Kames, Lord, *Elements of Criticism* (London 1762).

Kallich, N., *Horace Walpole* (New York 1971).

Kaufmann, E., *Architecture in the Age of Reason* (Cambridge, Mass. 1955).

Kendall, J., *Elucidation of the Principles of English Architecture. Usually denominated Gothic* (London 1818).

Ketton-Cremer, R. W., *Horace Walpole* (London 1940); *Thomas Gray* (London 1955); *Felbrigg: The Story of a House* (London 1962).

Kielmansegge, F., *Diary of a Journey to England 1761–1762* (London 1902).

Kirby, J. J., *Perspective of Architecture* (London 1761).

Kitz, N. and B., *Painshill Park: Hamilton and his Picturesque Landscape* (London 1984).

Kliger, S., "The Goths in England: An Introduction to the Gothic Vogue in Eighteenth-Century Aesthetic Discussion", *Modern Philology*, Vol. XXXXIII (November 1945), 107–17; "Whig

Aesthetics: A Phase of Eighteenth-Century Taste", *ELH, A Journal of English Literary History*, Vol. XVI (1949), 135–50; *The Goths in England* (Harvard 1952).

Krinsky, C. H., "Romanesque Architecture and Some Eighteenth-Century Critics", *Gesta*, Vol. II (1964), 20–1.

Ladd, F. J., *Architects at Corsham Court* (Bradford-on-Avon 1978).

Lambert, E., "Historic Architecture: Strawberry Hill, The Eighteenth-Century Beginnings of the Gothic Revival", *Architectural Digest* (June 1981), 144–50.

Lane, J., "Emerging from the Shadows; Robert Moore of Warwick (1711–1783)", *Country Life* (28 June, 1984), 1912–4

Lang, S., "Principles of the Gothic Revival in England", *Journal of the Society of Architectural Historians*, Vol. XXV, No. 4 (December 1966), 240–67.

Langley, B., *Ancient Architecture Restored and Improved* (London 1742); *The Art of Designing and Working the Ornamental Parts of Buildings* (London 1745).

Latimer, J., *Annals of Bristol in the Eighteenth Century* (Bristol 1893).

Lawson, J. and Waterson, M., "Pritchard as Architect and Antiquary at Powis", *The National Trust Year-Book 1975–1976*, 8–11.

Leach, P., "In the Gothick Vein", *Country Life* (26 September, 1974), 834–7; "A Pioneer of Rococo Decoration", *Country Life* (19 September, 1974), 766–9.

Lees-Milne, J., "John Chute at the Vyne", *The Connoisseur* (June 1960), 47–50; *Earls of Creation* (London 1962); "Hartlebury Castle Revisited", *Country Life* (23 September, 1971), 740–3; "Stout's Hill, Uley and Hardwicke Court, Gloucestershire", *Country Life* (5 July, 1973), 16–20.

Lennard Barrett, T., *History of the Families of Barrett and Lennard* (London, for private circulation, 1908).

Lever, J., *Catalogue of Drawings in the Collection of the Royal Institute of British Architects*, Vol. L–N (London 1973).

Lever, T., *The House of Pitt* (London 1947).

Levy, M., "Le premier renouveau gothique et la sensibilité anglaise au milieu du XVIIIe siècle", *Etudes anglaises*, Vol. XIV (1961), 349–50; *Le roman "gothique" anglais 1764–1824* (Toulouse 1968).

Lewis, G. R., *The Ancient Church of Shobdon* (London 1852).

Lewis, L., *Connoisseurs and Secret Agents* (London 1961); "Stuart and Revett; Their Literary and Architectural Careers", *Journal of the Warbourg and Courtauld Institutes*, Vol. II (1938), 128–46.

Lewis, W. S., "The Genesis of Strawberry Hill", *Metropolitan Museum Studies*, Vol. V, No. 1 (1934–6), 57–92; *Bentley's Designs for Walpole's Fugitive Verses* (London 1936); *The Library of Horace Walpole* (Cambridge 1958); *Horace*

Walpole (New York 1961); *Thomas Gray 1716–1771* (Cambridge 1971); *A Guide to the Life of Horace Walpole* (New Haven 1973); *Rescuing Horace Walpole* (New Haven 1978).

Lewis, W. S. (ed.), *Horace Walpole's Correspondence* (New Haven 1933–83).

Lightoler, J., *The Gentleman and Farmer's Architect* (London 1764).

Lindus Forge, J. W., "Kentissime", *Architectural Review*, Vol. CVI (1949), 187–8.

Lindsay, I. and Cosh, M., *Inverary and the Dukes of Argyll* (Edinburgh 1973).

Lines, R. C., "Arbury Gothick and the Newdigates", *The Connoisseur Year-Book 1960*, 11–17.

Little, B., *James Gibbs* (London 1955).

Longueil, A. E., "The Word Gothic in Eighteenth-Century Criticism", *Modern Language Notes*, Vol. XXXVIII (1923), 453–60.

Lovejoy, A. O., "The First Gothic Revival and the Return to Nature", *Modern Language Notes*, Vol. XLVII (1932), 419–46; *Essays in the History of Ideas* (Baltimore 1948).

Lowth, T., *Essay on Architecture* (Oxford 1776).

Lyttelton, G., *A Gentleman's Tour through Wales* (London 1781).

Macaulay, J., *The Gothic Revival, 1745–1845* (Glasgow 1975).

Macaulay, R., *The Pleasure of Ruins* (London 1953).

Macmillan Enclyclopedia of Architects 4 Vols. (New York 1982).

Malden, H., *An Account of King's College Chapel, Cambridge* (London 1769).

Malins, E., *English Landscaping and Literature 1660–1840* (Oxford 1966).

Malins, E. and The Knight of Glin, *Lost Demesnes* (Newton Abbot 1976).

Malton, J., *Essay on British Cottage Architecture* (London 1798); *A Collection of Designs for Rural Retreats, principally in the Gothic and Castle Styles* (London 1802).

Manwaring, R., *The Carpenter's Compleat Guide* (London 1765); *The Cabinet and Chair-maker's Real Friend and Companion* (London 1765)

Mason, G., *Essay on Design in Gardening* (London 1795).

Mathias, G., *The Works of Thomas Gray* (London 1814).

McCarthy, M., "Tracy of Toddington Manor", *Transactions of the Bristol and Gloucestershire Archaeological Society*, Vol. LXXXIV (1965), 164–71; "The Work of Hanbury Tracy, Lord Sudeley at Hampton Court", *Woolhope Transactions*, Vol. XXXVIII (1964), 70–5; "Sir Roger Newdigate and Piranesi", *The Burlington Magazine* (July 1972), 466–72; "Documents on the Greek Revival in Architecture", *The Burlington Magazine* (November 1972), 760–9; "Sir Roger Newdigate: Drawings for Copt Hall Essex, and Arbury Hall, Warwickshire", *Architectural History*, Vol. XVI (1973), 26–36; "The Rebuilding of Stowe House 1770–1777", *The Huntington Library Quarterly*, Vol. XXXVI, No. 3 (May 1973), 267–91; "James

Lovell and his Sculptures at Stowe", *The Burlington Magazine* (April 1973), 281–92; "Eighteenth-Century Amateur Architects and their Gardens", *The Picturesque Garden*, ed. N. Pevsner (Washington 1974), 33–55; "John Chute's Drawings for the Vyne", *The National Trust Year-Book 1975–1976*, 70–80; "Eighteenth-Century Cathedral Restorations: Correspondence relating to St. Canice's Cathedral, Kilkenny", *Studies*, (Winter 1976), 330–43 and (Spring 1977), 60–76; "The Building of Hagley Hall", *The Burlington Magazine* (April 1976), 214–25; "The Education in Architecture of the Man of Taste", *Studies in Eighteenth-Century Culture*, Vol. V (1976), 337–53; "Johann-Heinrich Müntz: The Roman Drawings 1749–1776", *The Burlington Magazine* (May 1977), 335–40; "Sir Thomas Robinson: An original English Palladian", *Architectura*, Bd. 10, No. 1 (1980), 39–57; "Thomas Wright's 'Designs for Temples' and related Drawings for Garden Structures", *Journal of Garden History*, Vol. 1, No. 1 (1981), 55–65, "Ireland Ancient and Modern: The Sketches in Architecture of Thomas Wright of Durham", *The Connoisseur* (February 1981), 158–61; "Art Education and The Grand Tour", *Art the Ape of Nature: Essays in Honor of H. W. Janson's 65th. Birthday*, ed., M. Barasch and L. F. Sandler (New York 1981), 477–94; "Soane's Saxon Room at Stowe", *Journal of the Society of Architectural Historians*, Vol. XLIV, No. 2 (1985), 129–45.

McParland, E., "Trinity College, Dublin", *Country Life* (13 May 1976), 1242–5.

Middleton, R., "The Abbé de Cordemoi and the Greco–Gothic Ideal", *Journal of the Warburg and Courtauld Institutes*, Vol. XXV (1962), 278–320 and Vol. XXVI (1963), 90–123.

Miles, E. G., *Thomas Hudson 1701–1779* (London 1979).

Miller, G., *Rambles Round the Edge Hills* (Kineton 1967).

Miller, J., *The Country Gentleman's Architect* (London 1787).

Miller, N., *Heavenly Caves: Reflections on the Garden Grotto* (New York 1982).

Milliken, S., "The Tribune in English Architecture", *Burlington Magazine*, Vol. CXII (July 1970), 442–6

Moir, E., *The Discovery of Britain: The English Tourists 1540–1840* (London 1960).

Momigliano, A., "Ancient History and the Antiquarians", *Journal of the Warburg and Courtauld Institutes*, Vol. XIII (1950), 285–315.

Monk, S. H., *The Sublime* (London 1935).

Morris, J. H. and Crunden, J., *The Carpenter's Companion for Chinese Railings and Gates* (London 1770).

Morris, R., *Essay in Defence of Ancient Architecture* (London 1728); *Lectures on Architecture* (London 1734); *Rural Architecture* (London 1750); *The Architectural Remembrancer* (London 1751); *The Qualifications and Duty of a Surveyor Explained in a Letter to the Rt. Hon. The Earl of . . .* (London

1752). *A Second Letter . . .* (London 1752).

Mowl, T., "The Case of the Enville Museum", *Journal of Garden History*, Vol. III, No. 2 (1983), 134–43.

Mowl, T. and Earnshaw, B., "The Origins of 18th Century Medievalism in a Georgian Norman Castle", *Journal of the Society of Architectural Historians*, Vol. XL (1981), 289–94.

Müntz, J. H., *Proposals for Publishing by Subscription on a Course of Gothic Architecture* (London 1760); *Encaustic: or Count Caylus's Method of Painting in the Manner of the Ancient* (London 1760).

Murphy, J. C., *Plans, Elevations, Sections and Views of the Church of Batalha* (London 1795).

Musgrave, E. J., *Inverary Castle* (London 1955).

Namier, L., *Personalities and Powers* (London 1955).

Namier, L. and Brooke, J., *The House of Commons 1754–1790* (London 1964).

Nares, G., *Arbury Hall, Warwickshire* (London 1970).

National Trust, *The Vyne, Hampshire* (London 1983).

Neale, J. P., *Views of the Seats of Noblemen and Gentlemen* (first series, 6 Vols., London 1818–23; second series, 5 Vols., London 1824–9; reissued as *Jones's Views of Seats* in 2 Vols. London 1829–30, and as *Neale's Mansions of England*, London 1847.

Nichols, J., *Literary Illustrations of the Eighteenth Century* (London 1858).

Noble, P., *Park Place* (London 1905).

Nutter, N. E., *Carlisle* (London 1835).

O'Connor, C., "Gardening at Marino", *Moorea: Journal of the Irish Garden Plant Society*, Vol. II (Spring 1983), 29–38.

O'Connor, C. and Cooke, B., "A Greek Stele in Dublin", *The Antiquaries Journal* Vol. LXI, Part 1 (1981), 29–34.

Over, C., *Ornamental Architecture* (London 1758).

Overton, T. C., *The Temple Builder's Most Useful Companion* (London 1766).

Pagan, H., Wrightson, P. and Chafee, D., *Church Architecture and Architects in Britain* (Weinreb Cat. 31, London 1973).

Palmer, W. M., *William Cole of Milton* (Cambridge 1935).

Pearce, E. H., *Hartlebury Castle* (London 1926).

Penny, N., "The Taste of Richard Payne-Knight", *Country Life* (28 January 1982), 218–21.

Perkins, T. S., *The Churches of Rouen* (London 1900).

Perry, F., *Series of English Medals* (London 1762).

Pevsner, N., *The Buildings of England* (London 1951–74); *Studies in Art, Architecture and Design* (London 1968); *Some Architectural Writers of the Nineteenth Century* (Oxford 1972); "Rococo Gothic: Walpole, Bentley and Strawberry Hill", *Architectural Review*, Vol. XCVIII (December 1945), 151–3.

Phillimore, R., *Memoirs and Correspondence of George Lord Lyttelton, from 1734 to 1773* (London 1845).

Phillips, H., *The Thames in 1750* (London 1951); *Mid-Georgian London* (London 1964).

Physick, J., *Design for English Sculpture 1680–1860* (London 1969).

Piggott, S., *William Stukeley* (Oxford 1985); *Ruins in a Landscape: Essays in Antiquarianism* (Edinburgh 1976).

Plunkett, Count, "James Cavanah Murphy", *The Irish Builder and Engineer*, Vol. LI (15 May, 1909), 295–7.

Pococke, R., *Travels through England* (Camden Society, London 1888–9).

Pownall, T., "Observations on the Origin and Progress of Gothic Architecture", *Archaeologia*, Vol. IX (1789), 110–26.

Pye, J., *The Patronage of British Art* (London 1845).

Rackham, B., *Early Netherlandish Majolica with special reference to the Tiles of the Vyne in Hampshire* (London 1926).

Raine, J., *Historical Account of the Episcopal Castle or Palace of Auckland* (Durham 1852).

Ralph, J., *Critical Review of the Buildings of London and Westminster* (London 1734).

Ramsay, A., *The Investigator* (London 1755).

Richardson, A. E. and Gill, C. L., *London Houses from 1660 to 1820* (London 1911).

Richardson, A. E., "Gothic Revival in the Early 18th. Century", *Journal of the Royal Institute of British Architects*, Vol. XLV (1938), 140–1; *An Introduction to Georgian Architecture* (London 1949).

Richardson, G., *Book of Ceilings* (London 1776), *Designs for Chimney Pieces* (London 1781); *Treatise on Architecture* (London 1787); *Designs for Country Seats* (London 1795); *New Vitruvius Britannicus* (Vol. I London 1802–8; Vol. II, London 1808–10); *Designs for Ornaments* (London 1816).

Riely, J., "The Castle of Otranto Revisited", *The Yale University Library Gazette*, Vol. LIII (July 1978), 1–17; "Shenstone's Walks: The Genesis of the Leasowes", *Apollo*, Vol. CX, No. 211 (September 1979), 202–9.

Riou, S., *The Elements of Fortification* (London 1746); *Short Principles for the Architecture of Stone Bridges* (London 1760); *The Grecian Orders of Architecture* (London 1768).

Roberts, S. C., *An Eighteenth Century Gentleman* (London 1930).

Rouquet, J., *The Present State of the Arts in England* (London 1755).

Rowan, A., *Garden Buildings* (London 1968); "Batty Langley's Gothic", *Studies in Memory of David Talbot Rice*, ed. G. Henderson (Edinburgh 1975), 197–215; "Lo Stile Castello", *Accademia Dei Lincei, Problemi Attuali di Scienza e di Cultura*, Quaderno no. 241 (Rome 1978), 19–38; "Gothic Restoration at Raby Castle", *Architectural History*, Vol. XV (1972), 23–50.

Rowe, R. R. and Scott, G., "The Octagon and Lantern of Ely Cathedral", *Proceedings of the Royal Institute of British Architects*, Vol. XXVI (1876), 60–85.

Royal Academy, *English Taste in the Eighteenth Century* (London 1955).

Rushfort, G.McN., "Painted Windows in the Chapel of The Vyne in Hampshire", *The Walpole Society*, Vol. XXV (1936–7), 167–9.

Rykwert, J., *On Adam's House in Paradise: The Idea of the Primitive Hut in Architectural History* (New York 1972); *The First Moderns: The Architects of the*

Eighteenth Century (Cambridge, Mass. 1980).

Sambrook, J., "Parnell's Garden Tours; Hagley and the Leasowes", R. P. Maccubin and P. Martin (eds.), *British and American Gardens in the Eighteenth Century* (Williamsburg 1984), 51–64.

Savill, A., and Sons, *Belhus, Essex* (sale catalogue, London 1923).

Sayers, F., *Miscellanies* (Norwich 1805).

Sigworth, O. F., *The Four Styles of a Decade 1740–1750* (New York 1960).

Simpson, D., *The Gothick* (Brighton 1975).

Sitwell, S., *British Architects and Craftsmen 1600–1830* (London 1945).

Smith, H. C., "Henry Keene, A Georgian Architect", *Country Life* (30 March, 1945), 556–7.

Smith, W. H., *Architecture in English Fiction* (New Haven 1934); *Originals Abroad* (New Haven 1952).

Smyth, W. H., *Addenda to the Aedes Hartwellianae* (London 1864).

Stanton, P., *Gothic Revival in American Church Architecture* (Baltimore 1972).

Steegman, J., *The Rule of Taste from George I to George IV* (London 1936).

Stewart, D. E., "James Essex", *Architectural Review*, Vol. CVIII (1950), 317–21.

Stokes, G. T., (ed.), *Pococke's Tour in Ireland in 1752* (Dublin 1891).

Stokstad, M. and Gill, L., "Antiquarianism and Architecture in Eighteenth Century Ireland", *Irish History and Culture*, ed. H. Orel, (Kansas 1976), 165–87.

Stroud, D., *Capability Brown* (London 1975).

Stuart, J. (attributed), *Critical Observations on the Buildings and Improvements of London* (London 1771).

Summerson, J., *Georgian London* (London 1948); *Heavenly Mansions* (London 1949); *Architecture in Britain 1530–1830* (London 1953); *The Life and Work of John Nash, Architect* (London 1980).

Summerson, J., (ed.), *Concerning Architecture* (London 1968).

Swan, A., *Designs in Architecture* (London 1757); *The British Architect* (London 1758).

Swan, A., *Talboy's Collection of the Oxford English Prize Essays* (Oxford 1836).

Tayler, I., "Bentley Bids the Pencil", *Woman in the 18th Century and Other Essays*, ed. P. Fritz and R. Morton (Toronto 1976), 201–15.

Taylor, J., (ed.), *Essays on Gothic Architecture* (London 1800).

Thomas, W., *Original Designs in Architecture* (London 1783).

Thompson, P., "The Survival and Revival of Gothic Architecture", *Apollo*, Vol. LXXVI, (May 1962), 284–7.

Tipping, H. A., "Belhus Essex", *Country Life* (15 and 22 May 1920), 650–60, 690–3; "Lacock Abbey, Wiltshire", *Country Life* (17 March, 1923), 357–9.

Tipping, H. A., and Hussey, C., *English Homes—Period IV* (London 1928).

Titchmarsh, P., *The Parish Church of St. Peter, Kineton,*

Warwickshire (Kineton, 1983).

Toynbee, P., *Journal of the Printing Office at Strawberry Hill* (London 1923); *The Strawberry Hill Accounts* (Oxford 1927).

Toynbee, P., (ed.), "Horace Walpole's Journal of his Visits to Country Houses etc.", *The Walpole Society*, Vol. XVI (1928), 9–80.

Toynbee, P. and Whibley, L., *Correspondence of Thomas Gray* (Oxford 1935).

Trevor, R., *Life of Richard Trevor Lord Bishop of Durham* (Darlington 1776).

Troide, L. E., (ed.), *Horace Walpole's Miscellany 1786–1795* (New Haven 1978).

Turner, R., *Capability Brown* (London 1985).

Vardy, J., *Some Designs of Mr Inigo Jones and Mr William Kent* (London 1744).

Verey, D., *Gloucestershire: The Cotswolds* (London 1970); *Gloucestershire: The Vale and the Forest of Dean* (London 1970).

Verney, Lady, *Verney Letters of the Eighteenth Century* (London 1930).

Verney, Lady and Abercrombie, P., "Letters of an Eighteenth Century Architect", *Architectural Review*, vols. LIX and LX (1926), 259–63, 1–3, 50–3, 92–3

Vernon, W. F., *Notes on the Parish of Harefield* (privately printed, London 1872).

Wade, E. F., "Notes on the Family of Prowse", *Miscellanea Genealogica et Heraldica* (New Series Vol. III), 162, 165.

Wallis, N., *A Book of Ornaments in the Palmyrene Taste* (London 1771); *The Complete Modern Joyner* (London 1772); *The Carpenter's Treasure* (London 1773).

Walpole, H., *Anecdotes of Painting in England*, ed. R. Wornum with Notes and additions by J. Dallaway (New York reprint 1969); *Description of Strawberry Hill* (London 1784).

Ward-Jackson, P., *English Furniture Designs of the Eighteenth Century* (London 1958).

Ware, I., *The Complete Body of Architecture* (London 1756).

Warton, T., *Observations on Spencer's Faerie Queene* (London 1762).

Watkin, D., *The Rise of Architectural History* (London 1980); *The English Vision: The Picturesque in Architecture, Landscape and Garden Design* (New York 1982).

Watts, W., *The Seats of the Nobility and Gentry* (London 1779–86).

Way, T. R., *Architectural Remains of Richmond, Petersham, Twickenham, Mortland and Kew* (London 1900).

Wayment, H. G., "The Stained Glass in the Chapel of The Vyne", *National Trust Studies 1980*, 35–47; "The Stained Glass in the Chapel of The Vyne, and the Chapel of The Holy Ghost, Basingstoke", *Archaeologia*, Vol. CVII (1982), 141–52.

Whateley, T., *Observations on Modern Gardening* (Dublin 1770).

Whibley, L., *Correspondence of Richard Hurd and William Mason, and Letters of Richard Hurd to Thomas Gray* (Cambridge 1932).

Whiffen, M., *Stuart and Georgian Churches outside London* (London 1947–8); "Shobdon Church, Herefordshire: an Unnoticed Example of Rococo Gothic", *Country Life* (2 February, 1943), 315–16.; "Rickman and Cambridge", *Architectural Review*, Vol. XCVIII (1945), 160–6.

Whistler, L., "The Authorship of the Stowe Temples", *Country Life*, (29 September, 1950), 1002–6.; *The Imagination of Vanbrugh and his Fellow Artists* (London 1954).

White, R., "Saved by the Landmark Trust: Laughton Place, East Sussex", *Country Life* (5 May, 1983), 1184–90. "The Influence of Batty Langley", *A Gothick Symposium* (London Georgian Society, 1983), unpaginated; "Wiston House Remodelled", *Architectural History*, Vol. XXVII (1984), 241–54.

Whitely, W. T., *Artists and their Friends in England 1700–1799* (London 1928).

Wiebenson, D., "Greek, Gothic and Nature 1750–1820", *Marsyas* (1965), 187–94.

Wiggin, L. M., *The Faction of Cousins* (New Haven 1958).

Wight, M., *The Churches of Shobdon and their Builders* (Hereford 1961).

Williams, J. D., *Audley End: The Restoration of 1762–1797* (Chelmsford 1966).

Williams, M., *William Shenstone* (London 1935).

Williams, M. (ed.), *Letters of William Shenstone* (London 1939).

Willis, B., *Survey of Cathedrals* (London 1742).

Wilson, M. I., *The English Country House and its Furnishings* (London 1979); *William Kent: Architect, Designer, Painter, Gardener 1685–1748* (London 1984).

Wilton-Ely, J., "The Genesis and Evolution of Fonthill Abbey", *Architectural History*, Vol. XXIII (1980), 40–9.

Wittkower, R., *Palladio and English Palladianism* (London 1974).

Wood, A. C., "Diaries of Sir Roger Newdigate", *Transactions of the Birmingham Archaeological Society*, Vol. LXVIII (1962), 40–54.

Wood, A. C. and Hawkes, H. W., "Sanderson Miller of Radway and his work at Wroxton", *Cake and Cockhorse*, Vol. IV, No. 6.

Wood, R., *The Ruins of Palmyra* (London 1753); *The Ruins of Balbec* (London 1757).

Woodbridge, K., *Landscape and Antiquity* (Oxford 1970); "William Kent as Landscape Gardener: a Re-appraisal", *Apollo* (August 1974), 126–39; "William Kent's Gardening: The Rousham Letters", *Apollo* (October 1974), 282–91; *The Stourhead Landscape* (London 1982).

Woolfe, V., "Two Antiquarians: Walpole and Cole", *The Death of the Moth* (London 1942), 45–51.

Wotton, H., *Elements of Architecture* (London 1624, Amsterdam reprint 1970).

Wragg, R. B., "John Carr: Gothic Revivalist", *Studies in Architectural History*, Vol. II, ed. W. A. Singleton (London 1956), 9–34.

Wright, T., *Louthiana: or an Introduction to the Antiquities of Ireland* (London 1748); *Book of Arbours (1755) and Book of Grottoes (1758)*, edited with an introduction by E. Harris (London 1979).

Wright, W., *Grotesque Architecture* (London 1767).

Yvon, P., *Le gothique et la renaissance gothique en Angleterre 1750–1880* (Paris 1931).

Index